DESERT FATHER

DESERT

James Cowan

FATHER

A Journey in the Wilderness with Saint Anthony

Shambhala · Boston 2004

Shambhala Publications, Inc.
Horticultural Hall
300 Massachusetts Avenue
Boston, Massachusetts 02115
www.shambhala.com

9 8 7 6 5 4 3 2 1
First Edition

Printed in the United States of America
♾ This edition is printed on acid-free paper that meets the
American National Standards Institute z39.48 Standard.
Distributed in the United States by Random House, Inc.,
and in Canada by Random House of Canada Ltd

Library of Congress Cataloging-in-Publication Data
Cowan, James, 1942–
Desert father: A journey in the wilderness with Saint Anthony/
James Cowan.—1st ed.
p.   cm.
Includes bibliographical references.
ISBN 1-59030-145-5 (pbk.: alk. paper)
1. Anthony, of Egypt, Saint, ca. 250-355 or 6.   I. Title.
BR1720.A6C69 2004
270.1'092—dc22
2003027431

O desert, bright with flowers of Christ! O Solitude, whence come the stones of which the Apocalypse, the city of the Great King, is built! O Wilderness, gladdened with God's especial presence! What keeps you in the world, my brother, you who are above the world? How long shall gloomy roofs oppress you? Oh, that I would behold the desert, lovelier to me than any city.

—SAINT JEROME

The desert is a question to All and horizon of Nothing.

—EDMOND JABÈS

CONTENTS

CHRONOLOGY

THE CHURCH OF THE WORLD	MONASTIC EGYPT
249-251 Persecution by Decius	
	251 Birth of Anthony; Paul of Thebes retires to the desert
	271 Anthony embraces the ascetic life
284 Reign of Diocletian begins	
	285 Anthony to Pispir
	ca. 290 Birth of Pachomius
	293 Birth of Macarius of Alexandria; Birth of Athanasius
	ca. 300 Birth of Macarius the Egyptian
303-311 Persecutions	
	304 Birth of Pambo; Birth of John of Lycopolis

	311 Anthony to Alexandria to assist the martyrs
	313 Edict of Milan; End of persecutions
	313 Anthony to Mount Colzim; Baptism of Pachomius
315-325 Arius preaches in Alexandria	
325 Council of Nicea condemns Arius	
328 Athanasius becomes patriarch of Alexandria	
	330 Amoun to Nitria; Macarius the Egyptian to Scete
	333 Baptism of Macarius of Alexandria
335-337 Athansius's first exile	
	338 Anthony to Alexandria and to Nitria; Foundation of the Kellia
339-346 Exile of Athanasius to the West.	
	340 Macarius the Egyptian ordained a priest
	341 Anthony meets Paul of Thebes; Death of Paul of Thebes
345 Death of Gregory of Alexandria	
	346 Death of Pachomius; John becomes a hermit at Lycopolis

	353 Death of Amoun
	356 Death of Anthony
357 Arian heresy openly declared	
	357 Hilarion visits Mount Colzim; Sisoes leaves Scetis and goes to Mount Colzim; Athanasius writes the life of Anthony
361-366 Emperor Julian the Apostate reigned	
	361 Julian the Apostate becomes emperor
	373 Death of Athanasius
	373-375 Rufinus and Melania in Egypt
380 Christianity declared the official faith of the Roman Empire	
381 Second Ecumenical Council in Constantinople	
	383 Evagrius to Nitria
	385 Theophilus becomes patriarch of Alexandria; Evagrius to the Kellia
	388 Palladius to Alexandria; Cassian in Egypt
	ca. 390 Death of Macarius the Egyptian; Palladius to Nitria
	391 Palladius to the Kellia
	394 Death of Macarius of Alexandria; Arsenius to Scete

395 Emperor Theodosius the
Great dies

398 John Chrysostom becomes
bishop of Constantinople

399 Death of Evagrius;
Palladius and Cassian leave
Egypt

400 Synod of Alexandria
condemns Origenism;
Postumianus in Egypt

402 Deposition of John Chrysostom
by the hastily convened Council
of the Oak

406 *History of the Monks in Egypt*
written

407 Death of John Chrysostom

407-408 First devastation of
Scete

412 Cyril becomes patriarch of
Alexandria

419 *Lausiac History* by Palladius

422 *Institutes of the Monastic Life*
of Cassian

430 Doctrine of Nestorius
condemned by council of bishops

440 Cyril of Alexandria dies

446 *Conferences of the Egyptian
Monks* of Cassian

DESERT FATHER

INTRODUCTION

Few people inspire us more than those who remove themselves to the wilderness. They awaken in us an urge to abandon normal society so as to pursue a free and open life. Moreover, instinct suggests that we might be better off living outside the constraints of the law. It is as if we know that at some point in our development we have lost the gift of living at one with nature and the world. Of course, this is a fallacy; nonetheless it has remained a powerful impetus for change since the Renaissance. Navigators, explorers, travelers, and merchants have all ventured forth into the unknown in a bid to discover what is loosely understood as Shangri-la. The American Wild West was less a place than an attempt to fashion a retreat where the rugged individualist could flourish. Gauguin's sojourn in Tahiti gave credence to Rousseau's idealization of the lonely man in paradise, while Robinson Crusoe, living on his own desert island, became the prototype for many a disillusioned hermit existing on the fringe of society.

The life of Saint Anthony of Egypt conforms to this model. He proposed a radical new way of living that was both asocial and adventurous. He sought to distance himself from late antiquity's loss of belief in the classical ideal in order to explore his own spirituality. In doing so, he sounded the death knell on Caesarism and the cult of personality that had so dominated the classical world since the days of Alexander the Great. *Civitas*, the Holy Grail of Rome and the basis of its imperial expansion, was all but neutralized by one man bent on questioning the role of the state as an arbiter of human values. Anthony preferred to live as a "society of one" in the desert of Egypt rather than submit to the coercive nature of imperial edict. The rise of the state represented for him the diminution of humanity itself.

Early Christian asceticism was therefore as much a political gesture as it was spiritual. Anthony had found a way to return to his origins by escaping the net altogether. By setting himself up as a lonely bastion of flesh in the desert, he served notice on how his body would in future be governed. Christ may have propounded this new governance during his ministry in Palestine, but none since had seriously put it into practice. Early theologians were still in thrall to their classical teachers, after all. Even Saint Jerome admitted that he found it difficult to give up his library of classics in favor of those "barbarous" writings then circulating in Palestine and the East. In those years Christianity was just another cult struggling to be heard. The distance between thought and practice was still very great.

It would take a spiritual genius to fashion an alternative life. It would take an artist to recognize the desert as the perfect representation of his own loss of self. No man before Anthony, not even Paul of Thebes, had so deliberately chosen to turn aridity into a positive value. The desert became his metaphor for being, his ageless encounter with lifelessness as a principle of rectitude. No wonder he was such a threat to Rome. This lonely man living in the desert imposed a new valuation on human endeavor: that people had a right to an inner life over and above their responsibilities as social beings. Such a premise went far beyond any that Socrates had proposed, even at his death. A new force had entered the world. By his retreat into the desert, Anthony paved the way for others to take their first step on the road to selflessness.

I had been drawn to this haunting figure ever since I first read Helen Waddell's *The Desert Fathers* when I was a struggling young writer in London during the 1960s. The image of this bearded man living in a cave high up on Mount Colzim captivated me. Then it was an image, no more. Here was a man who defied logic. He proposed dirt, hunger, loneliness, demonic battle, antisociability, nonambition, nonmaterial aspiration, asexuality, and the denial of all family affections as the basis of a new kind of adventure. It was almost as if he wished to deny everything that made the human experiment worthwhile. Did he really think that such complete identification with stones, with sand, and with thirst could produce a more luminous presence? Even then, in that unheated flat in London in the middle of winter, Anthony taunted me with his subversive vision.

For the next thirty years his memory claimed me. I saw his portrait in paintings, his emaciated figure sitting on a ledge outside a cave. Here was a man who had abandoned books, who was suspicious of words, who regarded knowledge as a tool of the devil. Everything that I was as a writer, he sought to undermine. He pitched me into a world where the very integrity of the image became suspect. Under his auspices every work of art, every expression of beauty became the handmaid of appearance. I began to suspect that I had come under the baleful influence of a shade that had quit life because of its encounter with the greatest of all human fears, the failure to enjoy life.

But still Anthony's presence remained. Over the years I returned to his story again and again in my attempt to understand his significance. It was not enough to see him solely as an ascetic, because he was more than that. It was not enough, either, to regard him as a recluse, because he was more than that too. As understanding slowly dawned on me, I started to see Anthony as the primeval encounter I had always wished to have with my selfhood. He was a kind of gnomic being imbedded in my psyche, there to activate my dormant spirituality the moment I allowed him to do so. A trip to Egypt in 1999, ostensibly to study hieroglyphs and pharaonic tomb painting, precipitated his reemergence from the hall of memory.

He came in the guise of a man that I met at Mount Colzim, on Anthony's mountain. I had gone there to pay my respects to an old obsession, believing that I had finally put it behind me. To meet Lazarus in his cave not far from the master's was to bring into focus the vitality of the ascetic ideal once more. Here was a man living like Anthony, who had forsaken the world in the pursuit of what the Desert Fathers called *apatheia*, holy stillness. The very word *apatheia* exploded in my mind with the full force of revelation when I first heard Lazarus utter it. He challenged me to step back in time with him, to abandon the illusion of distance that I thought separated me from Anthony, and begin the journey all over again. He made me aware that essential experience, whenever it occurs, never passes away. It is the vein of gold that lies buried underground for countless millennia, waiting to be unearthed.

My early version of Anthony, my Anthony of literary apprenticeship in London, was now transformed into an Anthony of the imagination. Lazarus alerted me to a thought I hadn't considered before: that this man was a minimalist. He was a figure as if sculpted by Giacometti in the fourth century, if that were possible. He had reduced himself, and his body, to the lowest—no, the lowliest, level. He was a man who had set out to reverse the process of human aspiration from one of expansiveness in the domain of the physical (man as owner, possessor, achiever, acquirer) to one who inhabited the least possible space. The Anthony that I slowly began to know and understand was someone content to occupy an inner space, the space of the spirit. He had made me aware that one could live a nonspatial existence in the midst of temporality.

Far from being a trip back in time, my journey to Egypt turned out to be a voyage into the future. The old pharaonic ideal of man as the supreme solar exemplar was now being supplemented by another—that of man as a generator of his own solar heat. Lazarus, the man I met living the anchorite's life at Mount Colzim, had shown me that it was feasible to live as Anthony had done, without in any way losing contact with the present. He taught me that asceticism is not an historical phenomenon but a way of life. Ascesis is none other than the science of the spirit. By following its practices diligently, and with due respect for the past, one could begin to perceive a reality unencumbered by the burden of images. This quality of perception is open only to those who are prepared to live what Ruysbroeck called "a ghostly life."[1]

Saint Anthony's monastery in the Eastern Desert became my laboratory. There I came in contact with ancient writings that inspired me to make the long journey inward. My journey through Egypt became an encounter less with events of history than with those of the spirit. The monastery library housed some of the earliest forays into ascetic and mystical literature that I had ever read. Thinkers subsequent to Anthony had taken up the challenge laid down by the master to fashion a new sense of interiority for everyone. It was this world that I had come to explore. With Lazarus's help I was able to investigate a region of the heart not accessible to me before.

This book is about an unusual journey. There were no maps, timetables, or travel arrangements. The destination was also unclear. While making this trip I allowed myself to be consumed by a thirst for the ineffable. In addition, there was one piece of advice that Anthony gave me that I assiduously followed: don't expect resolution but, rather, accept the path as wayless. Learn how to lean out of yourself and gaze back at who you are. It was good advice. With Lazarus as my guide, I was able to sojourn in countries not recorded on any map. With Anthony as my invisible companion, I was able to transcend time and keep him company in his cave. There he taught me that ascesis is a mysterious elixir capable of rendering insensible the self. All I had to do was drink this concoction and wait until it worked its miracle.

James Cowan
Mount Colzim, Egypt

one

TOWARD THE INNER MOUNTAIN

The hike up the mountain was steep and rough. At every step of the way stones dislodged, to trickle like water down the slope. I grabbed at rocks to steady myself. Whenever I looked up to ascertain my progress, all I could see was the same stony ridge above. Behind the ridge a high plateau, implacable and remote, stretched southward, its ridges glowing red in the afternoon sun. Desiccated, Mount Colzim was indeed forbidding. I had stumbled upon a place of bones, prayer, and memories.

This was the home of Anthony, the first Christian anchorite and solitary. He had lived in a cave on this mountain for the last fifty years of his life. Why he chose such a spot in preference to another was one of the reasons I had come to Egypt in the first place. I wanted to discover what might inspire a man to forsake the world with all its opportunities and pleasures in order to pursue a life of self-abnegation. It just didn't make sense. Either he had been mentally ill or else he knew something that I didn't.

The path I was climbing, however, did not lead directly to his legendary cave. On my arrival at the Monastery of Saint Anthony the previous day—located as it was at the foot of Mount Colzim in the Eastern Desert of Egypt, and several hours' drive from Cairo—the guest master, Elias, a youngish man who happened to speak good English, welcomed me with the news that Anthony's reincarnation had only recently taken up residence on the mountain.

"It is true," Elias said, a hint of pride in his voice. Or was it awe? "One man actually lives alone on the mountain to this day. He is the last anchorite."

I was struck by his remark. The last anchorite. It sounded so final, as if an entire subspecies of bird or insect were about to die out. This place that had spawned the monastic movement of Europe since the fifth century AD was now little more than a fossil. As well, an ancient spirituality was on the verge of extinction.[1] No wonder Elias was pleased. Someone had resolved to take it on himself to halt the decline of the solitary life before it was too late.

Out of a real sense of interest I decided that on my initial ascent of Mount Colzim I would seek out this lonely soul—even before I visited Anthony's cave. Elias had kindly given me permission to climb up to the anchorite's retreat, provided that I agree to carry a week's supply of bread for the man. Of course I readily agreed. A backpack full of bread was a small price to pay for the opportunity of meeting one of the world's last solitaries.

"When you see the man," Elias advised, "wait for him to give a

8

signal for you to continue your climb. If he thinks you are from Babylon, he may well decide not to wave you on up."

"And if he does, what city have I come from?" I asked.

"Why, Jerusalem, of course."

Such were the two psychic poles of an anchorite's world. One hailed either from Babylon, the city of material entanglement, or from Jerusalem, the celestial city. If one were disposed toward the former, there was no use climbing Mount Colzim in the first place. But if one had some yearning to enter the celestial city, it was possible to climb this track indicated by a few haphazard cairns. Somewhere up there a man had settled for a life of untroubled calm, or *ataraxia*. If he had managed to find the secret to such a life, I was interested to know how he had done it.

Finally, I recognized a low wall above. It was the first sign of habitation that I had seen on the mountain. As I shaded my eyes to gain a closer look, a man dressed in a black habit and bonnet, the kind worn by Coptic monks, peered down at me with unwavering eyes. I stood there, waiting for him to make a sign. Then he raised his hand and waved to me to come on up. I had passed my first test. Babylon, it appeared, was not my home.

Out of breath, I struggled up the track until I had reached a terrace built on the side of the mountain. The man stood before me at the center of a terrace, his face all but lost in his beard. Lines of fatigue and premature age creased his forehead. I could see little more of him except his hands, sunburned and gnarled, emerging from the folds of his habit. His bonnet, decorated with embroidered white crosses, was tied under his chin. He radiated a genuine, almost guileless warmth, however, as he extended his hands in welcome.

With my heart still pumping, I managed to introduce myself, hoping to hear a familiar response. The monk replied in perfect English. He told me that he wasn't Egyptian at all, but Australian. It seemed the last anchorite shared the same nationality with me.

"Lazarus is my name," he said, and then added: "because I am . . . reborn."

His final word fell like a pebble into a pond, intimating hidden circles of suffering and joy.

Lazarus invited me to sit on a bench that he had fashioned from stones on the terrace. While he disappeared into his cell to prepare a mug of tea on a gas burner, I sat there and gazed at the view. The desert below was expansive and steeped in its own aridity. I felt strangely elated. I was on top of the world, gazing down at something mysterious. Pharaohs and gods had looked on this ancient wasteland before me. Saracens and desert nomads had crossed it in their caravans, traveling between the Red Sea and the Nile River with precious stones and silks. It was clear that history had conducted a dialogue with these coruscated hills since the beginning of time. No wonder men like Lazarus and Anthony before him had come here. This was the land of *apostasis*, the ascetic renunciation of the world.

Presently Lazarus appeared on the terrace with two mugs of tea and a loaf of bread. This he broke into pieces before offering me a jar of honey to sweeten the morsels. We sat there and sipped our tea without talking. Between the desert and Lazarus's silence I tried to think of some way to begin our conversation. I guess I wanted to know what had driven him to take refuge in this remote spot in the Egyptian desert. What had driven him to seek a life of solitude with only a few deer and Coptic monks for company?

At last, Lazarus told me his story. A university lecturer, he had worked in a provincial city in Australia teaching literature. Life had been fairly normal for him until that point. He had owned a house and enjoyed all the advantages of a suburban life, including marriage. He wanted for nothing, so he informed me. He would have been prepared to continue living like that, even to the point of raising a family should the opportunity have presented itself. But something happened to change all that for him. His mother contacted incurable cancer.

Nursing his sick mother during the last months of her life affected him deeply. Her subsequent death prompted him to consider his own mortality. Gradually his way of life struck him as being less than fulfilling. He began to realize that he had indentured himself to things, to the promise of illusory happiness. His mother's untimely death destroyed his belief in all that. Without knowing it at the time, she had revealed to him the true paradox of existence: that it cannot be ordered or forecast.

One day in Melbourne, Lazarus found himself wandering the streets in an unaccountably distraught state. It dawned on him that his life held no meaning, that he had lost all sense of the value of being. Nothing meant much to him other than as an extension to his feeling of inadequacy and failure. His mother's death was like the tip of an iceberg submerged in a dark ocean. She had died without ever experiencing any feeling of calm in the face of death. Lazarus vowed then that this would never happen to him. He must discover a proper way to die, even if it took him a lifetime.

A guiding hand drew him into a Serbian Orthodox church that day. There he watched an elderly woman kneel before an icon of the Virgin Mary. Prostrating herself before the Holy Mother, and oblivious to everything but the glow of candles in front of the icon, the woman prayed.

At that moment Lazarus heard the voice of the Holy Virgin. She was calling to him, as if from the depths of her compassion, answering his unspoken entreaty: "I have nowhere to go. Please help me."

The voice of the icon replied: "Poor man, place yourself in my care, just as this woman has done. I am that light of your body."

Dazed, Lazarus left the church and soon found himself wandering the streets once more. Everything had been turned upside down. He could hear the noise of traffic as little more than a distant roar. The votive candles still shone in his eyes, however, all but blinding him. He knew then that he must make a change in his life. The Holy Virgin had spoken to him. She had heard his plea.[2]

The years that followed became a pilgrimage. He quit his job at the university and joined the Orthodox Church. In time he asked permission from the authorities to retire to a monastery on Mount Athos, in northern Greece. This was duly granted to him, and he traveled to the fishing village of Orionoupolis, on Chalkidhiki Peninsula, before boarding a boat sailing to the Holy Mountain. For some years he resided in the Serbian monastery of Chilandari, where he experienced at first hand the life of a monk. Later he moved to Philotheo, a Greek monastery, to further his studies in the eremitical life. He had finally quit the world. Such was his response to the comforting voice of the icon.

Over the years the ordered regime of the monastery, with its daily liturgy, its feasts and fasts, satisfied him less. He wanted to experience the solitary life more deeply. Of course he had read about Saint Anthony in Egypt and his lonely existence in a cave on Mount Colzim. Something inside made him want to emulate this man. Anthony became the prototype for a new and risky life: if he, Lazarus, could attain to a spiritual knowledge that was simple and not dictated by psychic deliberations, then might not he penetrate the greatest mystery of all—that of receiving what the Syrian Fathers knew as *maggenanutha*, the receipt of the holy gifts?[3] Surely it was worth a try.

Lazarus's decision prompted him to leave Mount Athos and journey to Egypt, to the homeland of the solitary life. Throughout the third and fourth centuries of our era a select band of men and women had taken on themselves the task of renovating consciousness by a deliberate act of withdrawal. The life of an anchorite became a demonstration of resistance and disavowal at a time when most men were content to serve the Roman state, pay its taxes, and fight its wars. The deserts of Egypt became a true laboratory of the spirit: men from diverse backgrounds and nationalities, both the educated and the illiterate, escaped their humdrum lives and took ship to Egypt, or left cities such as Alexandria and Thebes, in order to found small communities in the arid land west of the Nile, a region known as the Nitria Desert. These men pioneered a new way of thinking that transcended the weary dialectic taught in the philosophic academies of Alexandria or Athens. They became, in the words of one observer of the time, the "God-borne."

Lazarus soon found himself living in the Nitria Desert, south of Lake Mareotis, in the Monastery of the Syrians. He spent a number of years there before asking his spiritual advisor for permission to travel to the so-called inner mountain to join the community in the Monastery of Saint Anthony. When he arrived, he immediately felt at home. Something about Mount Colzim and its austere landscape inspired him. The stars that he saw when he stood on the rampart at night instilled in him a sense of the supreme singleness and adventure of his life. Here at last he could weave the carpet of his dreams.

"Solitude is the elixir of eternity," Lazarus remarked as he described his first years at Saint Anthony's.

He was directed to the bakery to serve out his ascetic apprenticeship. There he came under the influence of a deeply pious man who taught him how to practice discretion. Making bread drew him into complicity with a life of self-mastery and the spirit of ascesis. His Egypt was no longer an Egypt of pyramids, obelisks, and animal-headed gods; it had become a land steeped in the memory of the past endeavors of men who had wanted to overcome their faults and limitations, to realize what Isaac of Nineveh called a genuine "chastity of the mind."

It was heady stuff. Glancing at Lazarus as he related his story, I realized at once that I was encountering someone unique. It's not often that one escapes to a mountain to hear the words of a master of solitude. Such men usually remain out of sight, living as they do in a more luminous realm. We often journey to their ashrams in India in the hope of becoming one of their disciples. But in Lazarus's case, I was fortunate enough to discover a man from a background similar to mine—who, moreover, had deliberately chosen to forsake the tumult of modern life. I now recognized him to be a deeper echo of me. Yet he provoked a question I had never asked before: Was it possible, even in this fractious age, to embark on an ascetic life?

I couldn't escape its inference, however: that I had failed to heed the call of the spirit, except as some exotic aftertaste no different from a new suit or the latest recording of my favorite artist. In contrast, Lazarus's gesture of abandonment struck a chord in me. He had deliberately chosen to exile himself from the febrile structures of today's existence. Just as Anthony's "inner mountain" became less a place than a way of thinking, so did Lazarus's retirement to the desert to be near his hero's cave. He wanted to duplicate the saint's age-old encounter with what he had called "the still state of his soul."[4]

By good fortune, I found myself in the presence of someone who actually considered his soul to be an important field of investigation. It seemed hard to believe. Only a few days earlier, I had flown into an overcrowded airport and later stood in a smoke-filled bus shelter in a city mired in gridlock, breathing in my fair share of fumes, waiting for a bus to take me to Suez. I wondered then whether this were not hell. What sustained me was the hope that out there in the Eastern Desert somewhere, in a remote spot girded by stones, I might meet a man like Lazarus. Why? I don't quite know. Perhaps I wanted to believe that his existence might be sufficient cure against this contagion. Lazarus represented the last line of defense in the battle against meaninglessness. I had read somewhere that true spirit resides only in discovering for oneself the simplicity and nakedness of being. Right at this moment I probably felt too well dressed.

But why would one want to live in a desert? It was the question I asked myself as I gazed into the wadi below. Lazarus had made his choice, just as Anthony had made his seventeen centuries earlier. These men, and others like them, had decided that only in a full and irrevocable break with their past could they begin the slow process of recovery. They were men on a mission, it seems: to integrate what they perceived to be their own aridity with that of the desert. The Greeks described such an event as *akrothtes isothtes*, meaning "when extremes meet." Two aspects of dryness, the physical and the spiritual, are drawn to one another by a powerful attraction that confirms their natural magnetism. The Sahara of the mind was a perfect place to retire to in order to do battle with these forces.

The truth was that I considered myself to be living in a half world. Lazarus must have felt so, too, when he wandered aimlessly down that Melbourne street all those years ago. *I don't know who or where I am, or what to do* was the cry he had heard from within. It was the voice of his own impotence confronting the least armed of opponents—that of his self charged with its own annihilation. Confronting such a threat, our first instinct is to escape. Martyrdom doesn't offer succor either, except to those who wear the hair shirt of belief. Like Lazarus on that fateful day outside the church in Melbourne, I was a victim of my own inability to believe or to understand.[5]

Now I had come to Mount Colzim, to the very heartland of the solitary life, in a bid to change all that. I sensed at once that I was overlooking a battleground. The helots of despair were already retreating in disarray. Chariots of light blazoned forth, their drivers flailing their horses. Who would have imagined that it was I who held victory in my own grasp? Certainly it hadn't occurred to me before my encounter with Lazarus. Mount Colzim was to have been merely another destination on the itinerary I had planned for myself in order to escape boredom. What afflicted me most was the thought that *I did not have the courage to believe.*

I needed to understand the world that Lazarus had managed to recover from the shipwreck of Anthony's achievement. He probably believed that it had sunk without trace. Like him, I, too, needed to plunge deep into the life of this great ascetic in order to understand its meaning. This also meant that I needed to explore others like him who had escaped into all the deserts of the world in an effort to wrestle with their conscience. It is what makes them true athletes of the spirit. They had honed their bodies and minds into finely tuned instruments capable of detecting the faintest of spiritual vibrations. They had been men sensitive to what Evagrius Ponticus regarded as the richest of goals—the moment when the spirit begins to "see its own light."[6]

I made a pact with Lazarus that day. If he would allow me to climb up to his cave from time to time, in return I would commit myself to studying the works of the Desert Fathers in the monastery library. When questions arose, he would attempt to answer them. When doubts invaded my deliberations, he would try to allay them. In this way we pledged ourselves to becoming like two "Sons of the Pact" in emulation of the so-called salted ones who allowed themselves to be seasoned by knowledge. Such men inhabited the desert of Syria as late as the seventh century in their attempt to attain a purity of heart.[7]

It was a unique challenge. I was aware of my own inadequacies. Meeting Lazarus, however, filled me with new confidence. Not only did he invite me to enter his cell and see his rudimentary living arrangements (a piece of foam bedding on the ground in one corner, a low table made from boxwood covered with books, a number of icons hanging from stones in the cave wall, bottles of water in another corner) but he also allowed me to climb onto another small terrace above the entrance to inspect the place where he prayed.

"Sometimes I crouch here in the lee of this rock when the wind blows hard, particularly in winter," he explained. "It protects me from being tossed into the valley."

I looked down at the precipitous drop into the valley. So this is what awaits an anchorite when he retires into the desert, I thought: none other than a prolonged and unwavering descent into himself.

I had come to Mount Colzim to find Anthony. I could have gone elsewhere, I suppose. In the end, I asked myself whether there was any place left on earth that still retained the savor of such a heroic encounter with absolutes. It could be said of these anchorites that endurance was a succession of stones they took it on themselves to carry. If this were so, their actions echoed what Meister Eckhart once said: "If my mouth speaks and declares God, so does the being of a stone." Rocks retain their own spiritual intensity, in spite of what theologians might argue. Obviously Anthony and his friends thought so too—or else why did they spend their lives hiding among them? They knew that wandering the world is little more than a long circling of a word. That word is *release*.

two

WELCOME, THE STRANGER

In spite of his reputation, Anthony is the most enigmatic of saints. Though there are a small number of letters attributed to him, these were likely written by his followers. He was born to Egyptian parents in a village in Middle Egypt called Coma, near Heracleopolis, around AD 251. His father and mother were Christians, and relatively wealthy, owning more than two hundred acres of rich farming land. We can presume, then, that he was not illiterate, though we know that he could not read Greek, as in later life a man named Cronius joined him as his loyal interpreter. His biographer, Athanasius, informs us that he "could not bear to learn letters." This did not mean that he was entirely ignorant, as in those days reading and writing were the preserve of the relatively few. We know, for example, that Socrates never wrote down his thoughts, and no one has ever suggested that this man lacked discernment.

In his youth Anthony probably worked the land with his father and a few servants. The annual inundation of the Nile, the "ineluctable discipline of the water," would have been the determining event in the life of farmers like him, as it has been until quite recently. The harvest over, he often went to church, where he listened attentively to the sermons. Abstemious by nature, he spurned luxuries and excessive food. What we do know is that he enjoyed home life more than most. In fact, if one reads between the lines of Athanasius, he may have been what we know today as a mother's boy. Certainly he spent very little time playing with friends. One gains the impression that Anthony was already deeply conversant with *parresia*, a certain intimacy with God.

When Anthony was near the age of eighteen, both his parents died within a short space of time. Anthony was left with a young sister to care for and a fairly large holding of land to oversee. Under normal circumstances such an event would have been considered not unusual, given the precarious nature of life in those days. But rather than knuckle down to his duties, Anthony seemed to bear his grief longer and more intensely than most. He attended church frequently, while at the same time wandering alone through his fields deep in thought. Something was troubling him. He became obsessed with what he perceived to be the courage shown by the apostles, who forsook all that they owned to follow in the footsteps of Christ. They had given up everything in pursuit of the dream of transcendent life. This made him consider his own predicament, burdened as he was with property and the premature responsibilities of parenthood.

Athanasius vividly describes the next event in Anthony's life:

He entered the church pondering these things. Just then it happened that someone was reading from the Gospels, and he heard the Lord saying to a rich man *If you be perfect go sell what you possess and give to the poor, and you will have treasure in heaven* [Matt. 19:21]. It was as if by God's design that he held the saints in his recollection, and as if the passage was read on his account. Immediately Anthony went out from the Lord's house and gave to the townspeople the possessions left to him by his parents, so that they could not disturb him or his sister in the least. And, selling all the rest that was portable, when he collected sufficient money, he donated it to the poor, keeping a few things for his sister.[1]

The die was cast. Anthony had engaged in his first act of *anachoresis*, of social disengagement.

This is not so revolutionary as it sounds. Egypt of the mid to late third century was in a time of transition. Late Roman mores had created a climate of acute social tension brought on by increasing tax demands and religious upheaval. The old gods of pharaonic Egypt were still in evidence; philosophers such as Plotinus, Porphyry, and Iamblichus were plying their trade in Alexandria; and the early Christian bishops were busily engaged in doing battle with heresies such as Arianism and Gnosticism. At the same time, the smaller peasant-proprietors were struggling to make a living under a burden of taxation that applied to the village as a whole. Thus, when an individual like Anthony might have hoped to "go it alone" more than in the past, perhaps, he found the tensions and frictions of communal living being asserted in a particularly abrasive manner. We can feel this tension at work when Athanasius wrote in the text just cited, "so that they [his fellow villagers] could not disturb him or his sister in the least." One senses that Anthony wanted to disentangle himself from the oppressive nature of village life.

Thus disengagement, *anachoresis* (Gr., "to withdraw"), may well have been a reaction by Egyptian farmers to a difficult position. Of course, it may have been possible to move to another village in the hope of disengaging oneself. A desire to turn inward, to disassociate himself from his neighbors, is evident in the story of Aurelius Isidore, a near contemporary, who was also a comfortable farmer of the new style. Though he was illiterate, he nonetheless possessed a handsome collection of legal documents and complaints in his own interest, and his holdings had increased from 299 to 310 *arourae* (213 acres). Throughout his career he weathered the storms of village life by a canny insistence on noninvolvement. He was, he insisted "a man of means." When his house was attacked in 316 by a mob, he knew exactly how to protect himself: "Although I possess a good deal of land and am occupied with its cultivation, I am not involved with any person in the village, but keep to myself."[2] Here we see the seed of Anthony's bid to break with his predicament. While Isadore's *anachoresis* was a political withdrawal, we note how close to the surface noninvolvement lay. Though Anthony may have found an ideal justification for his action in the behavior of the apostles, we sense that there were other motives behind his desire to sell up and retire from village life.

Heeding the injunction of yet another reading in church one day, in which Christ said, *Do not be anxious about tomorrow*,[3] Anthony's mind was finally made up. He gave away his remaining possessions, placed his sister in the care of friends noted for their propriety, then retired to a hut outside his village. He had turned the political act of noninvolvement into an audacious, elemental, and purifying move. He had given up his social entity in favor of something less tangible. What possessed him to do so? What fundamental disillusionment, and at such a youthful age, urged him to break with his sister, his few friends, his village, and ultimately with his era? This is the question that drove me to want to visit the place known as

Mount Colzim, which in later life Anthony chose to call his inner mountain.

But I am drawing ahead of my story. During the next few years Anthony sought out fellow recluses who lived in the district. At one point he took up residence with an older man outside a nearby village who taught him his first lessons in ascetic technique. The old man was Anthony's first *geronte*, or spiritual advisor. From him he learned how to fast, how to pray, how to suppress mental discursiveness. It was at this point that he recognized that his mind was an anvil on which some sort of instrument of discernment needed to be hammered out. In Athanasius's words, Anthony did not return to his hut without receiving from the man "certain supplies for travelling the road to virtue." Clearly other men besides Anthony were engaged in ascetic practice, because we know from Athanasius that Anthony's *geronte* had lived the solitary life since his youth. Anchoritism, therefore, was very much a statement of rebellion not unlike the hippie movement of the 1960s.

The ensuing years saw Anthony deepen his commitment to the spiritual life. We see him wandering about the towns and villages of the region looking for different *gerontes* from whom he might learn. He had given himself over to a life of spiritual vagabondage, the life of the "stranger." It was the classic program of the holy man in antiquity that, by a long drawn-out and solemn ritual of dissociation, he was able to transform himself into the total stranger. The holy man was he who stood outside the ties of family and economic self-interest. In late classical times his type was known as *Theos Anir*, the "divine man," usually because he was able to perform miracles.[4] This is a superficial allusion, for these men usually drew on a bottomless well of occult wisdom to bolster their power in the community, whereas a man like Anthony drew his power from outside the human condition—namely, from Christ's supernatural life. Nonetheless, he and his fellow

anchorites did conform to a type. They wanted to test the boundaries of being nonhuman in order to see whether this newly realized being might offer some solution to the progressive
materialization of society. The holy man, the "stranger," therefore,
was a man who lived beyond the boundary of society and thus
was able to offer to many an alternative to the drudgery and seem-
ing aridity of material existence.

The truth was that men like Anthony usurped the position of
the oracles in late antiquity. Because they couldn't be appropriated
by any one section of society, including the emperor or the Church,
they were effectively able to act as mediators when required. Palladius, for example, spoke of how Anthony was often called on to arbitrate decisions on behalf of secular authorities.[5] The difference
between a Christian holy man and his pagan counterpart lay in the
fact that the former achieved his position as a stranger without being possessed by a god. The old *prophetus* tended to be dissociated
from his fellows by a loss of identity in the way that shamans often
are, whereas the Christian holy man never used trance techniques to
accomplish his goal. His objectivity as an arbitrator was drawn from
a lifetime of ascetic practice that made him, in a sense, "superhuman"
in the eyes of his followers. Moreover, his intimacy with God (*parresia*) assured him of a significant role in—or at least outside—society.
A holy man could often engage a crowd in a way that a classical
philosopher could not.[6]

Parresia was power to these Christian holy men, not unlike the
Islamic concept of *baraka*. Bishops and priests rarely possessed it.
They might wield the *mysterium tremendum* of the Eucharistic sacrifice, but the holy man, by his unassessable *parresia* with God, held
the keys to heaven. It was a spiritual power that flickered in and out
of the Church like Saint Elmo's fire. Anthony may have possessed it
from an early age, considering his willingness to associate with elderly holy men in his region, but we must assume that he could not

wield it with the same efficacy as he did when he, too, became an older man. With the decline of the oracles and the general loss of spiritual power among the old pharaonic gods, the rise of the holy man was inevitable. By acting out the role of the stranger, he was able to install himself as almost a "blessed object" in the midst of his fellows.

Anthony's early lessons in asceticism were confined to the discipline of his mind and his body. To accomplish this discipline, he first had to learn how to balance the needs of survival against those of contemplation. According to Athanasius, he "worked with his hands," which we know from other sources meant to weave baskets for sale in local markets or to passersby. The economics of basket weaving is interesting: if a man could reduce his needs by way of fasting and by living outside the Roman tax system, he could actually survive on weaving little more than two or three baskets a day. No wonder the holy man appealed to the common folk; he had shown them a way to throw off the shackles of secular oppression without in any way engaging in an act of overt sedition. *Apostasis*, the ascetic renunciation of the world, was soon regarded as not only a remedy against sin but also an act of liberation. Renunciation of all possessions was seen as essential to clearing away the psychological debris before a man could embark on the spiritual life. As Isaac of Nineveh said, "without renunciation of possessions, the soul cannot be liberated from the confusion of thought."[7] Anthony recognized that a "watchful life" entailed coming to terms with the carnal in himself: he knew, as Isaac did, that "in a full stomach there is no knowledge of the mysteries of God."[8]

Thus a holy man like Anthony was a professional in a world of amateurs. He alone could render safe the values of the Christian man of the world, the *kosmikos*, by allowing them to be absorbed into himself. For the piety of the average early Christian was essentially a piety of discontinuous moments of contrition. The holy man was able to allay anxiety and thus draw off the pain and guilt that lurked below the surface of collective consciousness. His blessing, or injunction against sinning, was tantamount to absolution. We know of a case of a patrician named Petronus who had been sleeping with a slave girl. He fell ill and turned to a holy man for advice. "Holy man, I am dying," he said. To which the holy man replied: "A Christian man does not die." "I am a Christian all right, but I have never behaved like a Christian. An evil-looking Ethiopian [devil] with a horrible expression on his face came up to me in a dream, and said: 'You are mine.'" After this interview with the holy man, Petronus enjoyed his first good night of sleep. And from that time onward the two men became inseparable. They even died on the same day.[9] In this way the holy man was able to draw up and place in the hands of the penitent a safe conduct to heaven.

From Athanasius we gain an idealized picture of Anthony's early anchoritic life outside his village. The Alexandrian, of course, had his agenda. Although he wrote his *Life of Anthony* some years after the man's death, he does say that he met the saint on a number of occasions. Clearly he wanted to protect the fragile doctrinal orthodoxy of the Church from the Arian controversy that threatened to undermine the essential mystery of Christ's being.[10] To propose Anthony's life as the archetype of the new spiritual life was to intimate a way of living that was entirely different from the old classical view of *arête*, human excellence, which found its inspiration in justice *(dike)*. This view finds an echo in Hesiod's insight that the order allotted by Zeus to mankind was to follow justice and shun violence: "for to fish and beasts and winged birds he gave the rule *(nomos)* that they eat one another, since there is no justice among them; but to human beings he gave justice." Heraclitus, a pre-Socratic philosopher, enlarged this concept when he suggested that justice is conflict (strife), thus placing humankind in a more passive relationship to the prospect of realizing inner freedom. What Anthony represented, at least to his biographer, was a man who had successfully transcended his humanity, at least sociologically, and become the quintessential stranger who lived the life of an angel.

But all this was in the future. Anthony meanwhile lived in his hut, dealing as best he could with the difficulties of spiritual growth and the attentions of the nearby villagers. He soon encountered the devil in the form of wayward memories of his lost possessions and his sister and the bonds of kinship, thoughts of money, glory, and the pleasures of food. Athanasius suggests that Anthony attempted to raise these in his mind as a "dust cloud of considerations" in the hope of cordoning off from himself his true intention. In reality, Anthony's resolve was faltering. How could he continue to live such an extreme and lonely life outside society? What was he trying to prove to himself? What advantage was there in subjecting himself to such austere demands of asceticism? It seemed that the intellectual life of the soul wasn't worth all this hardship.

Anthony's dilemma was the conventional dilemma of the outsider. He had set himself up as a paragon of *antisociability* without being sure of its consequences. Self-control may have waged a war against excess in the interest of a more dynamic *arête*, but it was too early in his career for him to know whether he had achieved anything permanent. The devil might appear to him in the form of lust, gluttony, dejection, or boredom, yet even he was aware that such prevarication was merely shadow play. It was the manifestation of a "blackness of the mind" that could be overthrown only by particular acts of ascesis—those of fasting, going without sleep, and above all, engaging in prayer.[11] This was the behavior of a new kind of man not seen before, a man who engaged in spiritual warfare not out of defiance of his bodily demands but in defense of the soul's intensity.

Athanasius, of course, attempted to plot Anthony's career as being a struggle between the devil and his own demons. He saw the man more or less acting out a part in a theater of aridity that was both physical (that is, the desert) and spiritual. His performance was two-dimensional: a vertical one as defined by the relation between heaven and earth, and horizontal as reflected in the relation between the settled land of Egypt and its problematic cousin, the desert. In this context the devil's territory was clearly the desert. Anthony's incursion into it later in his life unleashed a battle of no mean order that brought into stark contrast the prospect of achieving heavenly ascent—or its converse, infernal damnation. Athanasius saw his man as a unique kind of hero capable of opening up the Pandora's box of his age, thus making it possible to come to terms with centuries of psychological anguish that had been suppressed by paganism. Doing battle with the devil was no metaphor; it was the foremost engagement that any man of *arête* could hope for.

Ecstatic contemplation became the new weapon. Unlike the shaman, who removed himself from his body in order to become a seer, Anthony did so in order to contemplate himself. His powers of discernment were turned inward toward the primary object of his quest, the revelation of his soul. He wanted to banish the forces of negation that pinioned him, like Gulliver, to materiality and the constraints of identity. We are left with a vivid picture of this encounter, a picture that has become permanently lodged in the European psyche through the works of artists such as Hieronymus Bosch, Grünewald, Veronese, and even Max Ernst. The apocalyptic imagery of the temptations of Saint Anthony comes to us via

Athanasius, who gave us a detailed account of one of the saint's experiences:

> Once when he was about to eat, rising to pray about the ninth hour, he felt himself carried off in thought, and the wonder was that while standing there he saw himself, *as if he were outside himself*, and as if he were being led through the air by certain beings. Next he saw some foul and terrible figures standing in the air, intent on holding him back so that he could not pass by. When his guides [protective spirits] accosted them, they [the demonic spirits] demanded to know the reason why he was not answerable to them. And when they asked for an account of his life from the time of his birth, Anthony's guides prevented it, saying, "The Lord has wiped clean the items dating from his birth, but from the time he became a monk, and devoted himself to God, you can take account." Then as they [the demons] levelled accusations and failed to prove them, a passage opened before him free and unobstructed. Just then he saw himself *appear to come and stand with himself*, and once more he was Anthony, as before.

I have italicized certain phrases in this remarkable passage be-cause they suggest a psychological dimension that we do not often grant to antiquity. What we see here is a man engaging in a genuine ecstatic experience that removes him from his body. At the same time he finds himself encountering deep spiritual and psychological trauma that might well be collective as well as personal. Indeed, it would seem that Anthony's ascetic technique has taught him how to free himself from those irrational elements that tend to make a man conform to a type. By "stepping outside himself," Anthony points the way to a new kind of self-analysis, one that is determined by spiritual rather than personal considerations. The demons of diminution are those that want to hark back to a time *before* he had mounted guard over himself. In this sense we are seeing a man deliberately setting out to reinvent himself. The old Anthony, the Anthony of the village, of ties and attachments, of disappointment and grief at his parents' untimely death, had been refashioned in the guise of one who is prepared to lay bare his weaknesses and faults *to himself* in order that he might dismiss the influence of the demons. It is conventional aversion therapy put to a more ingenious test: the renovation of man's spiritual being here on earth.

The desert, then, would become his testing ground. But in those early years Anthony contented himself with living in the vicinity of the village. He was not yet ready to part company with *civitas*, that solace of the established order. But a time came when he finally knew that he must make the next step and enter, quite literally, the dark night of the soul. At this point he left his hut outside the village in order to take up residence in an ancient Egyptian tomb that he had discovered. Locking himself inside, in darkness, he charged a few friends to supply him with food from time to time. His spiritual incarceration was now complete. Anthony had entirely removed himself from the world. His only company now was the legion of his thoughts, desires, and aborted expectations.

What occurred in that tomb was a further demonstration of Anthony's commitment to defeat, once and for all, the wily imprecations of the old Adam. The demons returned, this time with a vengeance. As Athanasius tells it, "they whipped him with such force that he lay on the earth, speechless from the tortures."[12] The blows were so severe that he thought that humans had dealt them. One can picture the man, old beyond his years, possibly with early flecks of gray in his hair, lying on the floor of his tomb, surrounded by crusts of bread and the detritus of past occupants (the dead in Egypt were always well cared for), confronting the anguish of his soul as the most bitter of opponents. Today it seems inconceivable that anyone might want to retire into a tomb in order to confront one's weakness and faults. Yet Anthony did so—and more. For it is clear that those "demons in the air" were much more than incarnations of private affliction; they were the very embodiment of his existential fear of death, and the moral paralysis that results from that fear.

It is at this point that Anthony's actions take on a new, more radical meaning. Not only had he become the "lonely man" par excellence, but his decision to live in a tomb (as later in his cave in the desert) gave reality to a long tradition of speculation on the lost simplicity of Adam. His withdrawal had taken place in a world that was exceptionally sensitive to its *social* meaning. The tension that existed between man and man had finally been annulled by his extraordinary ascetic encounter with the devil. Moreover, his power and prestige were realized in acting out, heroically, before a society enmeshed in oppressive obligations and abrasive relationships, the role of an utterly self-sufficient, autarkic man. Anthony had attained to a "vertical" existence that most men only dream about. The air may have been thick with evil spirits, but he, the lonely man, was prepared to fight them on behalf of everyone.

This battle is highlighted by the way his friend found him when he came to deliver bread at the tomb one day. He found him "as if lying dead on the ground." He picked up the insensate Anthony and carried him to the local church, where he laid him on the floor. "Many of his relatives [his sister perhaps?] and the people of the village stationed themselves beside Anthony, as if beside a corpse." Truly the man was dead to the world. It was only around midnight that he came to his senses and "seeing everyone sleeping, and only his friend keeping watch, [he] beckoned to him to lift him again and carry him to the tomb, awaking no one." One hears echoes of the risen Christ and the sleeping guards outside his tomb. Already one senses a desire on the part of Athanasius to identify his hero with the Suffering One.[13]

In his tomb once again, Anthony confronts the whole phantasmagoria of images that were a part of the repertoire of any Egyptian. After all, they had seen them painted on the walls of the tombs of their forebears since time immemorial. Lions, bears, leopards, bulls, serpents, asps, scorpions, and wolves accosted him, moving "according to their form":

> The lion roared, wanting to spring at him; the bull seemed intent on goring him; the creeping snake did not quite reach him; the onrushing wolf made straight for him—and altogether the sounds of all the creatures that appeared were terrible, and their ragings were fierce. Struck and wounded by them, Anthony's body was subject to yet more pain. But *unmoved and even more watchful in his soul* he lay there, and he groaned because of the pain he felt in his body, but being in control of his thoughts and as if mocking them, he said, "If there were some power among you, it would have been enough for only one of you to come. . . . It is a mark of your weakness that you mimic the shapes of irrational beasts."

It is hard to imagine such a devilish encounter. All the animals of the *Egyptian Book of the Dead* had come forth to taunt Anthony. He lay there in his cell afflicted by the wildness of nature and the ravenous, insatiable demands of his own passions, as surely this is what these creatures represented. The darkness of the tomb was the breeding ground for a new kind of insouciance—that of someone who had not only died a social death but was also prepared to confront and overcome the untamed nature of himself. Self-imposed sensory deprivation further produced such extreme emotional states that hallucinations were deliberately courted. It is evident, too, that Anthony's ascetic preoccupation with the demonic was merely the dark side of the third-century emphasis on the protecting spirit as an upward extension of the self. Anthony's personality wavered between the stable guardianship of Christ, and of his protecting angel, and the unstable, incoherent forces of the demonic.

At a critical stage in this crisis (shall we say, of identity?), Anthony, too weak to stand, cried out from the floor of his tomb: "Here I am—Anthony!" It is the statement of autarkic man, the man on the edge of existence fighting to remain outside yet "in" the world. His relationship with the demons involves something far more intimate than attack from the outside: to be tried by demons meant passing through a stage in the growth of consciousness that exists on the lower frontiers of personality. The demonic stood not only for all that was hostile *to* man but also for what was anomalous and incomplete *in* man. It was as if the demons, as incomplete creatures, sought completeness through complicity with Anthony. As Heraclitus remarked, "The fairest order in the world [may be derived from] a heap of random sweepings."[14] To understand and to reject the demonic was an act of self-exorcism analogous to the symbolic achievement of "simplicity." Complicity with negation was one of the first rules of apophatic behavior, and one of the goals of asceticism. The pursuit of nothingness made it possible to attain to a pure state of self-awareness.

In the end, after his initial period of seclusion, Anthony did receive some kind of vision. It came in the form of a "beam of light" (*aktina photos*) that descended on him through the open roof of his tomb. "Suddenly the demons vanished from view, the pain of his body ceased instantly, and the tomb was once more intact," wrote Athanasius. The vision spoke to Anthony, congratulating him on his victory over the forces of negation and promising to aid and comfort him in the future. "I will make you famous everywhere," the voice announced, thus heralding the beginning of his fame as the greatest ascetic of his age. According to Athanasius, he was about thirty-five years old at the time.

Anthony finally quit his tomb and returned to visit his spiritual advisor, hoping that the old man might come with him into the desert. But the old man refused, citing his advanced age. It seems strange that Anthony might wish for company after spending so long alone in his tomb. Was he anxious about his next move toward what he called the inner mountain? All we know is that he continued on his way accompanied by his constant companion, the devil. As he walked he noticed a silver dish by the roadside. To pick it up, he knew, would invite destruction, just as would the discovery of some pieces of gold farther on. Wherever he went he found himself "stepping over fire" in his bid to remain steadfast. Finally, after wandering for days, he came on an abandoned fortress by the Nile, where he took up residence. That was to be his last place of abode in the realm of men, though he lived there nearly twenty years.

It is hard to know, or to understand, quite what went on in this place. By now Anthony has undergone such a change from being a wealthy farm boy to being a half-crazed solitary living like an animal among the ruins of past civilizations that it is difficult to recognize him. To try to visualize him is to resort to all those images we possess of men living in extremis. But in the end we must be more circumspect: Anthony set out to do no more than create a new identity for himself. His prolonged introspection only increased his relationship with the supernatural. At the same time, he has given us a tantalizing glimpse at what must have been a desirable consequence of the ascetic life: the closing of the divide between the human and the divine. Moreover, the power gained from this knowledge was not to be used in the way of the old-style miracle worker. By withholding it, Anthony was able to enhance his own standing as an anchorite.[15]

The great silver dish of material seduction was finally put behind him. It did not mean that the demons had been defeated, merely that their attempts to destroy his will had become transparent. His final bout with them in the fortress was to take on a more intimate form, that of hand-to-hand fighting augmented by argument. Athanasius described the demons as "a clamoring mob" that emitted pitiful sounds even as they tried to turn him back from his endeavor. "'Get away from what is ours!' they cried. 'What do you have to do with the desert?'"[16] The real issue between him and the demons was out in the open at last: Anthony wished to invade and reclaim the devil's territory in the name of Christ. It was an offensive maneuver on his part in order to transform the desert into a "land of devotion and justice," thus making it into a heavenly commonwealth where all the mores of contemporary society might be inverted. Carelessness and conceit would be annihilated by the love of virtue, for example. The desert embodied all that was malevolent in human nature; to invade it was to *invade the self*. A man did not escape to the desert to find identity but to lose it, to eradicate his personality, to become anonymous. In a sense he made of himself the void, becoming in the process an embodiment of silence.

What Anthony had done at this point was propose an alternative to civic life that involved withdrawal, renunciation, and the reestablishment of a proper relationship between body and soul. The ancient philosophers of Greece may have discussed such a concept several hundred years earlier, but since then it had fallen into abeyance. Normal human society was governed by sex, food, and wealth. If a society of piety and justice were to be inaugurated, then these demons needed to be overcome. The desert of human nature had to be nourished, and to do this Anthony proposed a radical solution. He proposed that one set up

camp in the devil's domain, in the very heartland of human neg-
ativity and failure, and so reclaim it for gnosial man, the man of
knowledge. If one were to "breath Christ," then one had to possess a certain kind of knowledge that Anthony identified with
self-knowledge. In this context he wrote in one of the few letters
that have come down to us: "I write to you as men of understanding who are able to know yourselves: you know that he who
knows himself knows God."[17] One now sees that the desert represented a place of knowing all but denied to normal society. It
was, to use Meister Eckhart's haunting words, the "inner ground"
of spiritual experience. Only there could the wind of the spirit
begin to blow.

Anthony lived for nearly twenty years in the fortress by the
Nile. Friends visited him periodically to deliver bread, but otherwise he had little or no contact with men except the occasional
pilgrim. What went on in that hole in the wall is one of the great
mysteries of early Christianity. We may speculate on it, of course,
or draw sustenance from the words of Athanasius, but in the end
we are left with a question mark. The ascetic life is so remote
from us now that we wonder how a man could survive such a fa-
natical regime. The body reduced to skin and bone, the hair and
beard hanging down to the waist, the eyes so penetrating that
only madness seems to lie behind them—these are the images
that we retain. The truth is that we are so removed from the idea
of self-inflicted want that we would prefer to see insanity as a
probable excuse for Anthony's behavior rather than consider the
true reason behind such an existence. In the end, we have no idea
of what to expect from prolonged ascetic endeavor. It is a mystery
to us.

"Yet when his friends came and forcibly tore down the fortress
door," Athanasius wrote of his appearance to the world,

Anthony came forth as though from some shrine, having been led into divine mysteries and inspired by God. . . . And when they beheld him, they were amazed to see that his body had maintained its former condition, neither fat from lack of exercise, nor emaciated from fasting and combat with demons, but he was just as they had known him before his withdrawal. The state of his soul was one of purity, for it was not constricted by grief, nor relaxed by pleasure, nor affected by either laughter or dejection. . . . He maintained utter equilibrium, like one guided by reason and steadfast in that which accords with nature.

Here, then, was a man fashioned by nearly thirty-five years of ascetic practice, a man in whom a certain luminosity and perfection were already in evidence. The old image of the crazed starker had been put to rest. Anthony had transformed himself into a living image of Christ.

The war was over, at least for the moment. The stranger had come home to his people. Moreover, he had shown how it was possible to engage in spiritual warfare and survive. This fact alone inaugurated a new era in a man's relationship with himself. Anthony's example persuaded many to take up the solitary life. "And so, from then on, there were monasteries in the mountains," Athanasius wrote, "and the desert was made into a city by monks, who left their own people and registered themselves for citizenship in the heavens."[18] A new society was born: one that owed its allegiance to no man save he who was prepared to dedicate himself to cultivating the blue flower of ascesis.

three

LIFE OF AN ANCHORITE

Solitary confinement in a cave was not an activity invented by Anthony. Pagan Egypt was familiar with the idea of withdrawal from society in order to practice meditation. Men known as *katochoi* ("to be withdrawn" and "inspired") were priests in the service of the god Serapis, where they lived inside the great temple of Memphis—the Serapeum—never seeing the light of day. Though there is no direct link between *katochoi* and desert anchorites, one can assume that Egyptians understood why men chose to withdraw from the world. Their obsession with eternity and their concern to preserve the physical and spiritual integrity of man made caves and hypogea necessary adjuncts to a life that is dark, still, and silent.

Asceticism therefore was designed to invoke a condition of "living death." For a man to approach this frontier intimating the beyond, it became possible to penetrate its secrets and come near to a hidden understanding. To arrive at the brink of death was to enter a domain whereby one could re-cognize death. René Daumal, a French scholar and Orientalist, attempted to do so in 1924 by conducting a series of experiments on himself with tetrachloride. "I decided to confront the problem of death itself: I would put my body in as close a state as possible to physiological death, but would concentrate my attention on staying awake and recording all that presented itself to me."[1] Daumal wanted to arrive at death's door ready to ascertain what lay beyond the limits of conscious life. Unlike Anthony, however, he did not experience beatitude or the realization of an eternal moment—rather, the opposite. "I saw, with glaring certainty, that I was irrevocably lost, that I was nothing more than *a very simple vicious circle*." For Daumal, the metaphysical reality of death was not to offer him those insights familiar to the priests of the Serapeum or to Anthony. His "vicious circle" and Anthony's state of *parresia* were to remain diametrically opposed.

Thus the cave was always going to be the abode of the anchorite, and become in the process the prototypal Christian monastery. Lucian of Samosata described a pagan Egyptian sage called Pancrates in the second century in his *Philopseudes* as "a great scholar, versed in all the Egyptian doctrines, who had stayed for twenty-three years in an underground cave where he had been initiated by Isis into the mysteries of magic." The cave became the home of introspection where a psycho-spiritual transformation was able to take place. The Christian anchorite, in particular those who were Egyptian, would have naturally resorted to such time-honored techniques of ascetic behavior. They would have retired into the desert in the hope of realizing in themselves the *Theos Anir*, or divine man, certain that this condition might be achieved after overcoming the perennial demons of the self.

Pre-Christian monks were also said to have lived in caves among cliffs by the Dead Sea in Palestine. A mysterious sect mentioned by Philo Judaeus known as the Essenes practiced in this region. Pliny speaks of "a solitary people, stranger than any other, living without womenfolk, without love, without money, their only companions being the palm trees, their only means of survival the daily arrival of new converts." According to the historian, these men elected to live on the western shore of the Dead Sea, north of the oasis of En-Gedi, as a community of men who had taken a vow of celibacy, poverty, and solitude. It was these vows that became the bedrock of early Christian monasticism. Though Jewish, the Essene communities provided a ready model for the development of early Christian monasticism in Egypt under the guidance of Pachomius and Shenute.

We know of a monk called Chariton who founded the laura of Faran in the Wadi Far, a few miles from Jerusalem. He later fled to a spot outside Jericho in order to escape the hordes of visitors who wanted to meet with him. Anchorites throughout the fifth and sixth centuries who built lauras and monasteries in the Judaean deserts followed his example. The most famous of these have left their presence in the records as names of their respective monasteries: Gerasimo at el-Qalamun, John the Qozibite at Wadi Qilt, and Theodosius the Coenobiarch at Der Dosy. The most eminent of them were Euthymius and Saba, both Cappadocians, who played very different roles in the history of monasticism. Euthymius was the missionary of eremitism, while Saba became its organizing genius.

Equally, there were men who wanted to go further in their demonstration of ascetic endeavor. Perhaps the most famous of all was Simeon Stylites the Elder, a Syrian ascetic of the fourth century who chose to live much of his life on the top of a pillar near Antioch. Simeon lived thirty-seven years on his column, not once quitting it other than to climb onto a taller one! Over the years the height was extended from six cubits to twelve, then twenty-two, and finally thirty-six cubits (approximately fifty-four feet). It was at this last height that he lived for thirty years, standing upright without any shelter from the inclemency of the weather, dressed with no thought for the changes of season or temperature. This was a man who had taken spiritual elevation quite literally. His fame spread far and wide, and we hear of his name mentioned by Gregory of Tours in the middle of the sixth century in relation to a monk who introduced stylitism to the Ardennes in France. Unfortunately the would-be stylite nearly froze to death in winter: "I was so frozen by the freezing wind that my toe-nails fell out and icicles hung from my beard," he later wrote.[2]

Those early monasteries and lauras were created to formalize the ascetic life into a collective and collaborative routine able to be practiced by a larger body of men. John Cassian introduced it to Europe in the fifth century after making a pilgrimage to the Thebaid in Egypt. He, like Saint Jerome and Athanasius before him, had been deeply impressed by the fervor of the early anchorites. But he also recognized the difficulty of living the full anchoritic life in Europe, where the weather made it impossible to enact a solitary program without the support of others. In any event the Pachomian rule of cenobitic living—that is, communal activity—was far more appropriate to the European mentality. Cassian's writings, however, reflect a deep sympathy with the hermit's life in the desert, and he wanted to incorporate Pachomian's rule into that of monastic life through prescribed periods of silence and meditation interspersed with work activity. One is able to detect his enthusiasm for the desert life in his *Conferences of the Egyptian Monks*, written as a guide to monks on his return to France in 426:

When I was in the desert of Scete, where are the most
excellent monastic fathers and where all perfection flourishes,
in company with the holy father Germanus, I sought out
Abbot Moses, who was eminent amid those splendid flowers,
not only in practical but also in contemplative excellence, in
my anxiety to be grounded by his instruction: and together
we implored him to give us a discourse for our edification; not
without tears, for we knew full well his determination never
to consent to open the gate of perfection, except to those who
desired it with all faithfulness, and sought it with all sorrow of
heart; for fear lest if he showed it at random to those who
cared nothing for it, or only desired it in a half-hearted way,
by opening what is necessary, and what ought only to be
discovered to those seeking perfection, to unworthy persons,
and such as accepted it with scorn, he might appear to lay
himself open either to the charge of bragging, or to the sin of
betraying his trust; and at last being overcome by our prayers
he thus began.

Though monasteries did begin to spread throughout Europe after the fifth century, cenobitic life flowered more readily in the East,
in countries such as Syria, Iraq, Palestine, and Greece. Nestorian
monasticism flourished all over northern Syria, spreading into Cili-
cia and Mesopotamia, becoming in the process a rival to the Byzantine church in Constantinople. By the eighth century the Nestorian
church had reached Central Asia, Tibet, India, and China, bringing
to the Orient for the first time the legacy of classical literature. By
the tenth century Nestorian monasticism stretched from the
mountainous massif between the Tigris and Lake Urmiah, and
from Hakkâri to the Great Zab, thus forming the boundary of
Kurdistan.

Mar Awgin (Saint Eugene), a pearl fisher from the island of Clysma by Suez, was said to have founded the monastery on Mount Izla, to the south of Nisibis, after serving his novitiate in Pachomius's monastery in Egypt. He journeyed there with seventy-two disciples.[3] Though likely a fabrication, it tells us how important it was for Eastern monasticism to maintain links with the tradition of the Egyptian hermits. Unlike many of the Egyptian anchorites, who spurned learning, the Nestorians forbade entry to the monastery by a would-be monk unless he could read and write. This meant that the libraries of the cenobia were always well stocked with books of scripture or liturgy, generally bound in rich ornamental leather. This was an age of great intellectual curiosity, which in turn spawned the likes of Isaac of Nineveh, Babai the Great, Dadisho', and Joseph Hazzaya, some of whom will be met in these pages.

Nestorian spirituality, of course, was totally different from the practical spirituality of primitive monasticism in Egypt. Its source and roots lay in Christian Hellenism, whose most important representatives were Clement of Alexandria and Origen. It was these thinkers who gave knowledge of gnosis as man's highest aim. Evagrius Ponticus, however, managed to remove all taint of Origenism from Christian doctrine, and so made it palatable for Eastern Christianity.[4] The monks were then able to pursue this new doctrine to such extremes that they felt that a so-called Gnostic should have knowledge that ensured the removal of all barriers between subject and object by way of ecstatic visions. Discursive thought faded into oblivion, thus allowing an immediate contact between the knower and known.

Mount Athos in northern Greece is perhaps the preeminent exponent of monasticism in the Christian East. Founded, at least officially, in the late ninth century by a group of monks fleeing from Constantinople at a time when the use of icons was considered anathema, the first hermits on the mountain formed communities, initially in caves and then later in lauras or hermitages. Athanasius the Athonite, with the help of Emperor Nikephoros Phokas, his friend, founded the Great Lavra, the oldest monastery on Mount Athos, in 963. By 972 the first ritual had been edited and promulgated to the communities on a goatskin called *Tragos*. This ritual recognized an independent monastic state consisting of *kellia* (hermitages) and lauras (communities) as well as cenobitic monasteries. Thus men could live either alone as hermits, in a loosely knit community that permitted individual ownership of property (idiorrhythmic), or communally (cenobitic), thereby perpetuating the ideals first formulated by Anthony at Mount Colzim. Today there are twenty monasteries left on Mount Athos practicing idiorrhythmic or cenobitic living, as well as a number of hermitages.

Monastic life was central to early Christianity. The supernatural essence of Christian life was nurtured within the confines of its walls. In many ways the monastery replaced martyrdom as a method of exclusion from secular reality. The monastic tendency grew out of a need to preserve the high evangelical idealism of the primitive church, which by the fifth century was in decline. A desire to renounce the world permeated ancient society, even as early as Pythagoras. What Anthony and his successors did was find a way to create an "eschatological" environment in which they could exist as servants of Christ. Monasticism became a reminder that while the pledge and source of a new life may have been the Eucharist and the grace it bestowed, acceptance of it was still an act of a free man. Solitary asceticism was a self-imposed discipline designed to demonstrate certain absolute demands on the conscience of those whom it sanctified.

The ascetic, protected by monastic life, becomes the "salt" that prevents the world from sweetening Christianity and so making it subject to itself. By withdrawing into the desert he acts as an eternal reminder that some images simply do not pass. His face, unique in appearance, tested by experience and confirmed by thousands of examples, towers over the whole Christian world and illuminates it. Emaciated by fasting, vigil, and asceticism, washed by tears of repentance and illumined by spiritual vision, he represents the body transformed into spirit, superior even to that of angels.⁵ The ascetic's task therefore, by living outside the world, is to exemplify angelic behavior for everyone. He becomes the archetype of *Theos Anir*, the perfect man.

These ideas, first promulgated by Anthony at Mount Colzim, found their most profound exponent in Dionysius the Areopagite. We know nothing of the man except that he was possibly a Syrian monk of the late fifth century with a deep understanding of Platonic thought. Some argue that Dionysius may have been the philosopher Proclus (d. ca. 486) in disguise, though this is unlikely. But we can say that many of his ideas have an affinity with those of Plotinus and even with the ancient philosophies of India. After his works first came to public notice in 533 at a council held in Constantinople, his mystical teachings quickly spread throughout the Eastern and Western churches. Erigena's Latin translation of *The Divine Names* in the ninth century was eagerly welcomed in places as far away as England, where one chronicler wrote, "*The Mystical Divinity* ran across England like deer." Thomas Aquinas read him avidly, as did the Flemish recluse John of Ruysbroeck. In the twelfth century, Abbot Suger of Saint-Denis outside Paris readily acknowledged his debt to Dionysius when it came to designing the first Gothic cathedral in Christendom.

It is not easy to encapsulate the complex theogeny of Dionysius. His notion of divine darkness, for example, argues that knowledge of God can be attained only by going beyond every visible and intelligible object. It is through ignorance (*agnosia*) that we know the one who is above all that can be an object of knowledge. It is not divine gnosis that is the supreme end but the union that surpasses all knowledge. For Dionysius, *theoria* (knowledge) is not the summit of the climb toward God; rather, we grasp the unknowable nature of God in ignorance, by detaching ourselves from all his manifestations and theophanies. This is the divine darkness and represents an understanding that surpasses every level of intelligence:

> For even as things are intellectually discerned cannot be comprehended or perceived by means of those things which belong to the senses, nor simple and imageless things by means of types and images, nor the formless and intangible essence of unembodied things by means of those which have bodily form, by the same law of truth the boundless Super-Essence surpasses Intelligences, the One that is beyond thought surpasses the apprehension of thought, and the Good that is beyond utterance surpasses the reach of words.[6]

Clearly we are dealing here with a graded reality that includes the material world; the spiritual world of truths, personality, and so on; and the domain of the Godhead, which, so to speak, is superspiritual. This is precisely the reality that Anthony and his successors attempted to engage while living alone in the desert. For them, God makes himself known by distinctions existing outside his nature. By calling him God, Life, or Substance, they knew that the deifying, vivifying, and substantiating powers by which God communicates himself, though remaining incomprehensible by nature, enable him to make himself known while still remaining unknowable in his essence. His superessential nature oscillates between movement toward distinction and the impetus toward unity. For Dionysius, as for Anthony and his friends, this dual aspect of knowledge (that is, revelation and inaccessible superessence) corresponds to the double current that runs through all of creation.[7]

Of course, Anthony would not have been conversant with such complex interpretations of mystical theology. Nor was he aware of the theories of his contemporaries in Alexandria and elsewhere, most of whom were Greek. As an unlettered Egyptian, grasp of such theological hair splitting would have been essentially beyond him. But this does not mean that he hadn't experienced what Dionysius called the Super-Essence of Godhead while living in his cave on Mount Colzim. One must assume that in the depth of his spiritual experience he had little to say. Through his actions, how-ever, he was able to turn the world upside down. It was his humility, his gentleness, and his heartbreaking courtesy that were the seal of his sanctity to his contemporaries, far beyond abstinence, miracle, or sign. There may be a great gulf between the "stone-quarried" wis-dom of Anthony and Erigena's vision of the "light inaccessible," but this does not mean that he hadn't experienced what John Cassian called the "fire of divine contemplation" many times during those long years in the desert.[8]

The entire monastic movement, both East and West, is depend-ent on the work of these early Christian mystics. The corpus of their writings was forged in remote places, in conditions of extreme abstinence, relying less on scripture than on existential encounters with the divine. These men lived a unique kind of spirituality that was utterly different from that prescribed by holy doctrine. Men such as Saint Jerome, for example, who were familiar with classical writings as well as theology, readily acceded to the authority of the early Christian anchorites. Jerome acknowledged how difficult it was to rid himself of his classical upbringing in order to inhabit the psycho-spiritual landscape of those men. But he knew he must. Re-treating to the desert of Chalcis for five years, he somehow man-aged to tame the Virgilian romantic in him:

Oh, how many times did I, set in the desert, in that vast
solitude parched with the fires of the sun that offer a dread
abiding to the monk, how often did I think myself back in

the old Roman enchantments. There I sat solitary, full of bitterness; my disfigured limbs shuddered away from the sackcloth, my dirty skin was taking on the hue of the Ethiopian's flesh.[9]

But no amount of ascetic endeavor could eliminate entirely the intolerable energy of his imagination. In order to overcome his yearnings for a past life, Jerome finally decided to learn Hebrew. This would be the rock on which he would break his mind open once and for all. "My mind was seething with imagination," he wrote, "so to tame it I gave myself up for training to one of the brethren, a Hebrew who had come to the faith: and so, after the subtlety of Quintillion, the flowing river of Cicero, and the gentleness of Pliny, I began to learn another alphabet, and meditate on words that hissed and words that gasped." His effort was finally rewarded when he translated the Old Testament into Latin for the first time. The desert had provided him with a new language, one that was to serve Christendom for centuries to come.

Anchoritism and monastic life were to become the major impetus in the spread of Christianity throughout Europe and the East. However much the Christian message might inspire men to adopt a new spiritual ethic at the end of the pagan era, it was the anchorite and the monk who became its shock troops. They provided a model of absolutism that classical philosophers had been unable to emulate. The age demanded a more austere encounter with the world, and a new approach to mystical expression. It is no accident that Jerome toiled hard to "reject my style" in his attempt to create a language that might express the profound nature of the desert experience. Words that hissed and gasped were a far cry from the polished diction of Virgil and his contemporaries. This was to be an experiment in both language and living that would realize the true nature of *Theos Anir*. All these men of the desert, whether they were aristocrats or plowmen, had embarked on a voyage without end.

Anthony's message to later Christianity was very simple: obedience coupled to abstinence offers a powerful break against excess. As he remarked, "Whoever hammers a lump of iron, first decides what he is going to make of it, a scythe, a sword, or an axe. Even so we ought to make of our minds what kind of virtue we want to forge."[10] There is nothing profoundly mystical about this observation, except that buried in it lies an injunction that for its time was revolutionary. The mind had become the new theater of spiritual exploration rather than the handmaid to rationality, custom, or tradition. Henceforth a person was in charge of his own inner life in a way that few before Anthony had foreseen.

four

CITIZEN OF HEAVEN

Saint Anthony's monastery, at the foot of Mount Colzim and on the edge of Wadi al-'Arabah, had become my temporary home, at least for as long as it would take me to fulfill my promise to Lazarus. It was a place steeped in history and the silence of the desert. I have always been drawn to such places, perhaps because they remind me of my youth. Then, I used to escape into the bush near my home to sit in caves overlooking moss-filled creeks and aging ferns, listening to what I believed to be nature's dialogue. Here at Saint Anthony's the sense of entering into converse with rocks, wadis, and a brown landscape of low hills was more than reaffirmed: the desert offered me a chance to experience my youth once more, a condition I knew that Anthony had sought to realize all his life.

I kept thinking of the image Athanasius left us of Anthony at the moment when he quit his fortress retreat by the Nile. In a state of equilibrium, utterly balanced in his demeanor, neither old nor young, he was a man who had learned how to defy time. He had been prepared to subject his body, and his mind, to such a rigorous self-examination that I wondered whether there might be anything left over of the old Anthony. Probably not. He had attained to a state of *diakrisis*, the gift of discernment, that rare spiritual gift of being able to see clearly what one is no longer able to possess. We might call such a state one of detachment.

The monastery where I stayed was home to men who also continued to pursue detachment in the wake of Anthony's achievement. A monastic settlement had already been established at the foot of Mount Colzim within a few years of the saint's death in 356. The original settlement included a few buildings in the form of a kitchen, a bakery, and a chapel in which the monks could worship. In those days the monks used to live in cells scattered across the mountainside, though within walking distance to the spring and the church, where they were able to celebrate liturgy once a week. It was a place of refuge during times of persecution.

Yet even Saint Anthony's was not immune from invasion. Various Arab armies pillaged the monastery, killing the monks and all but destroying its precious library. As late as the fifteenth century, bedouin who lived there as servants of the monks attempted to destroy the monastery and its library. Smoke stains in the Church of Saint Anthony still linger as a reminder of this attack. It's said they established their kitchen in the church, lighting their fires with ancient scrolls and documents. Time after time the monastery was rebuilt in the wake of such devastation, only to fall victim to yet another act of vandalism. It appears that Anthony's legacy was to subject men to a continual act of renewal of their chosen way of life. In each man asceticism needed to be fashioned from the ground up.

The guest master had provided me with a room overlooking the lower garden, just inside the monastery walls. A delightful scene of date palms, with rows of vegetables dispersed among them, greeted my gaze from my balcony in the mornings. To my right was a cluster of monks' cells, each one domed in the Arab fashion. Behind a nearby row of buildings was another palm grove. These palms were probably the descendents of those first planted by Anthony. For it was here that he came to draw water from the spring. Living inside the monastery walls was like inhabiting a piece of amber: the honey-colored buildings seemed to glow in the sunlight.

I spent most of my time in the library with its store of books, codices, and illuminated manuscripts. The librarian kindly allowed me the run of the place, so that I was able to peruse Coptic Psalters decorated in beautifully executed crosses or heraldic birds supporting ornate Arabic letters. It was a world of parchment and leather, of ancient texts that had managed to escape the ravages of time. I felt privileged to be in their company. They were the custodians of thoughts that intimated the mystery of Godhead: how men, some of them poets, had attempted to grapple with the unnamable and make it their own. Old books acquire sanctity simply by being associated with language, this much I soon realized.

When I was not reading or taking notes, I wandered about the monastery grounds familiarizing myself with its environs. The Church of Saint Anthony was one of those places I liked to visit—when it was not in use. It's said this church was built in the fourth century, making it perhaps the oldest in Christendom. It's also said that Anthony is buried beneath the floor in front of the iconostasis. The frescoes on the walls are barely visible through the smoke stains, but I was able to make out wall paintings depicting various prophets, such as Moses, David, and Elijah. The archangel Michael gazed at me from an arch. Saint Athanasius himself peered down from one narthex, his high forehead bulging with words, controversy, and the broad intellect of a rhetorician. Anthony, too, gazed out of the nave at me, his serene, though haggard, expression not at all off-putting. Of all those early anchorites, Anthony alone appears to have borne the marks of his ascetic fervor with grace. He is always portrayed in an elegant habit, with a full beard and gentle eyes and bearing a copy of the Gospels in one hand. Often he is shown using a *tau*, or staff, to support himself in his old age.[1]

At the rear of the monastery lies a tunnel reaching deep into the mountain. A steady stream of water flows from it into a shallow pool before being siphoned off into a larger cistern, where the water is stored. Anthony would have come here, perhaps weekly, either to drink or to collect water for his vegetables. For more than sixteen hundred years this spring has nourished a uniquely sacrificial life, the spiritual life of the desert. Men have journeyed here, thirsty beyond measure, eager to partake of its waters. They have probably sat on the same rough stones by the entrance as I, contemplating the reason they had made the journey from the Nile in the first place. Nothing has really changed. Men still kneel beside the spring, knowing that Anthony's example has inspired them to make this pilgrimage.

At other times I might visit an ancient chapel with the unusual title of Four Living Creatures. It is decorated with frescoes depicting a lion, an ox, an eagle, and an angel, all surmounted by the sun and moon. A fine Pantocrator figure looks down from the sanctuary, sublimely sure of himself in this desert enclave. I particularly like this chapel for its simplicity. Here it is possible to sit in the company of living creatures and know that nature is also represented within the pantheon. Nothing has been left out when it comes to celebrating humankind and its relationship with the creaturely aspect of being.

Farther afield the narrow, medieval streets of the monastery suggest a village. But it is no ordinary village, for only men inhabit its dark interiors, its olive press and mill, its keep and charnel house. There is real archaeology here dedicated to preserving an ancient way of life. Men still come to this monastery from the cities, hoping to realize a life that is different from the one they have left behind. They come with one thing on their mind—to learn how to transcend their predicament by a conscious act of letting go. No wonder the patina on the mud-brick walls of the buildings is so inviting; it reflects back at all who pass a timeless radiance. Here men know that they live under the protection of God whenever they climb narrow staircases to their cells after a long night's vigil.

This, fortunately, is my temporary home. Behind me lies Mount Colzim, with the cave of my friend Lazarus high up on the slope; in front, a wadi that probably sees water but once every ten years. I am somehow content. In fact, I don't think I've known such contentment. In a place where there is nothing to do but read and think, gaze into the distance, eat a simple meal each day in the refectory, and sleep on a hard bed in a room that is bare of furniture save for a stool and a desk, there's something to be said for solitude. It is less a condition of isolation than a state of mind. It becomes a journey into oneself, away from the cares of this world. I'm beginning to enjoy it. Here one is able to impose on the general disorder of one's thoughts a measure of gravity.

I tried to put myself back in Anthony's time in order to understand the conditions that prompted his flight into the desert. It was an age of persecutions and doctrinal conflict.[2] Fault lines of philosophic disputation had opened up between pagans and Christians. The age was in ferment. New ideas flourished in the Didascaleon, the Christian school set up in Alexandria, and in the homes of the wealthy. Alexandria was perhaps the most exciting intellectual center in the ancient world. Athanasius was not alone in propagating the new religion among Egyptians. He, along with Clement and Origen,[3] taught at the Didascaleon, along with other thinkers and theologians who championed the allegorical method of interpreting the Bible. Another group, labeled Gnostics by their opponents, men such as Valentinus and Basilides, also contended for men's minds, arguing for a more dualist approach to Christian belief.[4]

Derived from Iranian dualism, Gnosticism was superficially alluring because it propounded a belief that the unconscious self of man was consubstantial with the Godhead. Because of some tragic fall, however, man found himself thrown into a world that was alien, one that only revelation from above could alleviate. This could be realized through the redemptive power of esoteric knowledge that thrived on divine revelation. A person might discover his transcendent destiny *not* through reason or Christian revelation, because these were rooted in history; rather, it was a matter of man's using his intuition to discover the mystery of self. Since the world was produced by evil matter and possessed by demons, it could not be the creation of God. Therefore it was an illusion. These ideas helped a person to liberate himself from the chaos of creation derived from incompetent or malevolent powers.

Anthony was not immune from such influences, even if he did live in the back blocks of Egypt. To argue that he might have been an illiterate rustic defies logic, since he was a member of a new religion deeply committed to resolving its own theology and doctrinal differences. The tiny Christian communities along the Nile received their theology from the pulpit, of course, but they would also have been aware of Gnostic ideas through travelers and tax collectors (Saint Paul was just such a person) as well as passing boatmen. It is no accident that the largest body of Gnostic literature was discovered at Nag Hammadi, south of Coma and not far from ancient

Thebes, then headquarters of the Pachomian order of monks. Pachomius happened to be a contemporary of Anthony's.[5]

Anthony lived at a time of spiritual controversy. The old temple priests, the philosophers, the Gnostics, and early Christian theologians were all competing for men's minds. Far from being a period of social and political chaos as it has often been described, Egypt of the third century was a place where people from all walks of life were being challenged to reconsider their beliefs. Athanasius may well have wished to portray his hero as unlettered because it suited him to argue the case for a new kind of Christian. It was true that the Christianity of the second and third centuries was very much the preserve of city intellectuals who still looked back to their Hellenistic inheritance for inspiration. The rise of the anchorite and his flight from the city had not yet made its mark on the Christian way of life. Moreover, Athanasius became disillusioned with the arguments of his own kind and wanted to propose a more natural way for men and women to rediscover their original nature. Anthony became his ideal prototype.

Anthony's withdrawal into the desert in order to concentrate on ascetic practice echoed Athanasius's desire to reconfigure the individual's relationship to secular society and so restore a proper relationship between a person's soul and body. If a person could dispense with diversion, the very principle of urban existence, then he or she was on the road to salvation. The past eight hundred years of philosophic inquiry had nurtured in men a disposition toward reasoning at the expense of revelation. Athanasius, bold thinker that he was, recognized in Anthony a more pristine intellect than that produced by those who frequented the stoa in Athens, Ephesus, or Croton. He saw in this man, who had nurtured in himself an "unwavering life" of virtue, someone who had freed himself from the negligence that led to the fall of the original human beings.

The key to his thinking, and by implication that of Anthony, was the idea of developing a spiritual discipline that would enable people to reestablish the soul's control over the body. There was nothing new in such a desire, as Pythagoras as early as the seventh century BC, and later Plato, had espoused similar ideas. Even Philo mentions small sects of Jewish monks and nuns living in the neighborhood of Alexandria. The Therapeutae, as they were called, practiced an eremitical lifestyle that paved the way for early Christian monasticism. In his *On the Contemplative Life*, Philo wrote: "For six days they seek wisdom by themselves in solitude . . . never passing the outside door of the house or even getting a distant view of it. But on the seventh day they meet together as for a general assembly, and sit in order according to their age in the proper attitude. . . . Then the senior among them who also has the fullest knowledge of the doctrines which they profess comes forward, and with face and voice alike quiet and composed, gives a reasoned and well-reasoned discourse." So Anthony and Athanasius were not the first to argue the value of quitting the body politic in favor of the anchoritic life.

Nonetheless, Saint Anthony's monastery still exists today, and the hermitages of the Therapeutae have long since disappeared. This must say something about the ability of Christianity to survive persecution and the distortion of its message. The Romans, the Arabs, and heretical sects such as the Arians, Gnostics, Donatists, and Meletians, to name but a few, had all tried to erase or distort Christ's message. Rationally it had no right being there, but emotionally and spiritually it said something important to people desperate to realize meaning in their lives. Christ as God and man, as avatar, had finally overthrown the Egyptian gods Osirus, Isis, Horus, and Seth and his entourage of demons, to place before a thirsting populace the possibility of transcendence. It was a heady brew.

Living here at Saint Anthony's monastery made me realize that I was playing my own small part in this never-ending drama. It's not often that one can participate, if only imaginatively, in the evolution of human thought and belief. Unlike the high politics of kings and emperors, the politics of thought are often far more interesting. When one reads of Athanasius's numerous exiles to Rome, to the Rhineland, and to Upper Egypt, and his triumphant return to his native city, a sense of real adventure emerges. The frisson of intellect, the fact that men's lives might be physically changed because of conflicting theological opinion—such was the spirit of the age. Men were prepared to risk their lives and reputations in order to uphold what they believed. The complexity of belief has no end: people will always revel in the prospect of articulating a new point of dogma, a new equation, or the rightness of a new social program. In this sense Anthony and his biographer were no different.

Walking through the gate to the monastery, under the ancient pulley room through which visitors were once hauled into the monastery during times of siege, I always felt that I was quitting one kind of solitude in order to encounter another. Through the centuries the monastery and its inhabitants had developed a discipline of silence and a doctrine of emptiness. The early anchorites called such a state *hesychia*, meaning to enter into a state of stillness, tranquillity, a silence of the heart. Years of ascetic practice make it possible to realize a perfect void, an emptiness, in which no trace of consciousness remains. Even the sense of being unconscious has departed. All forms of mental activity are swept away, leaving the mind clear. *Hesychia* is acquired only after an upheaval that destroys the old accumulations of intellect, laying bare the foundations for a new life. It is this sense of stillness, this *hesychia*, that every monk strives to attain. According to Saint John Climacus, a seventh-century recluse, to achieve the solitary life one must "choose places where there are fewer opportunities for comfort and ambition, but more for humility. Otherwise we will be fleeing in company with our passions."[6] Men such as he knew and understood the dangers of embarking on the solitary life without paying attention to the habits of a lifetime.

Hesychia is a mysterious yet challenging doctrine. To become a hesychast meant that a man strove to enter the highest spiritual state possible, whereby he separated himself from everything created and changeable. In such a state a light from God illuminated him, a light that the early Fathers chose to call holy quiet. Gregory Palamas, a noted exponent of *hesychia*, wrote of it as a "standing still of the mind and of the world, forgetfulness of what is below, initiation into secret knowledge (gnosis) of what is above, the putting aside of thoughts for what is better than they; this is the true activity [of the hesychast], the ascent to the true contemplation and vision of God."[7] The object was to hold or "guard the mind" in order that it might regain its stability. To do so was no easy task.

All this made me feel inadequate. In a way, I thought of myself as someone who had been denied his heritage by an act of amnesia. Guarding one's mind? Choosing outlandish places to live? Denying myself every comfort? Were these the stuff of a normal life? So many questions crossed my mind as I wandered through the gates on an afternoon to take my evening walk in the desert. I kept thinking of the great mental and spiritual distance that separated me from those early solitaries. It was as if we lived on different planets, and yet when I read their work I understood what they said. It wasn't as if their thoughts were entirely alien.

To compound my confusion, I kept thinking about Lazarus high up on Mount Colzim. There was something ageless and yet unsettling about his very existence. Here was a man who wanted to engage in *hesychia* much as Anthony and his friends had done, at a time when the world was enthralled not by mental stillness but by a noisy and unstable fervor. Why have we distanced ourselves from the practice of *hesychia?* This was the important question—and one, I'm sure, that Lazarus addressed almost every day. If I, like so many others, had distanced myself from a life of "holy quiet," then it must have something to do with an inability to live an inner life.

Gregory Palamas rightly identified the problem when he said that the hesychast is someone able to maintain that which is "incorporeal" (that is, the mind or the intellect) *within* the body. "The sending of the mind," he went on to say, "*out* of the body, so that it may seek intellectual visions without, is the supreme illusion, and the root and source of all wrong-doing."[8]

The very idea of confining the intellect in or outside the body is an unusual concept. It suggests that the mind has the capacity for movement, that it can wander. Nor do I mean the idea of a "wandering mind." Gregory Palamas is alluding to a confusion between the nature of the mind and its activity. He saw the mind as inextricably linked to the soul. In order to penetrate one's soul, one needed to clarify one's thoughts. Clarification of thought could only be achieved by an act of mental cleansing brought on by ascetic practice. Probably the reason the intellect chose to quit the body, at least in terms of Gregory's argument, was that at some point we abandoned our belief in the soul as integral to being. Was this also the moment when we forgot the meaning of ascesis?

These were issues that both perplexed and challenged me. Moreover, living in the oldest monastery in Christendom made them appear more vivid. The solemn tone of the bell at times of liturgy, the sound of water trickling from Anthony's spring, and the knowledge that the surrounding walls had resisted for centuries those attacks of mindlessness from *without* only intensified their importance. What these ideas of Gregory Palamas represented (and by implication the people that adhered to them) was a belief that an exterior life is somehow better than a life of stillness, of holy quiet. I sensed in this attitude a failure of nerve, and a refusal to embrace the soul as being a part of us.

These were questions that I brought to Lazarus's attention on my occasional climb up the mountain. I did not make such trips often, believing that it was important to contemplate questions myself before inflicting them on my friend. I was conscious of not imposing myself on Lazarus in a way that might interfere with his life. He had a right to his solitude, as he had fought hard to acquire it. As a practicing hesychast, Lazarus deserved more than to have his world examined by someone like me. If Gregory Palamas was correct, and he makes a strong case for it, then anyone who partakes of the "divine substance," either wholly or in its "minutest part," would become omnipotent. If this was the goal, I suspected he meant something far more subtle than the idea of exercising power over persons.

In my desire to deepen my knowledge of Anthony and the Desert Fathers, I had wandered into a cenobium of spiritual masters. These men weren't recluses who had chosen the desert simply to escape Roman oppression. They were men in possession of a vision unique to the world. The fact that the desert was the place where they developed their knowledge was incidental. What they had been looking for was a metaphor to enter and inhabit. Here at the foot of Mount Colzim lay that metaphor: every stone and cave in the mountainside was testament to the life of men who had come here to test themselves in, and against, the desert. Most of their names were anonymous, yet their silence was like a chorus. I could hear them uttering the eulogy of the solitary: "We are the *katachoi,* the withdrawn, the God-possessed." It was a eulogy of promise.

five

THE LAW OF PROMISE

Anthony's autarkism was not in any way antisocial. At no point did he renounce his relationship with men, or with society. Though he had lived in his tomb by the Nile for close to twenty years, it did not mean that people were unable to make contact with him. Many would-be ascetics had joined him in the surrounding hills, and their cells were likened to "tents filled with divine choirs." It seems that a multitude had joined him in his endeavor, chanting, fasting, praying, and studying. "It was as if one truly looked on a land all its own—a land of devotion and righteousness," Athanasius tells us. Egypt was changing: the fertile fields along the Nile, for so long subject to the demands of the Roman state, and before that the pharaohs, had been transformed into a theophanic landscape. In the words of one observer, it had become "the imaginative antipodes of the sterile lands of the desert." Men like Anthony had become the new heroes, and for many pilgrims who made the journey from as far away as Rome and Constantinople to these anchorite communities, such men were believed to have touched, and to have realized for others, a palpable image of the paradise inhabited by Adam.[1]

The conflict between state and individual was nowhere more evident than in Anthony's decision to journey to Alexandria at the height of the persecutions conducted in the reign of Maximinus Daia. Maximinus, during his time as Caesar and later Augustus (308–313), was determined to renew paganism in the East and resorted to every means possible to achieve his ends, including publicizing the confessions of prostitutes alleging that they had participated in Christian orgies. Though personally against executions, he made sure that those who did not renounce Christianity would be condemned to the mines and quarries after being blinded in one eye. When Anthony decided to visit the capital and confront the authorities as an act of support for his Christian friends, it was clear that his spiritual authority would be challenged.

Athanasius tells us in his book *Life of Saint Anthony* that Anthony comforted those in prison and many who had been sent to the mines. He regularly visited the law courts to inspire others facing prosecution for their beliefs. One judge was so impressed by Anthony that he demanded that no more Christians be brought to him but rather that they be exiled from the city. It was in this climate of confrontation that Anthony stood in the path of the prefect of the city one day and thus demonstrated his indifference. Athanasius relates how Anthony blocked the official's passage dressed in a newly washed garment, a sign that he wished to die for his cause. So powerful was his presence that the prefect was reluctant to order him arrested. Anthony had shown the world that he was already dead to it and that the state had no authority to determine what he might choose to believe.

This was a significant moment in the history of Christianity. Of course, other men had chosen martyrdom before Anthony. We know that Bishop Peter of Alexandria was beheaded in 312. Anthony's defiant gesture represents a moment when the state, in the guise of the local prefect, no longer believed in what it was doing. Like Gandhi's in India during his resistance of the British, his very "calmness" in the face of the passing escort demonstrated the purposefulness that belonged to all Christians. Anthony had shown the world how important it was to "die a little every day" and so negate the fear of death.[2] The prefect was unable to order his execution because Anthony had already ordered his own.

One must try to picture Anthony at this moment. In his early sixties, with more than forty years of ascetic experience and demonic encounter behind him, here was a man who had modeled himself on Christ and was thus prepared to sacrifice himself on the alter of the state. There had never been a time during antiquity when the sacred and the secular were in such opposition. In the past, particularly in Greece, the gods had always acted in unison with society. They had complemented men's actions, whether at Troy or on the way home to Ithaca after the Trojan War, as depicted in the *Iliad* and the *Odyssey*. Anthony's action signaled a change in the way men—Christians, at least—viewed themselves and their beliefs in relation to the state. Now they were ready to put their spiritual aspirations before their civic responsibilities. The state had become secondary in the conduct of their inner affairs. By standing silently in the street as a sign of rebuke to the prefect of Alexandria, Anthony called on others to make their own choice. Either they accept secular control over their thoughts or they acknowledge the primacy of their beliefs by rejecting Rome's right to determine them.

Anthony's act of civil disobedience was a determining event for him as well. He returned to his cell near Pispir in Middle Egypt, knowing that his life as a famous holy man was over. Probably he sensed that the Christian life as one of subversion was also over. Maximinus had recently died, and the Christians were now left in peace. Suddenly there was no reason to stand in the street in defiance of the authorities. On the other hand, to return to his cell would not have given him the solitude he craved. Too many visitors, and too many demands for his intercession on behalf of those who were ill, made it necessary for him to flee. Derwas Chitty sets the stage beautifully: "In Middle Egypt, an aging ascetic, fleeing from fame, was waiting by the Nile in hopes of a ship to take him to regions where he was unknown."[3] One can picture this wiry old man, still vigorous in limb, seeking a passage toward anonymity. Finally he wanted to put himself beyond the bounds of society. The inner mountain beckoned.

We now see Anthony as the embodiment of the outsider. He joins a caravan, probably at modern-day Beni Suef on the Nile, and allows the Saracens to take him toward the Red Sea. After a three-day journey on camels, the party reaches Mount Colzim, where a spring and a few date palms are discovered. Anthony immediately decides that this is where he belongs. He takes leave of his companions, who offer him a supply of dried bread, and watches as they slowly move off down the wadi toward the Red Sea. From this moment on he is the solitary man par excellence. He has shed the world.

To drive to Mount Colzim even today is a moving experience. The dry hills and sandy wadis on either side of the road are confronting. You feel that the earth has been reduced to its original condition, that of an endless expanse of primeval matter. Certainly the Eastern Desert is forbidding. Except for the palm groves inside the grounds of the monastery itself, trees and herbage are nonexistent. There must be some form of plant life, however, because

Lazarus told me that a species of small deer inhabits the hills. Still, the place feels irreducibly to be the end of the road. Nothing is able to exist here except men whose sole nutriment is meditative life. They are the select few who are able to deal with the existence of rubble and meteor dust. Anthony had made it possible to be drawn to this wasteland, to this planetary dead heart. He was able to discover here the perfect metaphor for his life: to become that which he contemplated, the sheer emptiness of space.

We are enthralled, too, when we encounter such seminal places. I know I am. I have visited the tomb of Jalal ad-Din al-Rumi, the Persian poet, in Konya, and also Thermopylae, where a few hundred Greeks died defending their homeland. Both these spots radiate power, as if some residual drama were still attached to their narrow streets or stones. Word and warfare clamor for silence. Mount Colzim is no different in this respect: the cave of Anthony is the epitome of solitude and interior battle. One senses that only in such a cave, in such a remote place, could a man like Anthony initiate himself into the mysteries of *alter Christus*, of becoming another Christ. To be beyond perfection (*proteleios*) is a state few men aspire to, and even fewer attain. A cave in the desert is often the only place where "perfectionlessness" can be realized.

It was this place that Jean Coppin, a French traveler of the seventeenth century, managed to climb to and describe:

> The entrance is no more than two feet wide and four and a
> half feet high. This opening goes for some yards into the
> rock but does not widen out so that two men could not pass
> through it abreast. At the end of this passage there are three
> stones placed one on top of another in a crevice of rock to act
> as descending steps, and when we had gone down them we
> found ourselves in a cave almost circular in shape and large
> enough to hold about thirty people. The whole face of the

rock [outside the cave, overlooking the wadi] is very high and rises naturally as sheer as a wall. It continues in this way for a distance of some three or four hundred yards. The area is bare of wood, barren and rocky, traversed by a path, which makes several turns, since it would be impossible to climb straight up [to the plateau above]. From this spot we could observe the Red Sea lying to the east, but because it was so far distant it looked to us like a cloud resting on the ground.[4]

Today the cave is little different from when Jean Coppin visited it all those years ago. Inside, a brick table serves as an altar. Three icons, two of Christ and one of Anthony, grace the altar and the rock behind. Candles are attached to the rock face with wax. On the south wall we see examples of medieval graffiti, indicating pilgrims that have visited the place. Friar Bernardus (1626) is there, along with another date, 1641, though without an accompanying name. It is possible to imagine Anthony retreating to this cave in order to escape the demands of those who wished to share his grace, even as he struggled to maintain it in himself.

I know that when I first climbed up there via a track from Lazarus's cell, I had been fascinated by the loneliness of the place. Sitting on a rock outside the cave and gazing into the wadi below, it was not hard to picture Anthony taking a few minutes at dusk to contemplate the enormity of his solitude. On a hot afternoon, especially, he would have gazed out at a shimmering landscape, knowing that the haze before him was merely concealing the world beyond. Egypt, the Nile, its timeless pharaonic culture, the great pyramids, the countless regnal tombs in mountainsides, the innumerable hieroglyphics and frescoes depicting the procession of the dead into the underworld, the mummies in their faded wrappings, the withered carcasses of cats and other animals lying on the floors of tombs, the pagan temples, Roman baths and military barracks, the mud-brick villages and irrigated fields, the camels and donkeys drawing water from wells, the threshing floors and storehouses, the busy populace burdened with their duties—all was as if visible from his terrace, reflecting a multifaceted tableau. Egypt embodied the entire history of humankind, and he, the lonely man on his mountain, had chosen to live outside this panoply in a state of solitude.

I knew how he must have felt. All of us attempt to ascend to an Olympian perspective at least once in our lives. To look out over the world, whether it be physical or historical, sends a thrill to the very core of our being. We try to exercise some sort of superlative vision that allows us to see further, and deeper, into ourselves. Poets, of course, attempt to describe it for us. But we, constrained by our limitations, are content to experience this overworldly view as a sensation that transcends all our critical faculties. The world simply *is* in all its complexity and wonder. And we, rare birds on a branch, are able to absorb it with a glance. This is what Anthony's cave offers the visitor. He is able to gaze into the distance and see a reflection of himself as someone who has given up possession of his body.

It was wishful thinking after my first visit to his cave to think that I understood Anthony. I was conscious that I was dealing with an historical personage rather than anyone that I might know. To experience his presence inside the cave was to feel an energy that was in part the result of my own desire to understand. Anthony, this solitary hero, had made it possible for me to believe that a life lived *inside the earth* was less an act of turning one's back on the world than an attempt to unshackle the mind from its dependence on social values. Autarkism was a statement about humankind's capacity for freedom. It reminded me of Simone Weil's remark: "Society is a cave. The way out is solitude."[5] Anthony would have concurred. For him the universe was a compact mass of obedience. His cave was in stark contrast to society's cave because of the solitude he found there.

Mount Colzim is a sacred precinct. Standing on the terrace outside the cave, I tried to picture those starry nights that Anthony must have experienced. He would have witnessed the slow ascent of the constellations that marked the seasonal year. He was not so far from Sirius, the Dog Star, announcing the rising of the waters on the Nile. Scorpius and Orion would have kept him in contact with the celestial journeys of mythic heroes as they slipped below the horizon. Soundless, except for rocks splitting when temperatures plummeted, he would have contemplated life's origin spread out over a void, listening for its opportunity to rise up into the world. Ascesis for him would have been an act of wandering, suspicion, waiting, confluence, wound, exodus, and exile. At the same time, each day would have brought with it an encounter with the sublime.

This was the man I had come to meet. For all its austerities, the ascetic life will always prove to be attractive to some. We see in it something primal, life consuming, and altogether different from the life of the senses. As Evagrius remarks, it helps us to draw near to contemplative knowledge and so distance ourselves from the irrational nature of the soul. Such knowledge bears us aloft and separates us from our senses. Intuitively we know that this is a life-enhancing state whereby we are able to be more completely ourselves. *Ataraxia*, untroubled calm of spirit, becomes the health of the soul, which makes us hungry for contemplative knowledge. Anthony set out to make such knowledge his own here on Mount Colzim. He wanted to realize a state of moral and spiritual perfection that would allow him to arrive at a permanent level of calm. This was *ataraxia*, the mark of a true man.

We must remember that he was in his sixties by the time he took up residence in his cave. Descent to the spring was some thousand feet, down a track of uneven stones past the tiny cell of his good friend Paul the Simple, who later joined him in his retirement. He grew vegetables near the spring to supply food for visitors who made the journey across the desert from the Nile. For another forty-three years, from 313 until his death in 356, he lived here, if not entirely alone, then certainly removed from the kind of life he had known in Pispir. Anthony had found a place where he might practice an inner life that would forever change the way Western man addressed his own spiritual life. Though he wrote no books nor addressed crowds of acolytes, he managed to pass on a system of ascetic behavior that is with us today. We are heir to his unique encounter with desert places as a repository of spirit.

By good fortune rather than accident I found myself living in this environment. I had come to Mount Colzim as much out of curiosity as out of my interest in the anchoritic life. Past experience had taught me that any encounter with place is important. There is only so much that can be gleaned from books; it is also necessary to journey to places like Mount Colzim in order to experience them personally. Anthony was concerned with what he called the resurrection of the mind, which he saw as an expression of a partnership with the spirit.[6] As a natural Platonist, he understood that the relationship between body, soul, and mind was a collaboration that allowed for a return to his original nature.[7] To achieve this condition he needed to refine and transform his body through ascesis. In "Letter One" he maintains:

First the body through many fasts and vigils, through the exertion and exercises of the body, cuts off all the fruits of the flesh. In this the Spirit of Repentance is his guide, testing him through them, so that the enemy does not bring him back again. Then the guiding Spirit begins to open the eyes of the soul, to show it the way of repentance so that it, too, may be purified.

The mind also starts to discriminate between them and begins to learn from the Spirit how to purify the body and the soul through repentance. The mind is taught by the Spirit and guides us in the actions of the body and soul, purifying both of them. . . .

The body is thus brought under the authority of the mind and is taught by the Spirit.[8]

Like Plato, Anthony regarded wisdom as a purification that could be achieved only by engaging in ascesis.

This was the program that Anthony had set out to put into practice during his time at Mount Colzim. The sense of alienation that humankind feels when confronted by a lack of meaning in life he likened to the "great wound." To heal such a wound it was important for a person to return to the Law, which he saw as the first stage in the common history of humankind. It was the law of oneness, which he called the law of promise, as distinct from the law of multiplicity, which he argued came as a result of mental deterioration and a loss of spiritual insight. When the law of promise had grown "cold" or "withered away," it was a sure sign that the mental faculties had worn out. Men "had not been able to discover themselves as they were created, namely as an eternal substance" ("Letter Three"). Clearly the great wound represented a loss of perception on the part of humankind as to the true nature of being—that of attaining to what he called "a knowledge of one's eternal substance."[9]

I found myself sitting outside a cave where the law of promise had been inscribed forever on the desert's silence. Moses may have come down from Mount Sinai with his tablets, thus setting his people on a path toward dignity, but Anthony had gone one step further. He had shown a way of penetrating deeply into that primitivity which is our eternal origin. He had revealed to us that it wasn't enough to explore life as if it were a newly discovered wall of hieroglyphics whose meaning was lost. Curiosity can be a smoke screen, he seemed to be saying. What each of us is called on to attain is a true self-knowledge in order to help us "understand our time."[10] Self-knowledge, therefore, was the code breaker of that amorphous encryption of daily life.

The question I wanted to ask of Anthony, or indeed of Lazarus, was whether he had devised a system of ascetic practice applicable to the twenty-first century. Or were we too distant, and thus too removed, from the law of promise ever to attain to that ancient idea of self-knowledge? Anthony had spoken of three gates to repentance, but did these gates refer to a discipline, or were they another way of conveying the necessity to fast, to conduct vigils, and to impose restraints on the body ("cutting off all the fruits of the flesh")? I was conscious of how immersed we all are in the empire of the real ever to commit ourselves to an ascetic program that demanded quitting the world. We have been so heavily socialized that the mere idea of walking off into the Rockies, or finding a cave in the Tanami Desert of Central Australia, is no longer feasible. In effect, we have lost the gift of silence because we no longer understand, or have respect for, language. This alone expresses our fear of solitary places in that we are afraid of dealing with a reality that is expressible only through words. The silence of the desert, that silence which Anthony traveled into the Eastern Desert to discover, was more than a primal silence, a world of noiselessness. This was not the silence he wished to encounter. What he was trying to do was dwell in his own silence, whereby he might renounce his desire to rest in created things. The disclosure of words, in this case those of Christ, needed to transcend legend in order that the *silent word* might clarify its relationship to God. Such a condition, however, is alien to many; we feel at home in things even as we acknowledge our dependence. We no longer feel at home in the clarity of the word.

My dilemma was whether I might find a way back to the cave of Anthony's silence, or whether I was indulging in nostalgia. Could a person like me understand the ancient Greek concept of *eudaemonia*, the close relationship between God and humankind? While we might translate its meaning today as "beatitude" or "happiness," we would be missing its true meaning. *Eudaemonia* expresses the invisible and ungraspable nature of God. To experience *eudaemonia* is to enter the territory of the uncanny, a territory that Anthony sought at Mount Colzim. He wanted to know *eudaemonia* and so partake of divinity. I asked myself whether this was possible anymore. Could anyone, other than men like Lazarus, carve out his or her cave of the heart?

It was a question worthy of Lazarus. One afternoon on a visit to his cell, I put to him the difficulty of reconciling modern ways with the anchorite life. I also asked him whether Anthony or his contemporaries had ever detailed their ascetic practice other than in homilies. Did they write a manual for the solitary life? Or was such a life, as I had begun to believe, the outcome of a deliberate attempt to exclude the world, even if that world still existed. In other words, was it possible to practice a form of asceticism of the mind while pursuing a life in the city? These questions were in some way linked, even if I had no idea why.

Lazarus listened to my inquiries with an attentive ear. Before we commenced our discussions he usually prepared a mug of tea. We would sit on the bench in front of his raised prayer platform and contemplate the view before us. The colors of the surrounding hills often mirrored the tone of our conversation. One day they might be bright, untrammeled by shadow; another, they would be bland, indistinct, as if a hazy sun demeaned their contours. But we managed to raise our thoughts so that they conveyed what at first hearing was not related at all.

In answer to my questions, Lazarus often went off at a tangent. I received the impression that he disliked too much rational analysis. Years of prayer had taught him not to place reliance on intellectual perception. Like the Desert Fathers of old, he wanted to guide me away from disputation as the only means to understanding. He wanted me to listen with my heart rather than my mind. This was not so easy. Shifting one's understanding from the head to the heart, relying on intuition as a means of perception, was a difficult transition to make. I felt like an infant grappling with a new word: its sound was all I had to hold on to as I struggled to comprehend what it meant.

In reply to my questions Lazarus grew thoughtful, before answering by way of an allusion. Most of us, he said, have been driven from our homeland and are threatened to the core of our being. This loss of rootedness was not caused by accident or fate, nor did it stem solely from negligence or superficiality in the way we live. Rather, such a loss sprang from the spirit of our age. We have become victims of a desire to clutch at things, a desire to plan and calculate, to organize and automate. He saw our love of efficiency as one reason for uprootedness and our loss of self. In the process, we had lost the ability to reach toward the heavens and so converse with the spirit.

I was moved by his argument. Lazarus had spelled out the reason that people like me wander about the world. We are on the lookout for anything that might give meaning to our lives. Whether it is in a temple in India or in front of a painting of the Annunciation by Simone Martini in Florence or observing early Byzantine frescoes in the rock chapels of Turkey, are we not trying to discover a key that might release us from our prison? The beauties of the past ignite a yearning for something more intrinsic than the ease of present-day existence. We want to embrace what will not yield to the onrush of modernity with its penchant for change. This is what Lazarus stood for: a return to an ancient spirituality in order to reaffirm his relationship with the spirit.

But he did alert me to one important fact. The ascetic practice forged by Anthony at Mount Colzim was alive and well in the writings of those who succeeded him. The deserts of Egypt, the Sinai Peninsula, southern Palestine, Syria, and Iraq—all these regions had inspired thinkers whose work embodied the revolutionary doctrine of ascesis that Anthony had first promulgated. Men such as Dorotheus of Gaza, Isaac of Nineveh, Abdisho' Hazzaya, John Climacus, Dadisho' Katraya, Nilus the Ascetic and Gregory of Sinai, Simon of Taibutheh, and Joseph Hazzaya are but a few who absorbed Anthony's message. As anchorites, they were heir to a rich tradition of asceticism that had first been fashioned in Egypt. Lazarus's advice was to bury myself in the library at the monastery and study their works. There, he told me, I would discover what I was looking for—a way, a path, even a doctrine of transcendence. These men had devoted their lives to exploring the byways of the human spirit in their quest for *eudaemonia*, that deep relationship with God.

I thanked Lazarus for his advice. We said a prayer together, clinging like mollusks to the mountain made sacred by Anthony, before I kissed his hand and started down to the monastery. I was feeling exhilarated: our conversations always made me feel like this. The poetry of thought had taken on a new dimension. I could feel myself falling under the spell of minds that had journeyed forth into the desert, only to find that what they encountered there was different from what they had expected. I had to learn how to "turn toward the East," as Isaac of Nineveh urged his readers (see Wensinck, *Mystical Treatises of Isaac of Nineveh*, in the appendix). I had to learn how to embrace what Isaac called the "emotionality of discernment" that transformed ideas into angels. Climbing down the track that afternoon, I hoped I might one day gain some insight from my investigations and so join this unique company of "the Initiated."[11]

six

A WORDLESS JOURNEY

Journeying to an inner mountain is not something we feel entirely comfortable with, let's be honest. The thought of following in the footsteps of a man like Anthony, or indeed Lazarus, to the farthest reaches of the desert often leaves us with a feeling of unease. We sense that physical exile has its dangers—that to do so places us beyond the reach of human relationships. What is the point of abandoning all our allegiances to friends and family simply to experience *eudaemonia*, we might ask? And even if we did, would we be fortunate enough to experience such an abiding harmony anyway? The anchorites themselves often maintained that only one man in a thousand would ever achieve such a state. The stakes are high, it seems, and the prospects of reward are slim.

I kept recalling a few remarks made by John of Apamea whenever I asked myself such questions. He urged his fellow hermit Hesychius in a letter: "Be friendly to everyone, but do not seek for attachment to your loved ones, for your way of life does not require that. *You are a solitary, and you should not be tied down by anything*" (italics mine). This last statement always affected me profoundly, I don't know why. John seemed to be calling on all of us to acknowledge a fact of life, one that we would perhaps like to forget sometimes. According to John, in order to be truly free, one had to release oneself from every kind of destructive slavery, to throw off what he openly acknowledged as the "yoke of the world."[1] This man was clearly addressing every fear that we possess. Releasement for him was an annulment of all that we crave.

Still, there's no point in dismissing this conflict as the residue of some idle fancy. The ascetic impulse lies at the heart of all great spiritual disciplines, be they Christian, Muslim, Buddhist, or Hindu. No one can deny how important the monastic life has been in the growth and refinement of culture in so many lands. In remote mountain valleys in India and China, on the steppes of Russia, and in the teeming countryside of India we may witness temples and ancient walled monasteries, often with pennants fluttering from bamboo poles by their gates. These are home to a time-honored inwardness that has been carefully nurtured by generations of monks. As well, the men living in them know the risks they run. Satori, nirvana, or *apatheia* are not easy to achieve. They might spend a whole lifetime in meditation and prayer and not experience such bliss. But is this the point? Their job, surely, is to maintain the tradition out of which true geniuses of the spirit may ripen.

I would be the first to admit that my own life has been dedicated to exploring the ascetic impulse as it exists throughout the world. A youthful encounter with Zen in the monasteries of Kyoto in Japan has led me on a lifelong quest among the Sufi orders of Islam, among the monks on Mount Athos in Greece, to the ruined monastic communities of Turkey, and among those venerable monasteries of Sinai and Egypt, home to some of the wisest and most spiritual of men. Wherever I have journeyed in pursuit of this dream, I have always come away from the experience richly rewarded. The truth is that the monastery is a jewel in the crown of humanity's aspiration toward the infinite. In it one confronts not only that deep empathy we have with the things of the spirit but also aspects of ourselves. The monastery becomes a mirror; it reflects back at us all the contours of suffering and guilt that we think lie safely hidden from view.

I have found this journey to be more than worthwhile. In my early years I visited Cappadocia, in central Turkey, to observe the rock chapels there. How well I recall arriving in Goreme to be confronted by a town literally carved from cones of volcanic rock reminiscent of stalagmites rising from a cave floor. It reminded me of some childhood fantasy, a vision of a fairyland. Trudging out to the eight- to ninth-century chapels beyond town, I soon found myself enveloped in a rough-hewn world of pillars, cupolas, sanctuaries, and naves that had been tunneled from the tufa by monks eager to fashion a spiritual reality of their own. These tiny chapels, refectories, and hermit caves littering the landscape called to mind the existence of a visionary city dedicated to the celebration of Christ and his ministry. I had entered a valley where angels had once appeared, winged and radiant, to announce to those solitary men gathered there that their quest was worthwhile: the spirit did indeed emanate from their nightly vigils that they so diligently and so reverently filled with prayer, psalmody, and tears.

In the Church of the Sandals, a chapel filled with a delightful array of frescoes depicting scenes from the life of Christ, I remember noticing the imprint of a pair of sandals carved into the floor. These, apparently, were those Christ himself had made after one of his mysterious visits to the chapel. For a moment I thought of them as like two fish engraved in the floor. It was then that I realized how easy it was to slip into a state of unutterable joy at the way men are capable of surrounding themselves with the marvelous. The chapel represented a world created by men who believed not only in the reality of Christ but also in their own transcendent intuition. *They* had managed to carve out a chapel of visions, a chapel bedecked in frescoes portraying their understanding of the nature of the infinite, a place in which sandals had been engraved in the form of fishes. I had entered a rudimentary laboratory dedicated to the service of the spirit. The Church of the Sandals might not have been home to pipettes and Bunsen burners, but it was nonetheless a place where real experimentation had been attempted.

That night, I recall, I dreamed of a man entering my hotel room through the window. He had come to address what were then my nameless fears. This man, this unkempt angel who seemed to want to wrench from me some understanding that I was clearly reluctant to address, physically confronted me. His hands seemed to press against my temples, as if massaging from them some tiny homunculus of deceit. He wanted to extract from me an acknowledgment of my aloneness, and my wish to conceal this aloneness under the garb of normal existence. He seemed to be asking me to admit to the importance of detaching myself from normal daily affairs, the business of getting and having, and so to dedicate myself to a more transcendent existence. I found this hard to deal with and tried vigorously to resist his hands holding my head by thrashing about. But I was unable to do so; his hands held my head as if it were an orb of fire that needed to be held aloft. I awoke then, sweating profusely, to see the moon at my window.

This was my baptism into the realm of luminous reality. The rock chapels of Goreme with their phantasmal images and iconography were the pathway into what I now perceived to be the most mysterious landscape of all, that of our interior solitude, with all its forbidding contours and ridges. Inadvertently, or because of what I had encountered in the rock chapels, I had begun my own journey into this suspended universe of signs and symbols. Isaac of Nineveh called it wisdom's journey, a journey that has no limit because its end is truly unattainable. Earlier I might have regarded following such a path as futile, the result of some lingering nostalgia. But I now began to realize that what John and Isaac were really calling for was the adoption of a condition, a demeanor, perhaps, that helped to separate me from the entanglements of the world.

Years later I visited Greece, ostensibly to study Byzantine art. I climbed aboard a funicular train and was transported up a steep mountain valley to a place called Megaspelion, deep in the mountains of the Peloponnese on the shores of the Gulf of Corinth. The tiny train bore me through tunnels, over stone bridges, and through fields of spring flowers. About me the rough granite rocks appeared to have become fossilized in the shape of Gothic buttresses. A stream surged downward close to the track, tumbling over rocks. At last the monastery rose before me, attached like a swallow's nest to the side of a cliff. I looked up at this lonely aerie where men had chosen to isolate themselves for countless generations, knowing that I was in the presence of a particular kind of beauty, the beauty of solitude. It was only then that I understood how palpable such a state can be: men will always seek out certain places in order to meditate, to pray, and to simply allow their senses to be reinvigorated. I had journeyed to a place that one anonymous Syrian hermit called the "monastery of the heart."[2]

I spent some days in the monastery, attending liturgy with the monks and eating a frugal meal in the refectory. There I allowed my

inner eye to wander back over the mosaics I had seen in the church
of Hosios Loukas near Delphi, and at Daphni, outside Athens, before I had come to Megaspelion. I remembered walking through
the ruins of the monastery of Daphni one morning and entering
the church. High on the walls, in the dome and pendentives, I witnessed a series of dream images from another era. Gold mingled
with lapis lazuli and crimson to render in myriad small tesserae the
miraculous events of Christ's life. His birth, baptism, and transfiguration clung to the upper walls of the church like so many encrusta-
tions of coral. In the dome itself a giant Pantocrator gazed down at
me, the expression on his face redolent with severity and risk. These
were the images of a series of defining events in the history of consciousness, I felt. Artists were already grappling with something
truly awe-filled, something that hitherto had never been expressed.
Again I was reminded of what Isaac had said when he described the
Incarnation as a "treasure to the world":

> Truly this mystery is vast. . . . The flood of Christ's mysteries
> presses upon my mind like the waves of the sea. I wanted to
> be silent before them, and not to speak, but they proved to be
> like burning fire that was kindled in my bones. My mind
> rebukes me, revealing my errors to me. Your mystery
> stupefies me, but urges me on to behold it. . . . O my Hope,
> pour into my heart the inebriation, which consists in the
> hope of you. O Jesus Christ, the resurrection and light of all
> the worlds, place upon my soul's head the crown of
> knowledge of you; open before me all of a sudden the door of
> mercies, cause the rays of your grace to shine out in my
> heart.[3]

"Your mystery stupefies me, but urges me on to behold it"; this,
surely, was what I had experienced that morning in Daphni church.
The mosaics were so otherworldly, so steeped in what Isaac called

"inebriation" that I knew then why I had made this journey to Greece. I had gone there to renew my acquaintance with a knowledge that I had thought lost.

This sense of lost knowledge refound permeated all my journeys in the ensuing years. Once I climbed Mount Toubkal in Morocco, the highest mountain in North Africa. It was part of my desire to seek out remote places where men choose to center their own spirituality. I hired a mule and guide, and together we made our way through mounds of terminal moraine littering a dry riverbed outside a Berber village at the foot of the mountain. The peaks above reminded me of aging lion's teeth, so brown were their slopes. In some places we came on a mountain village of mud houses surrounded by terraces newly plowed. Sunlight shone on the damp, rocky slopes, giving the impression of patina on an old painting. Goats and sheep grazed on the sparse herbage. I had entered a world blessed by the monarchical nature of high mountains, those somber peaks of sublimity and indifference.

At one point we stopped for lunch on a track high above a river. I could see women below washing clothes and laying them out to dry on rocks. The colors of their garments reminded me of a rainbow. Here I was climbing into the Atlas, conscious of the increasing distance separating me from people. Yet this remote mountain community of farmers and shepherds had managed to fashion their own universe. They had woven into their existence the earth, the sky, the seasons, and the stark panorama of the mountains. What they had managed to create, which I felt suddenly a part of, was a piece of cloth shot through with a most vibrant of threads—that of the interdependence of men with their environment.

At one point we came on a shrine tucked away below an escarpment. The tomb, or *marabout*, belonged to Sidi Chamharouch, a local Muslim saint. Outside the walls of the shrine asses and mules were housed in straw-laid pens. Bright flags fluttered above the dome. Nearby, a group of women were sitting in a circle carding wool. All of them were wearing the same rainbow-colored clothing I had seen earlier. It seemed the genies of the mountains, so fearsome and so threatening, had been contained by the spiritual *baraka* of the saint and by this fixation with color. What the saint had generated in his lifetime, that now lay in his tomb like a nugget in the earth, was a power to resist the inchoate forces of nature. Meanwhile this great mountain before us, Mount Toubkal, shone like a beacon in the night. From where we stood its age-old radiance appeared to have been muted by the white-domed space of a saint's tomb and the brightly colored cloth being woven to cover our nakedness.

All these trips of mine impressed on me the importance of making my own journey to the inner mountain. In a sense, I had taken on myself the task of realizing what the Greek ascetic writers called *xeniteia*, or "living as a stranger." It is a curious term that means more than "exile" in that a nomadic existence is not implied. Its meaning pertains to a sort of journey *away* from the world, a withdrawal from its contingencies, in pursuit of a deeper awareness of the shortness and fragility of life. *Xeniteia* also suggests a desire to be unknown and of no account, and a willingness to be more flexible in one's approach to one's professional life. Isaac himself associates *xeniteia* with the acquisition of humility.[4]

I suspect that my own journeys, though more nomadic in nature, had taken on a quality of *xeniteia*, and I that of living as a stranger. It is a peculiar sensation, knowing that whatever you do is inspired by this need to enter into a more thoughtful relationship with the world. Everything that ones sees or touches, everybody one meets and with whom one shares some intrinsic experience, every moment of realization that showers forth from the very aloneness of the journey—these largely subliminal events go to make up *xeniteia*. I have often felt that I was engaged on the task of reconstructing something altogether different from a "life history" or a so-called past. What I had embarked on is best reflected in the words that I came across in an eighteenth-century Chinese novel known as *The Dream of the Red Chamber*:

> He had been dreaming and then woke up. He found himself in the ruins of a temple. On one side there was a beggar dressed in the robes of a Taoist monk. He was lame and was killing fleas. Hsieng-Lien asked him who he was and what place they were in. The monk answered:
> "I don't know who I am, nor where we are. I only know that the road is long."
> Hsieng-Lien understood. He cut off his hair with his sword and followed the stranger.

The idea that I don't know who I am nor where I am going is synonymous with *xeniteia*, I feel sure. Yet when I am surrounded by the journey—that is, when the journey has become my sole reality, erasing all memory of where I might belong in ordinary life—I find myself entering into another space, the space of the lame beggar killing fleas. Here I am able to practice what can best be described as the game of words, for this is what I retire to in the midst of my engagement with the exotic.

The game of words is the game all writers play, like others play at solitaire. It is a game born out of the knowledge that all experience and things do not attain to reality unless and until they are translated into words. Language brings things, realizations, and perceptions into being. In the act of exploring a city with its monuments, its churches, or its mosques, I find myself entering the historicity of my own thoughts. There they are appended to language, to words that describe the way I feel about what lies latent in them as impressions. I bring these impressions to the surface whenever I articulate their reality for myself. In a cheap hotel in downtown Suez or in a pension on a square in Córdoba or riding in a calèche along a back street in Marrakech, I am able to reiterate an interior language that only I have the ability to speak. It is the language of inner valuation whereby I am able to give meaning, a new meaning, to what is essentially an investiture of spirit on things. The world becomes in that moment not so much a place but an expectation, something that surmounts all distinctions.

In this game my thoughts may alight on a word such as *live*. I will ponder it with all the care of a jeweler assessing the perfection of a gem. As his eyes work the surface of a stone, so, too, do my thoughts caress the outer reality of the word. *To live* suggests a quality of aliveness, that being is predicated by some energy that we associate with life. I allow my thoughts to sink into this feeling even as I hear the sound of street noise outside my hotel window or my driver flailing his horse into a trot with a whip. I am conscious that no reality exists where the word is lacking; that *live* exposes something that is replete with spirit. It is the hidden essence, the unrevealed perfection lying at the heart of this word. Yet when I break it open, or peer deeper into it as the jeweler might do into a gemstone, I am made aware that other contingencies are at work.

Suddenly, when all the letters are thrown into the air so that they fall to earth in new configurations, I am presented with another set of realities. *Live*, or aliveness, has rearranged itself in my thoughts to reveal more negative aspects. It becomes *vile* and, more surreptitiously, *evil*. This word that had offered so much in terms of positive valuations has now shown me its darker side. I am disconcerted. I look out the window at some indecipherable street sign in Arabic and know that I have entered into the living hell of words. This, presumably, is where Anthony found himself whenever he confronted the demons in his cell. The benignity of existence was transformed into its demonic counterpart. He did battle, as I do, not so much with temptations, or the impulse toward diminution, but with his own inability to articulate the divine in himself. This is the real path of satanization. When a man like Anthony wrestles with the devil, he is doing battle with what he cannot express, and so with what he perceives as a nonreality. What he doesn't know is that in the end the Word subsumes spirit.

I suspect all those anchorites of the desert understood this game and this conflict. Reading what they have to say on the issue of the written word, one thing becomes evident: that they, too, saw *xeniteia*, the state of living as a stranger, as being in the service of language, of sacred script. How often did John of Apamea exhort men to "be constant in the reading of the prophets" or "toil at reading the Scriptures"?[25] He knew, as did others, that the games we play at the heart of the word often determine how we figure in the realm of the spirit. We are, at best, mere voyagers in the ocean of language.

Scrip-ture, the act of resacralizing words spoken by men and women engaged in the most valiant of battles, suggests to me the real task that lies ahead. I suppose, like most people, I have always regarded sacred writings as being somehow frozen in time, the product of ancient minds, scrolls of words sheathed in outmoded doctrine and prejudice. But when I sit in the library of Saint Anthony's monastery, gazing at the crumbling tomes on their shelves, I am conscious that these books contain material that is still explosive. They still have the power to ignite receptive minds. They still partake of that incandescence capable of dispelling the darkness we associate with subterfuge and convention. Scripture becomes an act of defiance in the face of our preference for the puerile, for the easily discernable, and the comfort of what is forever agreeably manifest.

The act of making script is therefore revolutionary. No wonder it is considered to be "sacred writing": certain arrangements of words that embody the transmission of the great questions serve as a counterweight to those kitelike perambulations that merely reflect how we think or feel. Scripture is a solid oak among groves of beech or ash. It radiates the slow growth of consciousness as it struggles to spread its panoply of shade. When we read the work of those old anchorites, we become aware that we are in the presence of men who have plumbed the depths of suffering, of doubt, and of joy. All their emotions have been placed at the service of rendering exquisite the inner workings of the spirit. What they are trying to discover is the way we might live and work in an altered state of consciousness wholly removed from the realm of appearance.

It is clear that all my journeys have been linked to this quest for the right word. I know, as did those old hermits, that one truly travels only when one crosses the frontier of language. To do so means traveling *through* words, through their marvelous inconsistency and ability to deceive. When I enter a rock chapel and gaze up at a crude fresco, or when I study a luminous mosaic in some Byzantine church, or when I allow my eyes to wander over the white dome of a saint's tomb, I know that what I am really encountering is my capacity to articulate the full depth of my feelings. These objects are but visible signs of what lies dormant within me: the ability to cut a furrow through the soil of some deeply imbedded experience that transcends all that I am. What I see conjures up a mode of expression tethered to something beyond words. Yet the intermingling of image and word in itself becomes a most perfect reality. I am transported out of myself into a world devoted to what Nietzsche likened to a wheat field on a summer's night. I think he meant that there is an aroma, a fragrance, a sense of invisible nutrient lying out there in the darkness that promises an ongoing enrichment of life.

The truth is I am secretly amazed at our ability to transform the things of this world into objects that reflect what Isaac of Nineveh called the "limitless powers and glory of Invisibleness." His own knowledge of the visible world around Qatar, where he was born, can be seen in the way he alluded to the difficulty of realizing what it is we all seek:

> If a diver found a pearl in every oyster, then everyone would quickly become rich! And if he brought one up the moment he dove, without waves beating against him [that is, temptations], without any sharks encountering him, without having to hold his breath until he nearly expires, without being deprived of the clear air granted to everyone and having to descend to the abyss—if all this were the case, pearls would come thicker and faster than lightning flashes!"[6]

How beautiful this is! The idea of lightning penetrating the oyster and so producing a pearl harks back to my *marabout* on Mount Toubkal housing the bones of a saint. Each is in the business of making manifest what lies below the surface. Moreover, meditation is about translating sensible experience into something that is non-sensuous. Thus we journey into stillness even as we adopt the cloak of silence. It is at this point that we deliberately abandon the gift of words for the sake of achieving inner silence. Isaac was clear on the relationship between words and silence when he remarked, "Silence is the mystery of the age to come, but words are instruments of this world."[7] He knew, as I had begun to learn during my years of wandering, that one must go beyond words if one wishes to understand what lies behind the skein of things.

Sitting in the monastery library each day is therefore another kind of journey. All that lies before me is the prospect of crossing on mental foot a broad meditational space. It is my desert. Tomes of vellum and parchment housed in glass cases surround me. Some are illuminated with tiny heraldic devices, others with the complex graphology of letters bearing the resplendency of the word. I am not alone here. The voices of countless ascetics alert me to the fact that I have joined a convivium of the spirit. Each one of them, it seems, has struggled to bring forth the right word, the right expression to describe that suspiration of air that accompanies the nearness of an angel. My task, if I am to heed Lazarus well, is to enter this experience of language, this quest for the *mot juste* of the spiritual life, if I am to understand the world of Anthony and his contemporaries.

I feel content at this moment. In no other place have I felt more content. Up on the mountain lives a memory and a man. The man emulates the memory. He is attempting to re-create the life of Anthony, his stability of character and purity of soul. Thus he is trying to fathom the greatest paradox of all: what comes first, thought or the word. One needs to turn to Anthony himself for some insight: "Which is first—mind or letters? And which is the cause of which—the mind of the letters or the letters of the mind?" Anthony's answer was unequivocal: "In the person whose mind is sound there is no need for letters."[8] Soundness of mind was related to the overcoming of language itself.

So I must read these thinkers. I must soak myself in their particular spiritual energy, their *parresia*. I must slowly learn to go beyond the paradigm of the word. It is something new for me. At the same time, by immersing myself in the thought of such men, I feel that I may be able to release myself from the tyranny of knowledge. Because somewhere in all of these ruminations I sense this to be the real issue. Anthony and his friends sought to go beyond the relativity of certitude, that urn filled with ashes, and so anoint themselves in an entirely new chrism. They wanted to become, each in his own way, the living embodiment of that completion, fulfillment, and perfection of death.

seven

CROSSING THE BORDER

"Prayer is the rejection of concepts," Evagrius Ponticus maintained. Already I hear some intimation of a mental terrain devoid of the idea of spokenness. Evagrius is an interesting and seminal figure in the history of early anchoritism, for he brought to this world a refined mind, a Greek mind, a mind that had suffered the ignominy of having to abandon what it loved most—dialogue, theological disputation, and the witty agenda of court life in the Byzantine capital. More than any other man—more even than Anthony, I suspect—he had been forced to denounce one kind of life in order to end up in the Egyptian desert. Evagrius Ponticus was a man of courageous intellect who was able to put aside all that he stood for in pursuit of the perfection and quality of peace (*katastasis*) that he desired above all else.

I was drawn to this man for a number of reasons. Here was a person who had managed to surmount his own deepest conflicts by an act of escape. Born in 346 into a noted Pontic family in the city of Ibora in Asia Minor, Evagrius was destined to occupy a senior position in the early Christian Church because of his education and family connections. Ordained a reader (lector) by Basil the Great, he became one of the greatest theologians of the early church. After the death of Basil, Evagrius was drawn to Gregory of Nazianzus, one of the three so-called Cappadocian Fathers, a wise and highly cultured man who introduced him to a more serious spiritual life than he had hitherto known.[1] He was asked to accompany Gregory to Constantinople in 381 to attend the first ecumenical council, there to argue against various heresies that threatened the Nicene faith. His skill in argument was immediately noticed by Bishop Nectarius of Constantinople, who invited him to stay in the capital, where he soon came to be known as "destroyer of the twaddle of the heretics."

Life in the capital appealed to Evagrius. What inclination he possessed for meditation, quiet, and prayer began to wane as he immersed himself in the social life of the city. He grew careless, worldly, and delicate, preferring to live in great pomp and allowing himself to be administered to by slaves. It seems, too, that the young Evagrius also succumbed to the allure of a married woman at the court who clearly adored him.[2] This secret liaison began to trouble him, however, for he knew that it called into question the veracity of his vocation. As a philosopher, a would-be ascetic, he now found himself "constrained by the chains of this servitude." In desperation Evagrius sought a way out of his dilemma. The answer came to him in a dream.

Let Palladius in his *Lausiac History* detail the poignancy of this dream, as it is one of the great dreams of antiquity, superior even to that of Saint Jerome, who once dreamed of being scourged for his love of classical literature, a scene so mysteriously portrayed by Piero della Francesca in a painting located in Urbino, Italy:

There appeared to him [in his dream] the vision of angels in the shape of soldiers of the governor, and they seized him and took him apparently to the tribunal and threw him into the so-called *custody*, while the men had accosted him, as it seemed, without giving a reason, having first fastened his neck and hands with iron collars and chains. But he knew in his conscience that for the sake of the above fault he was suffering these things, and imagined that her husband had intervened. So now he was extremely anxious. Another trial was going on, and others were being put to torture for some accusation, so he continued to be much perturbed. And the angel who brought the vision transformed himself to represent the coming of a genuine friend who said to him, tied up as he was among forty prisoners, and chained together: "Why are you retained here, my lord deacon?" He said to him: "In truth, I do not know. But I have a suspicion that so-and-so the ex-governor has laid a charge against me, impelled by an absurd jealousy. And I fear that the judge, corrupted by bribes, may have inflicted punishment upon me." He said to him: "If you will listen to your friend, it is not expedient for you to stay in this city." Evagrius said to him: "If God will release me from this misfortune and you see me in Constantinople (any more), know that I shall suffer this punishment justly. Except for one day, to give me time to put my clothes on board, I certainly will not remain." Evagrius then came out of his trance [dream] which had come on him that night, and he arose and argued with himself: "Even if it were a dream, I should act upon it." So, having put all his belongings in a ship, he sailed for Jerusalem.[3]

Of all the great anticipatory dreams of history, Evagrius's dream of his imprisonment for some unnamed crime strikes a chord. His guilt is palpable. And for a man who was later to set such store in the psychic power of dreams, this encounter with the angels of the prison draws on a vast range of material pertaining to the potency of redemption. Even as he fell into the arms of his lover, Evagrius was conscious of how close he was to damnation. Hell loomed not so much as a place or a sensation but as the failure of his own will to resist. The court lady was less his seducer than she was the final nail in the coffin of his spirit. He had to leave the capital and journey to the Holy Land if he were ever to regain his equilibrium.

In Jerusalem, at a hospice near the Mount of Olives, Evagrius met two people who were to become lifelong friends. Melania, an aristocratic Roman lady who had been widowed since the age of twenty-two, had herself journeyed to Egypt with Rufinus, once a friend of Jerome's. There she had met and talked with some of the great ascetics living in the desert of Nitria, before traveling to Palestine and establishing a monastery where Rufinus later resided. Evagrius found himself in the right company: Melania and Rufinus were both followers of Origen, a Christian philosopher who also influenced Jerome. He had entered a hothouse of spiritual, theological, and monastic experimentation. Palestine and Egypt, it seems, were the places where thinkers from all over the Roman world were congregating in order to explore new ways of conducting their spiritual life. Again Evagrius had landed on his feet.

Still he found it difficult to give up his old habits. Worldly ways once more seduced him. "The devil hardened his heart" and vainglory stupefied him, so Palladius relates. While he was in this condition of lassitude, Evagrius suddenly fell ill, and no remedy employed by physicians could help. In the end, Melania recognized the true cause of his conflict: his failure to honor the promise he had made to himself in Constantinople. After six months of illness she got him to confess to his failure, and within a few days he was cured. She urged him to remain true to his vocation and enter the monastic life. Evagrius consented. Wearing new clothes supplied by Melania, he departed for Egypt. The man of the court, this spiritual dandy, had finally made his commitment: he would give up everything in pursuit of *apatheia*, stillness.

Somehow I could identify with Evagrius. He was a man in transition. He had wavered between a successful life at court and a life governed by the mysterious sapience of the desert. On the one hand he had enjoyed the favors of women, while on the other, he sensed where this might lead him. He enjoyed the life of the intellect and the wonderful friendships that it offered. He had also known and shared ideas with the best minds of his generation—men such as Basil and the two Gregories, Nectarius, and Rufinus. These men had challenged him and made him recognize his own worth. His was a mind that had been honed in the foundry of civility and intellectual discourse. To enter the desert was, of course, to embrace a life that was more rusticated—a life that treated utterance with suspicion, since it partook of conceptuality at variance with the idea of *apatheia*.

Evagrius, therefore, was a modern. He wavered between opportunities and options. I liked him for that. I suspect that if Anthony had been alive and had been fortunate enough to meet the young dilettante, he would have seen in this man a magnificent conflict. What Evagrius did better than most was resolve his tensions in a way that was both deeply spiritual and productive. He set about absolving his past by a deliberate act of ascesis. For fifteen years he subjected his body, and his mind, to every conceivable form of denial. A pound of bread each day, a pint of oil every three months, nights standing naked in a well in winter so that his flesh was frozen in order to quell the demon of lust, days spent out in the open until his body was ravaged by ticks because of some blasphemy—these were the kinds of tortures he subjected himself to, until finally all the refinement and voluptuousness of his earlier life were eliminated. He had made peace with his past.

Evagrius spent the rest of his life in Nitria and later at Kellia, on the edge of the Wadi al-Natrun, south of Alexandria. There he composed his great work of mystical instruction that so deeply influenced people such as Cassian, the founder of European monasticism, as well as Isaac of Nineveh, whose thought we will study later. He was heir to the pioneering work of Anthony and Macarius the Egyptian and reflected their austere yet vigorous spirituality.[4] He was the first man to clearly articulate the ascetic experience as it has been developed by Anthony and his successors. It is to him, then, that we must turn if we are to understand the method (*theoria*) of the desert anchorites. Though forever the outsider in Nitria because of his cultivated background, Evagrius nonetheless gained a reputation for being a strenuous ascetic and loveable master. He was ever the stranger, it seems.

In a sense, Anthony lived on in the person of Evagrius. Though they came from vastly different backgrounds—the Coptic farmer and the Greek intellectual—together they embodied the spirit of early Christianity as it pertained to the ascetic life. To understand Evagrius was to enter into Anthony's cave at Mount Colzim and so draw nearer to the master's ascetic and mystical vision. For, according to Evagrius, if there was one true aim in life, then it was to transform one's image into the "resemblance of the archetype." To do so was to attain to an *apatheia* of the soul along with "true knowledge of things." This was the key.

My early encounter with his work in the monastery library made me realize that I was dealing with no ordinary thinker. Evagrius proposed some controversial ideas, not least of which was his doctrine of the *eighth day*, surely a dogma that would later leave him open to a charge of heresy.[5] According to Evagrius, the *seventh day* was marked by Christ's reign over all rational creatures, including the demons, since they, too, must pass through successive stages in order to attain, increasingly, purity of heart. When all creatures have attained to the stage of angelic purity and its proper contemplation, then the period of the seventh day would come to an end, thus inaugurating the period of the eighth day. Such a day marks the end of the reign of Christ, when all the intelligences return to the primitive unity of God. In the process, all rational creatures become *isochristoi*, as those fully equal to Christ. All of creation as we know it will be abolished, including bodily forms. Indeed, matter itself and all its implications, such as diversity, multiplicity, and number, will be eliminated from the face of the earth. The original form will thus be reconstituted. The great cosmic round dance would have come to an end.

What all this implies is rather challenging. Evagrius is suggesting that man, in becoming as Christ, releases himself from the need to identify with Christ. In other words, by following certain ascetic practices, man is able to go beyond belief, indeed beyond religion itself. One hears an early foreshadowing of Nietzsche's ideas in these remarks, as he too posited the idea that man might overcome himself if only he did away with a fixation with values.[6] Though with one proviso: Nietzsche wished to deny the metaphysical, whereas Evagrius seems to imply some form of eschatological completion in achieving equality with Christ. By becoming *isochristoi*, it seems, man overcomes his reliance on the material world as his bulwark against the actions of fate. As Evagrius so eloquently stated: "The perfect man does not work at *remaining* continent, nor does a man with *apatheia* work at being patient. For patience is the virtue of a man who experiences untoward emotions, and continence is the virtue of a man who suffers disturbing impulses."[7] One senses a more subtle initiative at work here: the act of becoming equal with Christ enables a man to go beyond the simple image of Christ as both an historical and christological figure. Man invents, to use Nietzsche's word, a new image of Christ that transcends his Christ-ness.

Evagrius was entering new territory. He had welded the ascetic experience of his years in the desert, as well as the spiritual theory that he had gleaned from his elders, onto those philosophic insights that he had acquired from his beloved Stoic thinkers. But unlike earlier theologians such as Tertullian and Clement of Alexandria, he did not wish to create a Christian dogma that might satisfy those eager to reinforce the idea of church hierarchy. He was more interested, it seems, in creating a genuine philosophy for living that took the best of Stoicism and grafted it onto the Christic vision. Perhaps his early contact with the "twaddle of the heretics" had taught him not to place too much emphasis on doctrinal orthodoxy. For him, the path to *apatheia* was a more devious route: it lay through the thicket of suffering and atonement, through the need to understand and accept the value of personal sacrifice over that of a simple allegiance to right belief. His lover in Constantinople had taught him well: from her he had learned how to distant himself from attachments in order to better know himself.

We are dealing, then, with a man who chose to remove himself from the society of the intellect in an attempt to discover new insights into the working of the spirit. In this sense he was a natural heir to Anthony, although for entirely different reasons. He understood better than most the importance of separating the soul from the body in a deliberate act of withdrawal *(anachoresis)* if one wished to acquire virtue. To do so, one needed to nourish the soul with "contemplative knowledge" in a bid to draw near to *apatheia*. "We call *apatheia* the health of the soul," he wrote, "since it alone is able to unite us with the holy powers."[8] Union with incorporeal beings, such as angels, follows quite naturally when the same deep attitudes are shared. One senses here a new and more refined psychology at work: Evagrius wanted men to realize how important it was to recognize the difference between these deep attitudes of the soul and the more passionate fever that lay on the surface of life. "Should you then be able," he went on, "as the saying has it, to drive out a nail with a nail, you can know for certain that you stand near the confines of *apatheia*, for your mind is strong enough to abolish thoughts inspired by demons."[9] According to Evagrius, in this moment contemplative knowledge overreaches the irrational part of the soul and so neutralizes the senses.

To read his *Praktikos*, a tiny book of some twenty pages, is to plunge into a cool stream of thought unsullied by turbidity or anguish. How acute is his psychological insight. "Sadness is the deprivation of sensible pleasure," he remarks, stripping away any illusion we might have that such an emotion is founded on loss of affections. His "Let us broach the question of whether the thought causes the passions or the passions cause the thought," refers us back to that age-old paradox of consciousness that Anthony alluded to. Evagrius answers this by arguing that the passions are stirred up by the senses, and that only charity and continence can ensure that they remain dormant. Charity, he maintains is the "killer of snakes" in the garden of anger.[10]

But he bestows most of his critical judgment and sympathy on the doctrine of *apatheia*. "*Agape* or love is the progeny of *apatheia*," he argues, the "very flower of ascesis." We are at once drawn into the shadowy space of that cave to where so many anchorites retired in the expectation of releasing themselves from the prison of self. This is the realm where men struggled to reach that state of tranquillity where all images of the sensible world were consumed by *apatheia*, whereby a man's spirit might begin to observe its own light. It is a remarkable observation: for one's spirit to "see its own light," a considerable transformation of one's being needs to occur. Evagrius seems to suggest that this can happen only after the intellect has been stripped of all its allegiance to self. The self, in a sense, must be abandoned; it has to be removed from the I-thouness of immediate perception. How the world is no longer determined by the self's interaction with it but by a supreme act of self-sacrifice, of detachment. I am immediately reminded of Wittgenstein's proposition, "The world is independent of my will. . . . For there is no logical connection between the will and the world, which would guarantee it, and the supposed physical connection itself is surely not something that we could will."[11] How beautiful is this premise: that in order for one's spirit to recognize the power and glory of its own radiance, it must be set loose from the bondage of selfhood.

There is another implication: this radiance is contingent on a man's accepting that virtue itself no longer bears the fullness of being. Evagrius put it well when he wrote: "A man who has established the virtues in himself, and is entirely permeated with them, no longer remembers the law of the commandment."[12] He is telling us that only in a state of *apatheia* is a man removed from all causality, from all recognition of his separateness. He has entered a region known only to those men who have dedicated themselves to a genuine renovation of spirit. Underlying this nonselfhood, too, is his concept of the eighth day. Man must go beyond even the concept of deity if he is to "know himself." A limitless life would then conform to that which Plotinus deemed as eternity, whereby a man knows nothing of past or future, since completeness possesses itself, intact, forever. Evagrius would have agreed.

Moreover, the idea of seeing one's own light calls to mind the doctrine of divine illumination and uncreated light so prevalent in the thought of the hesychasts on Mount Athos, and in the teachings of Gregory Palamas (1296–1359). Such a light belongs to the supernatural world of grace and is altogether different from natural light. We read in Gregory's *Hagioritus Tomus*:

> The light properly apprehended by the intellect is other than
> that apprehended by the senses. . . . Sensible light manifests
> sensible objects, whereas the light of the mind is the

knowledge contained in thoughts. Consequently sight and intellect do not properly apprehend the same light, but each acts according to and within the limits of nature. But when those who are worthy receive the spiritual and supernatural grace and power, they see with both sense and intellect that which transcends all sense and intellect."[13]

This light, often associated with the light given off by Christ on Mount Tabor (that is, the Transfiguration), was seen only by the disciples because their senses had so changed and therefore "passed over at that moment from the flesh to the Spirit." It seems that seeing one's own light, at least for Evagrius, partakes of a similar loss of sense.[14]

What is it about this man that I find so appealing? I suppose it is his philosophic integrity married to his abiding confidence in the profound ambiguity of truth. Only he could argue that out of prayer could come this confidence. More important, only he could maintain that we have the capacity to "walk with angels" and so learn from them the meaning of created things whenever we enter a state of pure prayer. Of course, this prayer is not a prayer of words. Only the spirit that has attained to complete unconsciousness (total insensibility) of all sensible experience at the time of prayer, becoming "free of all matter," can ever hope to enter into a state of *apatheia*.[15] It is at this point that we know how close we are to what Gregory Palamas called the "standing still of the mind."[16]

So the *eighth day* as a concept is less a heresy than it is an attempt to realize what is transcendent about Christ's message. Evagrius recognized that an ascetic life was the only kind of life that offered a man the possibility of breaking away from conditional existence in order to identify with this transcendence. He saw, as few before him had seen, that *apatheia* prepared a man's soul for a unique kind of experience. Plato's bifurcation of the universe into ideas and sensible things had met its match in this man's desire to see a correspondence between the material and the immaterial. In Christ, of course, he saw a bridge, someone who was able to make it possible for men to move between the inner and the outer without in any way impinging on self, since this had been defused of its opacity. Christ had shown how to eliminate death by embracing it, and how to make his life-and-death into a purely inward illumination mysteriously experienced by the heart. This, I think, is what Evagrius was alluding to when he expounded his doctrine of the eighth day.

Of course, when we explore such themes, we find ourselves dealing with a mystical experience that is not normally a part of everyday life. Critics of the ascetic life, and especially that of the early Egyptian anchorites, have concentrated their criticism on the physiological practices of these men while failing to acknowledge the illuminatory knowledge that flows from them. The endless tales of anchorites subjecting their bodies to lack of sleep, filth, poor food, excessive fasting, loneliness, a denial of intellectual discourse, suspicion of learning and of books,[17] suggests a lifestyle that reduces a man to both physical and psychological pulp. The opposite, however, proved to be more real. Men like Anthony and Evagrius transcended their psychophysical predicament through such ascetic practice and realized a new understanding of what it was to be human. Nothing like it had occurred in the history of mankind.

The unique blend of nonselfhood and spiritual insight that the early anchorites espoused represents a transition to a more subjective relationship between man and the outer world. Gone is the Neoplatonic view that purification of the soul is accomplished primarily through philosophy, as we see it especially in the work of Plotinus and Porphyry, where the emphasis was placed on intuitive vision being derived from a firm grounding in abstract reasoning. When we hear Plotinus' remark: "The Intellectual-Principle furnishes standards, the most certain for any soul that is able to apply them. What else is necessary Dialectic puts together for itself, combining and dividing, until it has reached perfect intellection,"[18] we know that we are still dealing with a disposition of the soul that can be realized only by the few. Evagrius's contribution to contemplative knowledge was to draw attention to the need to give up such reliance on abstract reasoning. He, the arch intellectual from Constantinople, ultimately came out in defense of Anthony's method because he knew that what Christian asceticism was directed toward was not the realization of a theurgy or power as practiced by certain Neoplatonists but the creation of a certain quality of being in man that went beyond philosophy altogether. As far as he was concerned, this is what Christian asceticism was all about.

Becoming equal with Christ, therefore, was a way of realizing man as *possibility* in contrast to that of man as sophic identity, as defined in the Plotinian view. His long years in the desert enabled Evagrius to discover a great deal more about man's potential spirituality than any of the earlier Greek or Alexandrian philosophers, who had rarely, if ever, ventured beyond the city. It may be argued that this was the flaw in Greek philosophy from the beginning: that it was essentially an urbane, and therefore abstract, method of reasoning. In contrast, Egyptian asceticism produced a more subtle method of detaching the mind from its reliance on reason. The truth was that it had undermined nearly a thousand years of patient philosophic endeavor by introducing the prospect of an eschatological event taking the place of the much-vaunted stoical calm of the ancients. This is why pagan philosophers so despised Christianity: it had subversively reintroduced the idea that metaphysics still had something to contribute to the refinement of consciousness, when all along they had sought to undermine this view.

No wonder I admired Evagrius. He was the first Greek thinker to cross the lines and join the enemy. Of course, men like Clement of Alexandria, Tertullian, Athanasius, Basil the Great, even Augustine (who was born two years before Anthony's death in 356), had expounded the new doctrine of Christianity. But none of these men had left their studies, classrooms, or monasteries. They had still attempted to put into practice this new doctrine by way of reason and dialectic. They were great writers, surely, and pioneer theologians. But they wrote as pagan philosophers, using all the rhetorical tools at their disposal. It's no accident that Augustine was himself a master of rhetoric, one of the subjects of the trivium, before his conversion to Christianity.[19] We may assume that Evagrius had also been educated in a similar fashion, since he possessed a firm grasp of the principles of reason and dialectic.

But for reasons stemming from his personal life, he had chosen the experiential path to spiritual enlightenment. By turning his back on court life and the city—and later the monastery—he had set himself on a more dangerous course. The captains of his fragile barque were, of course, Anthony and Macarius the Egyptian, two courageous navigators who had set sail in the Egyptian desert before him. Both these men came from the land; they were not city dwellers nor educated men. They were men who had perhaps instinctively recognized that philosophy had in the past denied men their rightful claim to a spiritual insight and understanding of their own. This is why Christ held such appeal for them: they knew that he, too, was, if not a man of the soil, then at least a working-class fellow like themselves. Evagrius's great contribution to Christian experience was to take onboard *their* method of reasoning as distinct from the one he was used to. It became clear to him that asceticism was as much a mode of thinking as it was a spiritual practice.

His end came prematurely, at the age of fifty-three. His health had begun to fail him in his last years, but still he maintained his austere regimen, only conceding to eat cooked food instead of raw vegetables at the last. He had reached such a profound state of spiritual calm that he was able to admit to those close to him how, during the final three years of his life, he was no longer troubled by disordered passions and thoughts. It seems the man had achieved complete *apatheia*, the goal of all anchorites. He had immersed himself in the observation of his own light to such an intense degree that even the meaning of the eighth day meant little to him. Later generations may condemn him as a heretic, but he would not be concerned. It's no accident that he chose to die on the Feast of the Epiphany celebrating Christ's transfiguration. The last thing we hear of Evagrius is of him being taken to the church for the feast, where he received the Holy Communion for the last time, and then peacefully dying. In a sense, the light had proceeded toward the Light.

This is the man I had come to know and to love during those days that I studied his work in the monastery library. He was a man after my own heart. He had put his great learning and intellect at the service of an ideal grounded in simplicity and existential truth. His cell in the desert made of mud brick and palm leaves was part of the great human architecture of the spirit. He was not the only man to build his retreat among the dunes, nor will he be the last— Lazarus is testimony to that. But he was one of the earliest to recognize that spirituality requires the whole man if it is to radiate and become as an inner light. He managed to bring together the intellect and the heart and so augment a new way of observing himself and the world. This is the Evagrius I admire: the man who found courage enough to give up everything in pursuit of his vision of truth. His desert, it seems, was filled less with demons and their destructive tendencies than with profound new insights into the relationship among spirituality, body, and earth.

eight

EYE OF THE OSTRICH

My understanding of the ascetic impulse as a result of my first weeks of study at Saint Anthony's had deepened. I felt like the traveler Robert Curzon, who made a journey to Egypt in 1837 to collect early Christian manuscripts from monastic libraries. The British bibliophile had toured the Wadi al-Natrun, where he managed to purchase several Coptic manuscripts from the impoverished monks. Though he sensed that these ancient manuscripts held untold secrets, he was never able to approach them as true sacred texts, such was his desire to amass a library of rare folios. This was the age of literary plunder, when an early Syriac Psalter was considered to be worth more than its weight in gold.[1] For my part, I was happy just to enter this world of spiritual discernment.

The fact that Evagrius lived in the Thebaid, where so many anchorites of the past had resided, inspired me to want to visit the region. I broached the idea with Lazarus on one of my visits to his cave, asking him whether he thought it would serve any purpose. A part of me wanted to visit this heartland of early asceticism, if only because I needed to see for myself this region that had lured so many there in the first place. Lazarus reminded me that he himself had lived in the Monastery of the Syrians (Deir al-Suryani) for a short time before coming to Saint Anthony's. It is one of Wadi al-Natrun's few surviving Coptic retreats. It appears that Curzon found valuable Aramaic texts hanging from pegs in individual leather satchels there, as well as masses of "loose vellum pages" in the keep's oil cellar. Today the monastery's few remaining antique volumes are lovingly maintained in a modern library, safe from literary predators. It boasts a number of ancient relics also, the most important being a lock of hair from Mary Magdalene.

It is there, too, so Lazarus told me, that an early anchorite named Bischoi used to fasten his hair to a chain hanging from the ceiling in order that he might remain standing in the *orante*, or praying attitude, throughout the night. It was said that Christ himself appeared before the saint, a redoubtable ascetic, and allowed him to wash the saint's feet. Ephraim the Syrian, one of early Christianity's greatest poets, traveled from his native land to converse with Bischoi. Though neither spoke the other's language, they each prayed and were immediately granted complete knowledge of the other's tongue. Ephraim's staff still stands in the grounds of the monastery in the form of a large tamarind tree, a memento to this profound meeting of minds.

Lazarus told me of another interesting custom associated with the monasteries of the Thebaid. Ostrich eggs are said to hang from the ceiling of the church as a symbol of spiritual dedication. According to Father Vansleb, a seventeenth-century visitor, this practice enabled monks to concentrate their devotions:

> I have read in an Arabian manuscript, a remarkable thing concerning the Austrich, which I cannot pass over without publishing.
>
> When it intends to hatch its Egs, it sits not upon them, as other birds, but the male and female hatches them with their Eye only; and when either of them hath need to seek for food, he gives notice to the other by crying; and the other continues to look upon the Egs, till it be returned . . . for if they did but look off for a moment, the Egs will spoil and rot.
>
> The church of the Coptics hath learn'd an excellent custome from the practice of the bird. They hang up a lighted light between two Egs of an Austrich, over against the priests that officiate, to advise them to be attentive to their devotions.[2]

It was this eye that made it possible for an ascetic to penetrate the mysteries more deeply than if he ignored the example of the ostrich. The bird had devised a method to intensify its level of concentration to the point where a genuine "hatching" might begin to occur. Whether the fact was biologically true was immaterial: the glow of the ostrich egg reflecting the light of candles in a church was enough to work its wonders on the monks.

I decided to make an excursion to the Thebaid. I needed a break from my researches anyway. The monastery food had begun to pall, too, restricted as I was to two meals a day and a supplement of chocolate from my own store. This required replenishing in Cairo. The excursion meant calling for a taxi to come down and take me back to Suez, then catching a bus into Cairo, before taking another bus out to Wadi al-Natrun, some seventy miles northwest of the

capital. I very much wanted to visit Old Cairo at the same time, so
the trip offered me the opportunity to do both.

My taxi duly arrived one morning, and I set off down the high-
way toward the Red Sea. On my right I could see Mount Colzim in
the distance, a solemn edifice of stone. It was strange to think that
for the first time since arriving at Saint Anthony's some weeks earlier, I had decided to take leave of the place. It felt unsettling, too:
the mountain and the narrow streets of the monastery, its smoke-
stained chapels and palm groves—to think that all of them had become so intimately a part of my life. To leave them was to place
myself at odds with what they stood for. Going back to the world,
even for a few days, was an act of abandonment: I could visualize
Lazarus sitting on the terrace outside his cave high on that mountain, utterly oblivious to my departure. As far as he was concerned,
no other world existed beyond what he lived for. So why risk oneself by quitting the preserve of Anthony's spirit in order to drive into
that maelstrom that was Cairo? He was right, of course, but I still
needed to reconnoiter "Babylon" and the land of the Thebaid first.

I reached Cairo early that evening—too late to take the subway
to Babylon (Old Cairo). I booked into a small third-floor hotel on
some anonymous street, not far from the Al-Azhar bus station. A
sleepy gentleman, who I gathered slept on the floor beside the
phone, manned the desk. On the walls of the foyer were large prints
of Swiss mountain scenes, typical of the type of decoration one
finds in such hotels the world over. These establishments are filled
with loneliness. They are like urban cells. It's possible to remain
firmly entrenched in the desert here, even as one hears the dull roar
of traffic from the street below into the early hours of the morning.
In a sense, one is surrounded by the solitude of old neon lights de-
vested of their radiance.

The next morning I took the subway to Masr al Qadima, or Old
Cairo. It was once known as Babylon because of Chaldean workmen

pining after their homeland on the Euphrates. They had been brought
to Egypt by Pharaoh Sesostris III to build public works around
1850 BC. It was during the reign of Emperor Arcadius (r. 395–408)
that the Copts began to build their churches in this quarter. At one
time forty-two were believed to have stood in the area. At the time
of the Arab conquest in 641, Babylon was such a sizeable community that walls to the newly founded capital of Fustat connected
with part of the fortress, including the towers and bastions. Today
it is a rundown quarter of the city, its narrow streets home to ven-
dors selling silverware and tiny wooden crosses woven from bamboo and straw.

Before visiting the Coptic Museum, I took a stroll through a
cemetery adjacent to the Church of Saint Barbara. There I noticed
a young man, a cripple, sitting on a gravestone reading from a small
book of piety. He was muttering the words to himself. He seemed
so self-contained, almost Christ-like, as he poured over his book. In
this vast Islamic city that awoke to the sound of *muezzins* calling at
daybreak each day, this young man had managed to find a place of
sanctuary where he could read in silence. The graves of countless
Christians enveloped him in their cloak of complicity as he read the
words of his favorite saint.

But it was to the Coptic Museum that I wished to go in order to
bury myself in the archaic spirituality from which Anthony and his
friends had first emerged. I had read that the museum contained a
fourth-century Psalter found under the head of a young girl in a
cemetery near Beni Suef on the Nile, not far from where Anthony
was born. The museum also contained textiles, stelae, sheaves from
the Nag Hammadi texts (the so-called Gnostic Gospels) discovered
on the Upper Nile near Luxor in 1947, illuminated manuscripts, cler-
ical robes, and some memorable icons depicting the saints Ahrakass
and Ohganny wearing masks like dogs' heads. These figures were

reminiscent of Anubis, the jackal-headed god of ancient Egypt. Somehow he had found a new incarnation in Christian garb.

Entering the airy rooms of the museum, I was struck by the freshness and vigor of the motifs and decorations on the textile fragments. They reflected a world that was not particularly pharaonic or Greek. They were more of peasant inspiration, the expression of simple men affected by their newly acquired religious beliefs. Of course, they had taken some of their inspiration from Egyptian statuary and hieroglyphics. The old Greco-Roman imagery could be seen in statues of saints dressed up in imperial armor. It was an art in transition, turning its back on the triumphalism of the past in its bid to express a different sensibility. Now it was an art wedded to the depiction of an inner landscape that gloried in the spirit of nature, rather than an art that celebrated human achievement. Gone were the images of pharaohs, emperors, or praetorian guards in full military regalia; in their place were the images of etherealized saints, Madonnas, and Christ figures bearing the Word in the crook of their arm. I had stumbled into the realm of the solitary, the stranger, the man who preferred to live within the desert of his own imagination.

One mural caught my eye. It was a fresco of the *Virgo lactans*, or Mary nursing the Christ Jesus. She was sitting on a pillow on a high-backed chair, baring her breast to the infant Christ child. He was suckling hungrily. It reminded me of a statuette of the Egyptian goddess Isis with her child Horus that I had seen in Paris. The Coptic Virgin had taken her stance from a much older tradition of divine motherhood—but with one difference: the statuette depicted the infant Horus as passive, his arms at his sides and seated on his mother's lap, whereas the Christ child was shown tugging at his mother's arm as he gratefully suckled her breast. The contrast between these two images was striking: Christ was clearly the New Man avid for the nourishment of divinity. His counterpart Horus, however, had grown tired in the wake of thousands of years of unthinking worship.

Another fresco that made a deep impression was one that I discovered in a niche taken from an abandoned monastery in Bawiti, in the Western Desert. It depicted Jesus Christ in majesty, seated on a stool holding the Gospels. In a land where leadership was idealized, and kingship, both on earth and in the afterlife, was understood by the people, such a figure suggested perfect benevolence. His dark hair and black beard emphasized his youthful strength. His open expression was reminiscent of someone who had encountered his own immortality and now glorified in it. This was no suffering Christ, no wounded being. This was Christ confident of his powers of rebirth and renewal, a God in whom the wounds of the crucifixion were absent.

Old Cairo had begun to yield up its secrets. Walking the back streets of the quarter, I soon found myself entering ancient churches, each with its own tale to tell. In Saint Barbara, for example, I discovered the relics of two martyrs, Cyrus and John, both of whom were commanded to be shot by arrows, burned in a furnace, bound to the tails of horses, then dragged to a neighboring city. Miraculously, they suffered no harm. Their bones lie in a chapel to the left of the sanctuary, contained in two velvet-covered cylinders decorated in silver inlay. The sanctuary screen in this church, which was of dark wood, ebony perhaps, and inlaid with ivory, impressed me. Each beautifully carved circle in the screen seemed to drive the next, so that the ivory inlay gave the illusion of being a series of cogs. The entire screen had been transformed into a celestial machine.

Every church that I entered generated its own sense of piety and age-old gravitas. They had withstood persecution, fire, and decay, so that their very walls had become a testament to their survival. They continued to stand, in spite of the ravages of history. I realized how central the Coptic Church in Egypt was to the story of

Christianity, for it was here that real oppression was experienced long after it had ceased elsewhere. The frescoes and artifacts in the museum emphasized something that is all but forgotten among Christians in the wider world: that belief can be renewed only when it is made aware of its own fragility in the wake of indolence and barbarism.

Later, when I visited the Church of the Holy Virgin at Ma'adi, a few miles south of Old Cairo, I came on a stairway leading down to the Nile River at a point believed to be where the Holy Family began its journey to Upper Egypt. According to tradition, the church marks the site where the daughter of Pharaoh discovered the infant Moses among the reeds when she came down to bathe. It is also the place where the Holy Family set sail for Middle Egypt during their flight from Herod. The tradition further says that they sailed south to Bahnasa in Middle Egypt. Near Gebel al Tair (Mount of Birds) on the east bank of the Nile, there is a hallowed site where Mary feared for the safety of Jesus because a large rock threatened to fall on their boat from the mountain overlooking the river. Apparently the baby Jesus extended his hand and prevented it from falling, so removing the threat of their being crushed. His imprint remains on the rock to this day, and the Church of Our Lady of the Palm nearby was built in commemoration of the event. It's said that the Holy Family spent three years in Egypt, although Muslims maintain it was longer.

Seeing the steps leading down to the river through an iron gate, I asked myself what Christ might have derived from his Egyptian sojourn. Not only had he taken ship from the very spot where Moses had been rescued, and so linked up two great traditions, but during his flight with his parents he had also traveled deep into the heartland of an ancient spirituality. The Egyptian gods would have been ever present, the priests of Amon still there performing their rituals in the great temples. Though an infant, would he not have soaked up at least a small part of this sacred ambiance? It is highly conjectural that he traveled so far into Egypt; nonetheless, the tradition remains, and we must respect it. The idea that Christ might have been affected by his Egyptian interlude is hard to dismiss. He may have carried back into Palestine, subliminally at least, something of its ageless encounter with divinity. For Egypt was, and continues to be, a landscape populated by gods. They seem to flourish here in this endless expanse of sand threaded by the most august of rivers. I suspect that the young Christ took back with him from Egypt something irreplaceable: its birthright as the home of man's idea of sanctity.

I came away from Old Cairo that day feeling that I had experienced something different. Coptic Christianity is permeated by a feeling of being able to survive against all odds. In this sense it harks back to an earlier age, the age of martyrs and men who were willing to give up everything for their beliefs. The old churches of Babylon were not built as fortresses but as enclaves of simple piety and repose. Yet many of their frescoes and icons continued to celebrate the desert experience. Asceticism, and the feats of men such as Anthony, Macarius the Egyptian, Pambo, Evagrius, and Paul, were never far below the surface. These men are the exemplars of the Coptic Church; they give it its flavor, its austere simplicity and sense of living on the edge. A Copt is a stranger par excellence.

In my room that evening I lay there listening to the din from the street. I felt estranged for the first time, as if my encounter with the churches of Old Cairo had reinforced my sense of alienation. Their continued existence acted as a reproof: the city, so steeped in history and forgetfulness, lay below me all but smothered in pollution and a state of agitation. This was the modern age, I told myself. We prefer to bury ourselves in the detritus of waste, of evil gases and collective stress, simply to say that we're alive. Yet when I thought of the bones of those martyrs lying in their velvet-covered cylinders, so silent and enfolded, I knew that something was amiss. The image of the celestial city no longer exists in our imagination because it reminds us of a time when restraint was considered to be a genuine spiritual value, not as it is regarded today—as some sort of pathological condition.

The next morning I took a bus out to Wadi al-Natrun, halfway to Alexandria. This was the place where the Christian monastic experience was largely realized in the fourth century. Although Pachomius founded the first monastery at Tabennisi in Upper Egypt in the early part of that same century, it is to the Thebaid that the bulk of anchorites were drawn during the time of Anthony, probably because of its proximity to Alexandria. During the persecutions it would have been easier to escape into the desert than to make the long voyage upriver to Thebes. Wadi al-Natrun is therefore a nodal point in the history of Western spirituality, for it was here that men put into practice the lessons taught by Anthony.

Of the four monasteries left in the region, the one I most wanted to visit was Suryani because of its venerable link with the school of translators in Edessa. The monastery was a key point in the long roundabout route by which the ancient knowledge of the Greeks reached the philosophical and scientific schools of Córdoba, Toledo, Salerno, and Montpellier. The Syrian Church gave rise to a veritable school of translators, of whom the greatest were Sergius of Resaina (d. 536) and Jacob of Edessa (d. ca. 708). Under their guidance the whole corpus of treatises on philosophy, mathematics, medicine, and grammar by Aristotle, Euclid, Archimedes, Ptolemy, Hippocrates, and Galen were translated into Syriac and subsequently into Arabic. Later still, in the thirteenth century, they were translated into Latin.

At one time Suryani possessed the oldest book in the world, a manuscript written in Edessa in AD 411. Suryani also housed fragments of a Bible written in Syriac at Dyarbakir in 464, as well as the works of Aphraates, the so-called Persian sage, made at Damascus ten years later. Because of its uniquely isolated position in the Egyptian desert, far from the many Middle Eastern political upheavals, the monastery ended up becoming the sole repository of all the knowledge and thought of those Mesopotamian monastic thinkers. Suryani was one of those placenta places in the history of mankind: it allowed the oxygen of ideas to be transmitted across linguistic boundaries to a wider world.

At the Wadi al-Natrun rest house I hired a taxi to take me out to the monastery. At once I was confronted by a rather forbidding landscape of sand and sparse herbage. We drove along a dirt track toward the monastic settlement that was said to lie half buried in sand dunes on the edge of a shallow wadi. On the way we passed by a number of ruins and heaps of stones nearly level to the ground, indicating the remains of numerous ancient monasteries. I asked the driver to stop so that I might take a closer look. Instead my driver decided to make a slight detour to show me a recent excavation overseen by a Swiss archaeological team in 1981 to 1983. Though it was some miles out of our way, he informed me that there were a number of interesting sites to see there.

He was right. At a place known as Kellia (the famous Desert of the Cells), where Evagrius himself had once lived (which Anthony was reputed to have founded in the company of Abbot Amoun),[3] today within sight of the Alexandria-Cairo rail line, we stopped near the ruins of a series of monastic compounds that reminded me of squares on a chessboard, so neatly ordered were they on the plain. Walking across the sand to the now flattened entry to one of these monasteries, I felt a strange sensation, as if I were about to enter something altogether primeval, the very first spiritual center on earth. I could almost see the ghosts of those fourth- and fifth-century monks entering the chapel or refectory, or sitting outside their cells in the late afternoon weaving baskets. They had entered this land in order to deal with their own lack. What they had managed to build there was a monument to the rejuvenating power of aridity.

My driver kindly directed me toward a recent excavation, where I was able to observe more intimately the life of those ancient monks. I wandered among the mud-brick rooms, gazing at the fragments of frescoes on the walls. In one room I came across a flower-decorated alcove dominated by an image of the cross. In another I discovered a well-executed painting of a fish surmounted by a cross with the inscription IC XC NIKA, (Jesus Christ triumphs) written beside it. In a third I found a beautiful cross painted in ochre, decorated with red and green gemstones and cabochons. Beneath the cross two delicately rendered birds in red ochre and white plaster completed the heraldic image.

Wherever I looked I was confronted by a wonderful feeling of celebration. This was not a solemn world but a world consumed by joy. Each image had been painted with such love and care. There was none of the anguish that I had come to associate with Christian iconography in Europe. There were no images of Christ on the cross, for example, no depiction of the God-man suffering for humankind. It was evident that pure graphic design married to bright colors had been placed on the walls simply to entrance. For all their silence, the ruins of Kellia were alive with a distant music: I could hear the monks chanting the office in the dawn light, knowing that they had sung into existence the deep spirituality of the Egyptian desert.

In one room I came across a Coptic inscription on the wall that brought to life the simple acceptance of life and death that often permeated those who lived the monastic life. There was no rancor, no sense of loss in what the words had to say:

Lord God Jesus Christ
giver of repose and happiness
brother Ptolemy

son of Ticoi and resident
of Psenetoni, [and] that our Lord
Jesus Christ gives repose to
his soul! Please remember him,
who was able to read
and write! Please remember him
to God that grants repose
with all those that are saints
with him!

Here indeed was a voice from the past, the silent message of a man who had managed to learn how to read and write. It said so much about the real value of literacy: to be able to inscribe a simple obituary on a monastic wall to the memory of a long-dead anchorite. Brother Ptolemy, where are you now?

I slowly made my way back to the car parked amid the rubble of ruined monasteries. As the driver started the engine, I looked back toward the mud-brick walls protruding from the sand. This was home to a courageous human experiment, I told myself. This was where men and women had chosen to flee in order to embark on a new adventure of the inner life. It didn't matter that these monasteries had not survived the ravages of time. It didn't even matter that their message had been buried under the relentless incursions of sand. What had survived, and would continue to do so, I felt sure, was the life they believed might be possible. For these men and women of the desert had perfected a model for existence, one that still has the capacity to blossom and render poems on walls in an age of secularism.

Meanwhile, as we journeyed back along the track to Suryani, I soon recognized the monastery in the distance. It looked so remote, so imprisoned within itself as we finally made our approach. Above the high walls I could just make out the towers on the chapel and a grove of palm trees. The general feeling of flatness in the surrounding landscape nonetheless imposed its own sense of isolation. It was a place where books had turned their backs on the world, there to meditate on the deep obscurity of the word.

Entering the courtyard, I asked to meet the guest master—a slim, hawk-nosed young man who wore a skullcap and a long habit that reached to his ankles. I had decided in advance not to visit the library, not wishing to arouse suspicions as to my purpose for being there. The names of Robert Curzon and Elias Assemani were probably very much alive in the minds of Suryani's monks.[4] When I told the guest master that I wished to visit the place where the founder Bischoi used to tie his hair to a chain, he agreed to accompany me to the Church of the Holy Virgin (al-Adhra), in which the monk's cave was located. Before we entered the cave down a dark passageway, the guest master showed me a superb ebony "Doorway of Prophesies" inlaid with ivory panels depicting the disciples and the seven epochs of the Christian era. It reminded me of the screen I had seen in Saint Barbara in Cairo. There was certainly an African feel about these decorations. I also noticed a fine fresco of the Annunciation in one niche.

I eventually climbed down a narrow staircase into the cave at the back of the church. In the ill-lit precinct I could just make out a soot-stained chain hanging in a bare room. There was nothing else in the room save a half-burned candle. The cave smelled of centuries of prayer and supplication, of austere asceticism wedded to a mystical vision of Christ.

Quitting the cave, I noticed two ostrich eggs hanging above the altar in the church. I recalled Father Vansleb's account of the strange stories associated with the bird's nesting habits. Sometimes one needs to look intently at the shell-like carapace that shelters the spirit, I thought. To take one's eye off it, even for a moment, is to condemn the heart to a Stygian existence in the catacombs of one's own sense of spiritual indolence and failure. The anchorites of the

Thebaid, though they no longer exist save as ghosts among the ruins of their monasteries out there in the Wadi al-Natrun, are still able to conjure up that aspect of God-possession that was their lifelong aspiration.

Their names ring out over the centuries: John the Dwarf, Pior, Agathon, Poemen the Shepherd, Abbot Zacharias, Xanthias, Theodore of Pherme—these are but a few who blend with and echo all the tens of thousands of anonymous ascetics who kept company with them in the caves and mud huts that littered the Thebaid. One can imagine, too, the great thinkers and spiritual athletes, men like Rufinus, Ephraim, Athanasius, Evagrius Ponticus, Macarius the Egyptian, as well as Anthony himself, joining them at different times, bent on forging a spiritual practice for the realization of eternity. They were a rare breed of men, these ascetics. Let no one say that they had not stared at the ostrich egg and hatched forth something hugely important for humankind. Their legacy remains with us today, for we are loathe to dismiss the spirit of ascesis that they stood for.

That evening I arrived back in Cairo tired but content. I had visited one of the most arid yet productive places on earth. Who can say whether such a land will one day generate a new impetus for renewal? Of course, the question must and should be asked: If late antiquity could spawn such a legion of spirituals, could not our own age do the same? As I pressed the elevator button to ascend to my hotel room, I tried to formulate an answer to this question. The whir of the cables above my head seemed like an eager response. Old radiances never die, I told myself, especially when they are forged in the fires of men's unending quest for spiritual understanding. Wadi al-Natrun was just such a fire, just such a radiance.

nine

IN THE CRUCIBLE OF FIRE

Arriving back at Saint Anthony's was like reaching an oasis after a long journey across the desert. The feeling of relief was palpable. I could feel the tensions of city life passing from my body within minutes of walking back through the gate. How easy it is to call a monastery home! I thought. Even the prospect of eating course gruel in the refectory did not seem all that bad anymore. Compared with the disorder and stress that I experienced in Cairo, the solitary calm of those high monastery walls and unruffled palm trees promised the sort of balm I needed. I wanted once more to plunge into the timeless omnipotence of the desert where every day seemed fashioned from itself, just like those tiny hieratic figures that parade across the walls of pharaohs' tombs. Each represents that sense of anonymity we find when eternity is accepted and acknowledged.

The following morning, after attending office in the Church of the Four Living Creatures (how the sun and the moon above the frescoes of the Living Creatures glowed as dawn invaded the sanctuary!), I resolved to visit Lazarus in his cave.[1] I felt that I owed him an explanation for my decision to visit Cairo at a time when it appeared that I was making real progress in my ascetic understanding. He would have regarded my dash to Suez and beyond as an aberration, as some sort of foolhardy attempt to revisit a contagion. But equally, Lazarus was a man of generosity and sympathy, and he would have accepted my decision with his customary forbearance and good grace.

I started up the track to his cell. The sun was not yet warm, so I rather enjoyed this solitary climb. The high plateau above was etched clearly against the sky. I kept thinking of Anthony's cave up there, its narrow entrance still enveloped in shadow. For some unknown reason, I felt close to the man at that moment as I began to climb the mountain. Anchoritism is like a stone, I told myself. It contains within it a primal sense of matter. Without the earth how could we support ourselves? The anchorite's life is a validation of the soil's role in our lives. It shows us how to cultivate those invisible energies that lie buried within us.

Eventually I neared Lazarus's cell. Since I had last visited it, he had managed to apply a coat of whitewash to the terrace wall and cave entrance. There was a rustic order about the place that I hadn't noticed before. Was it for my benefit? Or did he feel that solitude required a coat of paint occasionally? As soon as Lazarus heard me reach the step at the entrance to his compound, he came forth from his cell, greeting me with a warm smile.

"So the prodigal returns," he said, taking the supply of bread that I presented to him. In doing so, he touched his chest with his open palm as a gesture of thanks.

While Lazarus prepared a mug of tea for us both in his tiny outdoor kitchen, I outlined my trip to Cairo and to the Wadi al-Natrun. I told him also of my visit to Ma'adi to see the spot where the Holy Family had set sail up the Nile. Intriguing as the idea was that the infant Christ might have carried with him from Egypt something of its ageless wisdom, I was careful enough to suggest that because of his avataric nature he had, of course, wanted for nothing. In other words, Christ's completeness, at least in the theological sense, precluded him from being affected by his stay in Egypt. But as a man, I argued, couldn't the Nile have bestowed on him some hint of its cyclical convergence? Lazarus listened to me as he might a twittering bird caught in a thicket.

"What you speak of is part of popular belief," he finally admitted. "These stories help simple people preserve their link with the past. Egypt is an ancient land. It behooves everyone living here to accept that each layer of gods contributes to the next. The mystery of Christ's sojourn in this country can therefore be no exception."

I was taken aback by Lazarus's remarks. Far from reciting a litany of canonical sources to bolster any belief he might have in Christ's immaculate nature, he had been at pains to admit that almost everything was acceptable as part of the Christian mystery, including popular folk stories that might have no basis in fact. He seemed to be saying that Christianity had its roots in very ancient mythological material that went far beyond those events in Palestine seen as so important by Christians. Isis and Horus as the divine mother and child, the dismemberment of Osirus followed by his miraculous reconstitution, the sun god Amon bestowing his eternal light and warmth on men—these were but old manifestations of a mystery that Christ now embodied. What Lazarus appeared to be saying was that it mattered little how the divine clothed itself; the important thing was that men were prepared to wear a similar garb themselves.

I began to sense that Lazarus had staked out a territory for himself in this ancient mythic material. Living the life of an ascetic had helped him to discipline the eye of his imagination so that he could see things that were not apparent to people like me. That the Holy Family was believed to have wandered through the Nile delta region and proceeded into the wastes of the Wadi al-Natrun to visit the monasteries there, then trekked back to Old Cairo in order to embark south along the great river, before journeying inland to the monastery of al-Muharraq near Luxor, merely confirmed to him the need we all have of investing our religious heroes with a human dimension. Christ needed to be a product of a journey, a spiritual trek through the hinterland of some primary experience that was Egypt. He needed to partake of that pharaonic encounter with the other world, too, if ever he were to make it relevant as a place of repose for his own generation. Is not a voyage on the night boat of the sun, the legendary funerary barque of the pharaoh into the realm of Duat, an echo of Christ's magisterial descent into the underworld?

Lazarus made me conscious that I was also a part of this mythic interlude. By climbing Mount Colzim to be in his company, I had inadvertently entered a land rich in the subsoil of myth. It appears that Mary, too, reputedly quenched her thirst in the spring at the foot of the mountain that Anthony had finally chosen to make his home, presumably with Joseph and her son on their way back to Palestine. The linking of the first Christian family to the first anchorite only reinforces what we already suspect: that Christ's presence is always needed, whether miraculously or otherwise, to lend credence to the sanctification of certain places dedicated to the spiritual life. Asceticism itself required its own imprimatur if ever it were to play a role in the progressive interiorization of the Christian life.

"It is why you read so many remarkable stories about those early anchorites," Lazarus responded, anticipating my train of thought. "We hear how they did battle with demons in their caves, or conversed with animals, and were transported in clouds—knowing, I think, that such stories are designed to intensify our belief in the power of prayer to work miracles. The lives of those early anchorites represent one long encounter between fact and the supernatural. We like to think that these men were pioneers in a new way of investigating the inner man. They were attempting to break down eight centuries of Aristotelianism and its penchant for calling a spade a spade. Men yearned to break free from the constraints of the real. They wanted to renew their compact with a level of spiritual knowledge and understanding that offered them something more than the prospect of merely living out a succession of 'works and days,' as Hesiod so aptly phrased it."

Lazarus had made an interesting point, one that clarified for me why men like him retreated to the desert in the first place. They saw in a life divested of all comfort and diversion the very essence of mystical aspiration. In their heart they believed that the role of the imagination as a conductor of spiritual insight could be realized only by living a life of renunciation. This is why so much emphasis was placed upon living the ascetic life in what one writer called the "gymnasium of the intellect."[2] It alone offered what Joseph of Panephysis regarded as the opportunity to "become all flame." Such a condition, I suspect, was the goal of every would-be ascetic. Isaac of Nineveh was adamant that this kind of life was the only way to prepare the body for its encounter with the flame:

Fasting, vigil and wakefulness in God's service, renouncing
the sweetness of sleep by crucifying the body throughout the
day and night, are God's holy pathway and the foundation of
every virtue. Fasting is the champion of every virtue, the
beginning of the struggle, the crown of the abstinent, the
beauty of virginity and sanctity, the resplendence of chastity,
the commencement of the path of Christianity, the mother
of prayer, the wellspring of sobriety and prudence, the
teacher of stillness, and the precursor of all good works.[3]

In other words, *hunger* was the arbiter of the ascetic life. Going
without nourishment was designed to reduce physical vitality to
the point where the imaginative faculty could impose itself in a way
that previously it had not been able to do. The body was like an un-
bridled horse that could neither be directed nor controlled. By setting it to rein—that is, by curbing its passionate nature—it could
be put to the service of those deeper affiliations of the spirit. To do
so required a particular kind of training in the way the mind worked.
Not since the rise of the Pythagorean schools in Magna Graecia
during the sixth century BC had any group of men attempted to
modify thought in such a rigorous and uncompromising manner, at
least not in the Mediterranean world. The Pythagoreans, however,
had made their emphasis on ritual purification and the noneating
of certain foods. In contrast, the early anchorites went further; they
denied the importance of food altogether.[4] They had quit that zone
of food as represented by the fertility of the Nile valley in order to
create for themselves a landscape devoid of human nourishment altogether. This landscape reflected the shared weaknesses of a starv-
ing humanity.[5] It could be said that seldom, if ever in the ancient
world, had the body been more deeply implicated in the transformation of consciousness. Food became yet another facet of an as-

cetic's ongoing struggle to remove himself from a society that wanted to remain in contact with him for reasons of its own.

Such a modification of thought became the hallmark of early Christian asceticism. It was not simply an attempt to dispense with the old ideal of classicism, or the desire to transform a man into *homo philosophicus* as distinct from his predisposition toward irrationality. No, something more radical was being suggested. Lazarus and his predecessors had stumbled on the possible existence of an entirely different kind of spiritual urgency lying below the surface of classical gravitas. They recognized, as the ancient philosophers had not, that it was possible to become like a god on this earth. Instead of dismissing the gods as creatures of the imagination, as Plato and Aristotle had done before them, the early anchorites chose to inhabit these fabrications in the realm of their imagination. The gods became God and then became Christ, the first and only god to adopt the garb of the physical. The anchorites' argument was persuasive, as it was based on a logical imperative: if God could become man, why couldn't man become an angel? Their mode of existence therefore became obvious: it was one way of bringing about this supreme act of palingenesis in themselves. None other than John Climacus, one of Byzantium's ascetic masters, argued that a man might find himself in an earthly and defiled body, but nonetheless he was able to "push himself into the rank and status of the incorporeal angels."[6]

The problem, of course, at least for a person like me, was that I needed some clear articulation of ascetic practice so that it might mean something to me as a recognizable discipline. In this sense anchoritism is very much like Zen Buddhism, in that Zen monks, like their desert counterparts, are reluctant to talk or indeed analyze their religious thinking. Zen monks, when questioned about their practice, are apt to reply, "There is nothing to Zen," or "There is nothing to study in Zen," or "Zen is daily life." An ascetic in the desert would likely answer in a similar vein. The good Abbot Isaiah used to say, "Nothing is so useful to the beginner as insults." Or Abbot Zacharius, "He is a monk who does violence to himself in everything." Or as Anthony remarked: "Without temptation no-one can be saved." We are dealing here with an elliptical mode of expression as each ascetic attempts to bypass the obvious. He knows, as few of us do, that language can be a trap for the unwary. As with the Zen koan, or riddle, each anchorite is in the business of composing a series of irrationalities to mask what language hopes to isolate. The early Fathers often called this the "hidden activity,"[7] which was none other than a new alphabet of the heart.[8]

The daily life of an ascetic was entirely concentrated on cultivating his own "hidden activity." Solitude, and the reduction of life to as few practical activities as possible, were a part of the process. Since the induction of food had been reduced to a minimum, so too was the necessity to work. Many ascetics wove baskets or plaited mats in order to scrape together a few dinarii to purchase their food and clothing. According to Abba Megethius, all he needed to make were three baskets a day to ensure his survival. Others copied books or performed basic tasks such as offering their services as a barber. Yet even as they worked, anchorites were expected to pray without ceasing. Their whole being was always directed toward such an injunction. Prayer of the heart led to a spiritual displacement of self. This was the real business of the so-called hidden activity, it seems.

Finally I broached the subject with Lazarus as to his understanding of the "hidden activity" alluded to by those early ascetics. On a more personal level, I actually asked him whether he performed such an activity, or whether it was a practice that had all but died out.

"I can only allude to what Isaac of Nineveh wrote on the subject," he replied, going inside his cell to collect one of his books. He appeared again with a battered copy of the *Mystical Treatises of Isaac of Nineveh* bulging with snippets of paper containing his handwritten notes. I asked him whether a copy of this book might exist in the monastery library, to which he concurred.

"We must understand that the power of the mind has its limits," Lazarus began, opening the book at random. "Isaac tells us that during prayer, when a mind has reached this point, it finds itself with two options—either to turn back into the realm of psychic deliberations or to press forward to a point where prayer ceases altogether. Prayer, for him, becomes a mediator between the psychic and spiritual state. When prayer ceases, a man is usually engulfed in what he calls a 'delightful glory' whereby the mind forgets itself and all that's here and will no longer be moved by the thought of anything. Let me read something to you by the great man himself, to explain what I mean," Lazarus added, putting on his glasses:

> Man, therefore, may freely go so far as to say: all excellence whatever and all orders of prayer whatever, in body or in spirit, are in the realm of free will, as well as the mind that dominates the senses. But when the influence of the spirit reigns over the mind that regulates the senses and the deliberations, freedom is taken away from nature, which no longer governs but is governed. And how could there be prayer at that time, when nature does not possess power over itself, but is conducted by an outward force without knowing whither. Nature then does not direct the emotions of the spirit according to its will, but captivity reigns over nature in that hour, and conducts it there where sensual apperception ceases; because nature even has no will at that time, even to this extent that it does not know whether it is in or without the body.[9]

"I think what Isaac is saying," Lazarus extrapolated, "is that a point is reached in the practice of prayer where fundamental human impulses, which he classifies as nature, are put aside. These impulses that govern the mind in life and in the lower echelons of prayer are slowly dispensed with. In the process, nature loses its capacity to will anything. What takes over in its place is a state of 'delightful glory,' which we might regard as a state of ecstasy. A man, literally, leaves himself when he is in such a state."

I found Lazarus's explanation deeply moving. I was reminded of what Plotinus had said on the subject when he argued for what he called the loss of "intellectual shape" when the soul encounters the "straining love" that moves toward its object on the occasion when it apprehends Beauty.[10] What Plotinus calls intellectual shape is no different from Isaac's "nature," of course: both partake of form and the reality of conditional existence. But for Isaac, prayer embodied far more than Plotinus's apprehension of Beauty alone. In a sense, his was a more dangerous exercise in that it involved less the calm contemplation of Beauty as a divine archetype than it did the absolute loss of self. The idea that the soul in its aloneness receiving the Alone removes the self from the contemplative act is also central to Plotinus's belief, but his soul is a philosophic soul born out of the reason-principle, not a soul desiring a relationship with Divinity itself.

For Isaac, prayer was an act that went beyond meditation. We are dealing here with a select group of ascetics who had taken it on themselves to put into practice certain ancient philosophic observations in the form of an existential spiritual imperative. This would not have occurred, I suspect, without the advent of Christ. By his actions alone he had made it possible for everyone, at least potentially, to enter a different kind of space altogether. His virgin birth, miracles, and crucifixion imprinted on history a transcendent possibility that no philosophy in the past had ever been able to achieve. Christ became the mediator between the temporal and spiritual worlds. He became, in actuality, the world's prayer.

Clearly Anthony, Isaac of Nineveh, and now Lazarus were engaged in realizing in the act of prayer what Isaac himself called an "unconsciousness not to be surpassed." These men, like all the anchorites of the desert, had made it their business to go beyond the philosophic implications of Beauty or Soul, or whatever other label the Neoplatonists liked to place on their understanding of the ideal state. For the anchorites, such a state was essentially devoid of any human aspiration toward a genuine collaboration with the divine. What they were after was to in some way enter the spiritual domain in order to explore its mysteries for themselves, not merely to arrive at some philosophic acceptance of its existence.

On my journey to Wadi al-Natrun and the Thebaid, therefore, I had been able to explore what was once a genuine land of prayer. Over centuries those generations of men who lived there had fought with their personal demons in an attempt to realize their own state of "consciousness not to be surpassed." One can only say that this was a courageous endeavor. At places like Nitria, Scete, and Kellia the desert sands and scabrous ridges of stone that radiated such heat in the summer had encouraged men to retire into themselves like moles into the earth. They may have been living cadavers, but they were also, in rare instances, flaming torches visible to others. Lazarus was kind enough to read a description that Isaac gave of how Arsenius attained to this condition after many years of ascetic practice:

Once one of the brethren went to the cell of Abba Arsenius, looked through the window and saw the father standing *who was wholly burning as fire.* For this brother had gone to see the Father was worthy of this sight: he did not belong to the small but to the great ones. The blessed one was famous on account of his exalted behavior and all Fathers desired to see him. And because they especially desired to see him, it was as Abba Macarius said to him: "Why do you flee from us?" Therefore the strangers who came to Scete desired chiefly to see him and to receive his blessing. When that brother knocked at the door, the Father came outdoors . . . and when he saw that his visitor was astonished at what he saw, he said to him: "Was it time for you to knock? Have you seen anything?" The other answered: "No."[11]

Though not common in mystical literature, one does occasionally come across such references to ascetics adopting the garb of fire or light in their dealings with the outside world. It is a condition that we meet with in other traditions where it is perhaps described more explicitly. I am thinking particularly of Persian Sufism and the works of a certain Sheikh Samsoddin Lahiji. The learned sheikh expounded the theme of the existence of a "black light," which absorbed him in its pure essence:

> I saw myself present in a world of light. Mountains and deserts were iridescent with lights of all colors: red, yellow, white, blue. I was experiencing a consuming nostalgia for them; I was as though stricken with madness and snatched out of myself by the violence of the intimate emotion and feeling of the presence. Suddenly I saw that the *black light* was invading the entire universe. Heaven and earth and everything that was there had wholly become black light and, behold, I was *totally absorbed in this light*, losing consciousness. Then I came back to myself (italics mine).[12]

What do these observations have in common? Aside from what one writer called the "aesthetics of incandescence,"[13] I think it suggests that in some way a perfect human spirit partakes of an illumination, or a fiery warmth, that can be communicated only to those who themselves are in possession of certain unique qualities of spirit. Simeon the New Theologian goes so far as to say that this light comes directly from God, who communicates his brightness to those who are united with him, to the extent that they too are existing in a purified state.[14] Many ascetic writers, including Evagrius Ponticus, were at pains to dismiss the manifestation of this transparency of the soul as no more than the wiles of the enemy, since they felt that sensible apparition was a delusion. Nonetheless, Isaac maintained that Arsenius did indeed glow like a fire in his cell, and that a number of his neighbors observed it, and that those who were not of sufficient spiritual insight could not see it. It seems that men of Arsenius's caliber could radiate a fiery presence that was immediately perceptible to those with eyes to see. It's not for nothing that Palladius spoke of Elpidius, a Cappadocian ascetic living near Jericho, who attained to such a height of *apatheia* that his body dried up and the sun shone through his bones. His body had become transparent.[15]

I was dealing with a mode of thinking that defied the normal categories of philosophical inquiry. It was not rational but suprarational. It was not logical but deeply intuitional. Moreover, it sprang from ascetic practice rather than any form of intellectual analysis. The anchorites had made prayer the principal method by which men might break down the complex superstructure of rationality that had served Greek thought so well. These men had wanted more from their engagement with the world than simple recognition of its categories: they wanted it to reflect a purely inward illumination that could be mysteriously experienced by the heart as an apparently external radiance resembling earthly light, which at the same time inwardly illuminated the seer. This was the goal of the new theocratic knowledge; it was no longer a knowledge geared toward worldly considerations so favored by the ancient philosophers.

"In the end," Lazarus continued, his voice breaking into my thoughts, "we are dealing with a phenomenon that transformed the world. When Christ was transfigured on Mount Tabor, he bestowed on history what we now understand to be an uncreated and natural grace. It has affected the way we view the world ever

since. Anthony and his fellow anchorites were not just unedu-
cated peasants who felt the need to escape the clutches of Roman
authority. Many of them were deeply educated men who had
voyaged from afar to be a part of this great human experiment.
Nor is it right to describe them as killjoys who despised pleasure
as an agent of the devil. Rather, they were men who looked on
the body and the mind as objects that needed to be overcome, indeed modified, before any real spiritual progress could be achieved.
Asceticism was the means, not the end. I think, if you could ask
Anthony what he thought the ultimate goal was, he would surely
say that asceticism was no more than an inn on the road to salvation. A man needs to rest in it for a time—but that he must once
more take to the road and dispense with it altogether."

"But not prayer," I argued.

"No, not prayer. Prayer is the jewel in the crown, the luminous
center of all spiritual experience," Lazarus maintained. "Without it,
we are forced back on our reliance on things, on factual knowledge.
Prayer offers us the door to that deeply imaginative experience of
the workings of the divine. Meditative knowledge is derived from a
sharpening of all our faculties, physical as well as mental, in order to
create the right conditions for the manifestation of this immaterial
light that the early anchorites so much wanted to see."

"So you believe that it can still be realized, that this light has not
died out?"

Lazarus looked at me with a faintly quizzical expression. His
years of solitude had made him immune from the doubts that
might plague people such as me.

"You asked me earlier about the hidden activity, and whether it
survives today. Wait, I have something to show you," he responded.

Lazarus rose from the stone seat where we sat and ducked his
head through the doorway to his cell. A few moments later he reap-

peared, this time carrying what looked like a knotted rosary fashioned from black wool.

"I want you to take this as a gift," he said. "It was given to me by a monk on Mount Athos, just before he died."

I took the woolen rosary in my hands. It was tightly knotted and smooth from much rubbing over the years. Or was it from prayer? The black cross that seemed to emerge from the knots at one end reminded me of a human figure with his arms outstretched. He wanted to embrace me. He wanted to enfold me in his love.

"So the hidden activity is not dead after all," I remarked.

"When you have a tool such as this in your hands, the image of Christ will never die," Lazarus replied.

I had been handed a lifeline; it was up to me to haul myself aboard this fragile coracle of the spirit before I was washed away.

ten

THE LION'S MOUTH

These early ascetics in turn inspired later generations of ascetics to live the anchoritic life in Palestine, Mount Athos, Cappadocia, Sinai, Qatar, Syria, and faraway Persia. The arc of Christian asceticism had widened beyond the Roman frontier to reach men and women all over the East. Though sometimes familiar with classical thinking, many of this new breed of ascetics did not feel it necessary to compliantly follow its precepts. In many ways these Eastern spirituals were less doctrinaire, more mystical in their teachings. The classical models of thinking touched them less than their own intimate knowledge of an ancient landscape fashioned out of the fire worship of

Zoroastrianism as well as their encounter with Buddhist beliefs from India. The trade routes brought more than just merchandise from the Orient, it seems.

Lazarus made me aware that I should explore more thoroughly the rich field of writings that had emanated from the East if I were ever going to come to terms with the ascetic practice of men like Anthony. Perhaps because Anthony was, like them, more Eastern than Western, these thinkers and spirituals more readily understood the nature of the "hidden activity" that he espoused than did their Greek and Latin counterparts. Knowing, too, that Christ was born into their physical and intellectual environment, rather than that of the West, made me think their understanding of his message could have been more subtle. The early apologists from the Western empire were steeped in the classics. They were reluctant to give up their love of the poets and philosophers on which they had cut their teeth as students. I am reminded of the letter that Jerome wrote to his friend Eustochium, recounting a dream he had on precisely this subject. The dream described his flagellation for daring to read the so-called gentile authors in preference to the sacred writings of scripture:

> Even when I was on my way to Jerusalem to fight the good fight there, I could not forgive myself to forgo the library, which, with great care and labor, I had put together in Rome. And so, miserable man that I was, I could fast, only to read Cicero afterwards, I would spend many nights in vigil, I would shed bitterest tears called forth from my innermost heart by the remembrance of past sins, and then I would take up Plautus again. When I returned to my right senses and began to read the prophets, their language seemed rough and barbarous.[1]

The early Christianity of the West was therefore much influenced by classical ideals, even if only as a reaction to them. The

Eastern thinkers were never so indebted. They were able to read into the achievement of Anthony and the Desert Fathers something more intrinsic to their own needs. They saw in what the anchorites wanted to achieve something closer to their hearts: what a certain Abbot Isaiah called the supervirtues because they are higher than virtues, as they are neither accomplished through the body nor performed through the soul but are bestowed by grace before the mind even thinks of them.[2]

Thankfully, the monastic library at Saint Anthony was well supplied with the surviving works of these early Eastern spirituals. As soon as I dipped into their books, I found myself traversing an entirely different landscape from the one I was so far familiar with. I was now journeying through old Persia to places such as Nineveh, Nisibis, Qatar on the Persian Gulf, Nimrod, and Mosul on the Euphrates River, to the remote monasteries of Kashgar, Mar Mattai, Rab-Kinnare, and Beth-Abe. It was a land where so many different traditions intersected. I was now in the company of men who had forged their special brand of asceticism out of the heritage of Anthony and his contemporaries, wedded as it now was to the ancient mystical practices of the Magi. This was an Oriental Christianity that I was encountering for the very first time.

Had I known it, I had all but joined what these Syrian ascetics knew of as the "Sons of the Pact." Such men led an ascetic life near towns and villages, or in remote monasteries, and engaged in what was called mystical prayer. Many of their names have come down to us. Men such as Babai, Martyrius, Joseph the Visionary, John the Elder, join Dadisho', Joseph Hazzaya, Isaac of Nineveh, and John of Apamea. All of them have written on the ascetic tradition of the East in a way that is quite different from their Western counterparts. Moreover, they have chosen to elaborate on the "hidden activity," or prayerful meditation in such careful detail that one begins to suspect that their knowledge of such activity stems from an intuitive understanding of its mystical origins, which not even men such as Evagrius could fully explain.

My early reading drew me to a man named Abdisho' Hazzaya, the brother of Joseph Hazzaya. It appears that he died around 690, probably in the monastery of Maragna between the Tigris and Euphrates in central Iraq. We know nothing of the man's life except that he was born in Nimrod and wrote a treatise called *The Book of Questions and Answers*. His peers also knew him as "the Illuminated." In his treatise Abdisho' explores what he calls the fiery impulse, which he maintains can sometimes clothe a man in fire, from the soles of his feet to the crown of his head. Such is this fire that when a man looks at himself, he cannot see his own body but only the fire in which he is clothed. I was immediately reminded of the image of Arsenius in his cell in the Wadi al-Natrun surrounded by flames. Yet Abdisho' understood the nature of this fiery impulse, linking it to the attainment of a level of prayer that he called the sphere of serenity. When I first read the work of Abdisho', I was struck by the purity of his style and the ease with which he explored such refined conditions of the heart.

"No man is able to endure the workings of this fiery impulse," he maintained, commenting on its expansive qualities:

The soul will also change the order of its nature to an image that is above its nature, and from being up till then passable in its thoughts [that is, able to think in a cognizant fashion] it will, through that fiery impulse, draw near to these thoughts unto impassability [*apatheia*]. The mind will also begin to become intoxicated and enraptured, as with strong wine, in the vision of that fiery impulse through which it will undergo a change in the exquisite odor of that holy smell. The fiery impulse of which I speak is, therefore, a spiritual key which opens before the mind the inner door of the heart.[3]

These were the remarks of a man who had made a journey that few of us are privileged to make in our lifetime.

Abdisho' went so far as to describe what it felt like for a man to be filled with such ineffable light. Unlike his Western counterparts, he was not afraid to wrestle with language in order to draw nearer to what he wanted to express. Abdisho', it seems, found himself on the brink of saying what had never been said before: none other than the delineation of that state of *apatheia* that all ascetics sought:

The heart of the man will be filled with the holy light of the vision of this theory [practice] to such an extent that the mind will not even perceive and distinguish itself, because all the faculties of its spiritual nature will at that time become absorbed in it. There will neither be thought of anything, nor any consciousness and remembrance, nor any impulses or inward movements, but only ecstasy in God and an ineffable rapture. Blessed is the man who has been found worthy of this gift, the workings of which cannot be expressed with corporeal tongue. Indeed, there will then be made manifest mysteries and revelations, which only a mind can receive spiritually from a mind, because having no power over them a corporeal tongue is not able to express them.[4]

So this is what being in a state of *apatheia* meant, I thought. Moreover, Abdisho' spoke of a form of spiritual communication that transcended speech altogether. "Mysteries and revelations, which only a mind can receive spiritually from a mind" suggests a form of self-telepathy that can only be experienced when all other avenues of communication have ceased. When a man has achieved this wordless communication with himself, he has crossed what Abdisho' calls the boundary between his natural soul and the "sphere of perfection." It is the goal of all inner activity—to reach out toward the sphere of serenity where all lights, feelings, and images are concentrated on one glorious vision of Christ himself. Christ becomes the coalescing energy that makes *apatheia* possible.

This was indeed angel's food. Abdisho' had opened my eyes to an entirely new set of metaphors to bridge the gap between this world and the next. In the sphere of serenity he says that the soul is surrounded by the "blue color of the heavens" and the mind itself is hidden in a "cloud of crystal light." The mind has reached such a transcendent state that it is no longer able to distinguish itself from the glory of that light. In a sense, one's whole being is swallowed up in an all-consuming state of serenity that precludes any awareness of self.[5] Subject and object have been annihilated. It was as if Abdisho' wanted to suggest a complete reconstitution of the world, and of the human psyche, *before* they had fallen from the center into nature itself. Being in a state of *apatheia*, therefore, removed differentiation from the world altogether. Unity was thus regained.[6]

Abdisho' is careful, however, not to fall into the trap of seeing his images as anything more than allusions to the ideal state that he is exploring. "We say that we see light in the sphere of spirituality," he says,

> but this light is not a material light. We say also that we have there a spiritual food, but that food is not like the one we have here; we say further that our mind will perceive there the sound of glorification of the spiritual hosts, and it will there have speech and conversation, but that speech does not resemble the one we hold with one another. The sound that is heard there by our mind is so fine that our senses are not able to receive it, and a corporeal tongue is not able to utter

and describe that which is made manifest there to the mind, whether it be made through our sense of vision or through that of our hearing.[7]

Again we are made aware that "there" and "here" are but manifestations of an altered state of being and are not meant to refer to a physical place beyond this world. *Apatheia* brings into presence what is normally outside the purview of men in their natural state. What becomes visible are immaterial impulses that direct the soul to what can never be circumscribed. According to Abdisho', only seers and the illuminated can distinguish the identity of the mind from the vision of that glorious light. "The light which is not distinguished by any likenesses or images is a single light in a single vision," he says.[8] What we are dealing with here is a severance between the way men see the world in terms of its physical attributes, and the recognition of its mysterious inner properties.

At this point I encountered the principle of the Five Signs through which an ascetic must pass on the road to the sphere of serenity. According to Abdisho', the first sign is determined by a renunciation of the world brought about by a love of solitude. The second sign is perceived when a man has entered a state of complete humility whereby all sense of good and bad, just and unjust, is eliminated from the critical faculties. The third sign is determined when tears begin to flow spontaneously, like "fountains of water," so that the heart is kindled with the fire of the Spirit in a spirit of loving-kindness. The fourth sign is the sign of remembrance, when the key to the inner door of the heart is opened, thus revealing the hidden Christ, whose vision is an ineffable light. The fifth and final sign bestows on a man the illuminated vision of his own mind, which is able to see the firmament of the heart "like a sapphire sky." It is this vision that enables a person to perceive the difference between the material and intelligible natures. Abdisho' describes the fifth sign and knowledge of intelligible nature as a way of

> ascending to the revelations and mysteries of the divine judgment and providence. It is this gradual ascent that raises you up and makes you participate in the holy light of the vision of Christ. From this glorious and holy vision you will fall into ecstasy over that broad world, the benefits of which are ineffable. From this ecstasy you will derive a flow of spiritual speech and knowledge of both worlds: of the one that has passed and the one that shall pass, and also a consciousness of future things, together with a holy smell and taste; the fine sounds of spiritual intelligences [angels]: joy, jubilation, exultation, glorification, songs, hymns and odes of magnification; communion with the spiritual hierarchies; sight of Paradise; eating from its tree of life . . . together with other ineffable things.[9]

The Five Signs were thus a program for inner action that Abdisho' regarded as essential if any anchorite or monk were to attain to a genuine state of *apatheia*.

It became evident to me that Abdisho' Hazzaya had thought long and hard about the nature of ascetic practice. Moreover, his way of expression suggested that he had truly experienced the various levels of ecstasy that he alludes to on more than one occasion. Nor was he so reluctant as Anthony to speak of his experiences. Here is a man who is not afraid to articulate the deepest encounter a mind can have with the inner workings of the spirit. "I stand sometimes and examine my soul," he says, "and the mind is swallowed up in it."[10] Clearly I was dealing with a man who had managed to enter nature's beginning in order to refurbish in himself his own sense of eternity.

In a way, the desert had come alive for me while reading Abdisho'
Hazzaya. Whenever I looked out the library window at the
monastery walls and glimpses of the distant wadi beyond, I began
to feel that such an arid landscape nurtured a different kind of
herbage than the one we had come to expect of land, cultivated or
otherwise. The idea that the earth must and should be an extension
of our own need to exploit it for survival struck me as particularly
facile in the light of what men like Abdisho' were engaged in. In the
desert such men cultivated the seed of the spirit, which they perceived lay in the earth as something dormant but alive. What, to
me, looked like an absolute wasteland, a thing abandoned, to Abdisho', Lazarus, and Anthony must have seemed like an unwitting
garden of dreams and visions. As cultivators, they plowed back into
it the nutriment of their own need. This, in turn, helped to fertilize
the wild seed of the spirit, those fertile husks of mystical attainment, so as to bring forth the new man that they felt lay buried
there. The desert may have appeared to be a wasteland on the surface, but to those early ascetics it harbored the richest harvest of all.

"Enter your innermost cell," Abdisho' urges, "close the doors and
endeavor to respond *to what is being done to you*."[11] This is an interesting observation, for it implied that a man is in receipt of grace
whenever he prepares himself aright. Something occurs, a mysterious movement-toward, an interpenetration of the man, the ascetic,
by energies outside himself. Or are these energies generated within?
Abdisho' does not say, but he does suggest that there is some complicity between inner and outer, between the workings of the heart
and the desert beyond. It is all part of the hidden activity that anchorites were at pains to realize in themselves.

Abdisho' Hazzaya attempted to further clarify his theory of signs
in a letter that he wrote to one of his friends who, presumably, had
asked him to write down his thoughts on ascetic practice. The first
step, he maintained, was never to leave one's quietude, to remain

removed from men and even from the sound of birds. The second step he called the "workings of understandings," whereby one attempts to remove discursive thought from the mind, to retire into oneself and root out all distraction. When this state has been achieved, it is possible to arrive at the third step, that of a love of recitation. "The furnace of recitation of the Psalms and of reading will then be kindled in the heart to such an extent that if possible, even when a man is sitting at table in order to eat, his mind will be occupied inwardly with the recitation of the Psalms."[12]

The fourth step is characterized by a flow of tears and the need to make continual prostrations before the crucifix. These are spontaneous tears and are normally shed "through the fire which kindles the soul within and without the body." According to Abdisho', these tears constitute the boundary between purity and serenity. The mind is now poised at the gate leading to the sphere of serenity. At this point all sense of polarity ceases, male and female merge, freedom and bondage are seen as irrelevant, nor does it matter whether one is circumcised or not. "Christ will be seen all in all," he elaborates.[13]

The next condition that arises is that of "impulses stirring and rising in the heart." They are, according to Abdisho', like "light mixed with fire." In such a condition a man may hear the voice of a fine sound of glorification unperceived by the faculties. He will then be in a position to contemplate the "cloud of the intelligible Cherubim" surrounded by a choir of voices, which utterly silence the mind, leaving it ready to be "swallowed up in the light of the high and sublime Theory, like fish in the sea."[14] In this condition the mind is no longer able to distinguish itself from the sea in which it swims.

The sixth step finds one clad in fire from the soles of one's feet to the crown of one's head, similar to that state experienced by Arsenius. It is at this point that the ascetic's whole being has been transformed into what Abdisho' calls a "fine spiritual body." This state is both an individual condition and a collective one in that it partakes of the community of saintly bodies throughout time. One senses here that Abdisho' is alluding to the existence of a transcendent body that subsumes all spiritual entities into one great orb of light. He suggests that this orb sometimes appears as a "sphere or star," and that one should not be afraid. Moreover, he, too, was aware of how Arsenius appeared to his friends, acknowledging as a result that when a man entered into his inheritance as a fine spiritual body, he has become at last a seer.

The seventh step, or condition, Abdisho' confesses, cannot be expressed in a letter. But he tries anyway. What emerges is a commingling of the senses to the point where complete impassability (*apatheia*) has been attained. A man is enveloped in joy, without knowing where it is coming from. "He only sees it and is conscious of it, but why he sees it he does not know."[15] At first, touch and sight join together, then taste and smell, before the sense of hearing is stimulated by what he calls "spiritual speech." This commingling of the senses is all part of what the French poet Arthur Rimbaud was later to identify as a "derangement of the senses," though possibly with a less spiritual expectation in mind.[16]

Abdisho' Hazzaya, what little we know of him, evidently aspired to a state of realizing the highest level of consciousness that is open to men. Nor did he draw back from articulating what he had experienced in his innermost cell. His voice, I now realized, was so purely driven by years of ascetic practice that he was able to articulate a level of consciousness that no Western spiritual has ever attained—and I include men such as Saint John of the Cross and the anonymous scribe who wrote *The Cloud of Unknowing*. In Abdisho's case, I was dealing with someone who had managed to raise the level of verbal expression to a new height in order to bear the burden of his extraordinary mystical vision. He had found words to recount the great depth to which a mind could descend in order to plumb its own essence.

The memory of Christ as a prototype was contingent on the realization of *apatheia*. The idea of a God-man entering into the spiritual life of humanity was entirely new to antiquity. Not even those various Greek half-god–half-men (Hercules, Achilles, and so on) radiated their divinity on earth in the way that Christ did, even as he did in his own lifetime. Though they might have been born of an earthly mother and a god (as well as a goddess seduced by a man), the qualities they bestowed on humanity were entirely linked to physical supremacy in battle or in some other field of activity. They were not considered to be spiritual beings. They never proposed a new way of life that might lead to a revolution in human consciousness. This was Christ's unique contribution, and one that inspired men to aspire to more than victory in battle or the achievement of political success. The Christ of those early centuries after his death introduced men to the idea that they, too, were capable of achieving godlike status.

Abdisho' only rarely mentions the name of Christ in his work, as does Anthony. The desert ascetics were not men to dwell on the crucifixion or the Virgin birth as events that needed to be molded into their being, as later generations of theologians wanted to do. They accepted the historical reality of these events, of course, but they were seen as no more than an adjunct to Christ's miraculous life. What Abdisho' and Anthony were primarily interested in was Christ's luminous nature and his capacity to articulate humankind's spiritual potential in the face of the pervasive materialism of his time. Roman functionality, the decline of the gods, the rise of international mercantilism, excessive public ritual, the deification of emperors, as well as a decline in philosophic inquiry, all these had contributed to the pulverization of social values in late antiquity. There was little to live for save the continuation of the species. The classical ideal had simply run out of steam.

Christ had changed all that; and the men of the Egyptian desert were the first to devise a Christ-like modus vivendi that broke with the classical model. No matter what might be said about the early Christian theologians as intellectual and spiritual pioneers—men such as Clement of Alexandria, Tertullian, Origen, Jerome, Athanasius, and even Augustine—they were still classically motivated in their actions and still saw themselves as philosophers whose reputations were founded on the practice of dialectic. If they had been so inclined, they might actually have enjoyed a visit to the stoa to argue with their pagan contemporaries, thinkers such as Porphyry and Iamblichus. It's no accident that the Platonic Academy had been revived in the late fourth century in Athens in the face of Christian insurgence. Conversely, the early theologians were only ever able to engage in disputation in the time-honored manner of the philosophers, and so spent their time arguing points of dogma or rooting out heresy. They were never able to formulate a genuine Christian lifestyle in the way that Anthony and his contemporaries effectively did.

This makes the work of the Syriac mystics all the more important. They were uncontaminated by declining classical ideals and were free to incorporate Eastern nuances into their thinking. They were not afraid, either, to press the boundaries of emotional and psychic deliberation in their attempt to realize the intensity of Christ's inner ordeal. Thus they were able to devise a mystical tradition that in turn permeated Western Christianity. Dionysius the Areopagite, Isaac of Nineveh, John Climacus, Dorotheus of Gaza, Gregory of Sinai, Mark the Ascetic—the list of those whose ideas have come to rest in the Greek Orthodox and Latin canon goes on and on. Such men provided the mystical leaven to an often overly dogmatic and theological mode of expressing religious belief. Certainly, in the desert, there was no room for an Aquinas, Benedict, or Ignatius.

After my first foray into the heartland of old Mesopotamia, into this Persia of the imagination, I had come away fortified. Abdisho' Hazzaya had alerted me to something else lying buried in the ascetic process, something that did not concur with the harsh regime of hunger, lack of sleep, and poverty normally associated with anchoritism. There was a sophic quality about his thought—a sense that a man might dream dreams that were deeply transfiguring in their import. Abdisho' was telling me that Christianity was more than the sum of its dogma, its theology, and its dependence on a hierarchy of virtues. His Christianity was one that involved a process of thought committed to freeing a man from his own limitations. Prayer, of course, was central to his spiritual practice, but it was a prayer that reached beyond the structure of thought itself as it sped toward that holy orb of stillness.

Lazarus had pointed me in the right direction. Our discussions on his terrace on those late afternoons had yielded their first fruit: I had entered into the abode of what might best be described as mystical detachment, even if I hadn't yet experienced it myself. I comforted myself in the knowledge that on any journey one needs to know that the destination itself offers its own special incentive, even if one has yet to reach it. Abdisho' Hazzaya was the first to point the way. He had shown me that the desert experience was not just confined to Egypt, or to Anthony's cave, where the flame had first been struck. The ascetic impulse possessed its own momentum and had reached out to the world across every frontier. Rome and Constantinople were no longer the sole bastions of Christian life; places all over the East nourished the memory of Christ's sojourn on earth as well—but with one difference: Abdisho' and his friends, along with Anthony and his, often regarded doctrinal orthodoxy as an impediment in their lifelong pursuit of *apatheia*.

eleven

CONVERSATIONS IN THE DESERT

"Human nature has the potential for endless existence," wrote Isaac of Nineveh.[1] When I read this statement I was immediately struck by its modernity. He further went on to describe the five incomparable gifts that a man could possess: life, sense perception, reason, free will, and authority. Here was someone in whose company I could feel altogether comfortable, I thought. Though I was vaguely familiar with his name from other works in which he had been quoted, it was not until Lazarus reminded me of his importance that I decided to study him more seriously. Isaac of Nineveh is one of the great figures of Eastern spirituality. He, more than most, gave form and beauty to the discoveries of the desert anchorites. I suspect it was because he had been fashioned by a similar sort of desert himself.

He was born in Qatar on the Persian Gulf in the mid–seventh century, we know nothing of Isaac's early development, except that he was consecrated bishop of Nineveh around 670. It was evident from the beginning that the task would be beyond him, and within five months he had retired to the mountains of Kurdistan to live as an anchorite. His inability to deal with normal disputation between men was said to be his downfall. He simply did not have the mind, or the will, to deal with the petty problems of everyday life when people came to him and asked him to arbitrate. A story is told of how two men came to his residence to request his adjudication over a loan. "If this man refuses to pay back what belongs to me," one of the men said, "I will be obliged to take him to court." Isaac said to the man, "Since the Holy Gospel teaches us not to take back what we have given away, you should at least grant this man a day to repay." The man answered dismissively: "Let's forget about the teachings of the Gospel for the moment." To which Isaac responded: "If the Gospel is not to be present, what's the use of me being here?" Shortly thereafter he left for the desert.[2] Beyond this point, all we know is that Isaac went blind in his later years and died as one of the most venerated men of his age. The picture we have of him is that of a man who was "quiet, kind and humble, and his words gentle. He ate only three loaves of bread a week with some vegetables, and he did not taste any food that was cooked. He composed five volumes filled with sweet teaching."[3] Another writer called him the "master and teacher of all monks and the haven of salvation for the whole world."[4] Here indeed was a man in whom the spirit of Anthony had come to rest.

Lazarus, I know, regarded the man as one of his mentors. On more than one occasion he had quoted him from memory during our discussions. "Sapphire is the color of the new man," he once said.

"Why, I wonder?" I asked.

"According to Isaac, it was the color of heaven."

"And death? How did he view that?"

"He regarded death as being a product of the wisdom of the Creator, a way of releasing a tied-up energy in order to possess an energy that is free and capable of understanding our true relationship to things. At this point in the history of the world, it rules for a certain time over nature. Nature as we know it is therefore a creation of death. But one day it will vanish altogether. When this happens eternity will reign."

"It appears that contingency is a stage through which the world must pass," I reasoned.

"Isaac would argue that transience is a necessary transition, yes. Birth and death represent a defeat that we must somehow overcome," Lazarus replied.

"And evil? How did Isaac explain that?" I responded, hoping to find a weak spot in the great man's argument.

Lazarus gave one of his wistful smiles. "He saw the devil as the name we give to the deviation of the will from truth. He was adamant that the devil was not a real designation of a natural being."

"Satan exists in our minds only. He's therefore no more than a figment," I said.

"He is the deviance of our will. We attribute a name to this condition: we even give it a form, but Isaac saw this as a part of our natural tendency toward wanting to personify things."

Our conversations together high on Mount Colzim were like old-fashioned Socratic dialogues. My ignorance was like grist to Lazarus's mill: he was able to grind a more refined reality out of the raw seed I had managed to harvest in the monastery library. "What have you to do with the ways of Egypt, and with drinking from the Nile?" he often used to quote whenever I thoughtlessly drew our conversation back to issues of the world. We were like two men on watch as we gazed out over the desert, ever alert to the appearance of the enemy. Nonetheless, I found our conversations to be helpful; they sent me back to my studies with a renewed energy to know and understand more.

The idea that transience was a necessity struck a chord, however. Isaac considered that only when one was engaged in deep personal contemplation did the heart become, in his word, "subtilized" and thus torn away from any participation in decay. Decay was the result of a predisposition toward attending to the natural affections (which he called psychic service) rather than to a spiritual discipline that dispensed with the senses. Moreover, Isaac understood personal contemplation not as something psychologically engendered but, rather, as a way of entering into the creation of nature itself. This was not a nature of the senses, to which we are so addicted, but a nature steeped in the eternal nature of things. The object of such personal contemplation was the removal of the heaviness of the body. He wrote:

> From there, one is easily moved onwards towards what is called solitary knowledge, which is, according to a clear interpretation, *ecstasy in God*. This is the order of that high future state which will be given in freedom that lives on in immortality, in that way of life that will be after the resurrection. It will consist therein, that from that point on human nature will not be cut off from constant ecstasy in God, mingling itself with any created being. If there were any other thing equal to Him, nature would sometimes follow Him, sometimes as His equal. When, however, the beauty of all which exists in that future order of things, is inferior to His beauties, how should it be possible for the mind not to fix its gaze exclusively on Him? What then? Should mortality trouble it, or the heaviness of the flesh, or the remembrance of kindred, or natural wants, or adversities

which overtake it, or the distraction of ignorance, or the deficiency of nature, or the distraction caused by the elements, or intercourse with one another, or the influence of dejection, or the weariness of the flesh? If now in this world—while all these things are thus—the veil of the affections is somehow withdrawn from before the eyes of the spirit so that it gazes at the glory, and the mind is drawn away in ecstasy—then, without doubt, if God had not limited the duration of these moments in this life, man would not return from that state during his entire life, if it were possible. Now when all these earthly things exist no longer, and that endless order has been established . . . how then should the spirit find a way to remove itself from the wondrous sight of God, or dwell with any other?[5]

Of course, one might argue that Isaac is merely reiterating a popular eschatological viewpoint about the prospect of heaven on earth becoming a reality "after the resurrection." I had no quarrel with this as part of the doctrine and mythos of Christianity. But he was also saying much more—articulating, in fact, a complex idea about nature as a veil, and of the heart's heaviness contributing to the illusion of that veil. The idea that a man might quit himself altogether, dispense with every psychism, and through ecstasy in God mingle in the lives of any created being is a revolutionary thought.[6] No Hellenic philosopher had posed such an alternative in the past, not even Plotinus. It meant that a man might participate in "endless existence" after all—but not at the level of simply remaining alive in perpetuity. What Isaac meant by endless existence was something more subtle: he wanted to alert us to the possibility of a transmigrational life that allows for the opportunity to enter into the spirit of all created beings at their most principial level. He did not want to see us become a cow, a horse, or a mollusk. This would be to accept the veil of nature as the only reality. "After the resurrection" therefore becomes a metaphor for the moment when one gives up one's allegiance to psychic life, to appearance, and crosses over into "endless existence." "The future order of things" is thus not a condition bound by time so much as it is a consequence of just such an abandonment.

This is why Isaac pays particular attention to human affliction and adversity. He knows that these are the very thread that makes up the veil. While we continue to place these at the forefront of our lives, we will always be burdened with "heaviness of the flesh." In a sense, he is making a case for a life normally lived as a spiritual infant in contrast to one of deep and untroubled maturity. By dispensing with the heart's heaviness, with what he called the "preternatural affections," a man could be brought to a "nakedness of mind," which he likened to "immaterial contemplation." This can only be achieved by living a life entirely dedicated to the purification of the body:

> Body discipline in solitude purifies the body from the material elements in it. Mental discipline makes the soul humble, and purifies it from the material impulses that tend toward decaying things, by changing their affectable nature into motions of contemplation; this is spiritual discipline. It elevates the intellect above earthly things and brings it near to primordial spiritual contemplation; it directs the intellect toward God by the sight of unspeakable glory and its delight spiritually in the hope of future things, thinking of what and how each of them will be.[7]

Here Isaac is making a case for body purification (not cleanliness, as such) as being a prerequisite for any suspension in the process of decay. Death, therefore, is the culmination of this suspension, when finally the body is no longer able to continue its resistance to the material impulse. The affectable nature, however, can be influenced by mental discipline in that it elevates the intellect above earthly things.

Isaac's equation for resisting death is simple: one needs to utilize the will as a vehicle to initiate mental discipline in order to bring about a state of "primordial spiritual contemplation" that in turn realizes the "unspeakable glory" in the sight of God. In other words, a purely intellectual endeavor can suspend, or at least delay, the workings of the affectable nature toward the inevitability of decay and death. One needs to be wary, though, in regarding such a suspension as geared toward the physical only. Isaac wants us to understand that a state of primordial spiritual contemplation stands outside such a prerogative. He does not want to eliminate the physical nature of death, as he has already acknowledged it to be essential to the way the world works at this point in its evolution. Rather, he wants to alert us to a condition of unspeakable glory that awaits those who attempt to break with an excessive dependence on material well-being. Unlike the ancient Egyptians, who saw eternal life in physical terms (the pyramid as tomb is its exemplar), Isaac had proposed a new kind of eternal life that distinguished between physical immortality and its counterpart—the gradual overcoming of all dependence on the physical through ascetic practice. According to him, the "inner activity" of the anchorite was the only way to dispense with the elaborate funerary rites of the pharaoh and his ultimately futile bid to live forever.[8]

So "after the resurrection" is not so much a sign of thing to come or the "hope of future things" as it is the realization of a new inner dimension that Isaac says can be found only through spiritual contemplation. He wants us to accept that humankind's spiritual evolution has crossed its own Rubicon and entered a new life of freedom no longer dependent on bodily freedom. Man has, in a sense, dematerialized himself through his allegiance to Christ and the supreme sacrifice that he made of himself. Man lives now, not so much as a shade on the face of the earth, but as a figure capable of entering into the whole of nature by way of his mental and spiritual capacities. It may be argued that this is why man today is so

vigorous in his inquiry of nature, even if only at the level of observation and scientific analysis. While Isaac and his precursors may
have made it possible to see nature less as the embodiment of
mythic or psychological forces than it once was for archaic man,
they have also opened the way to the experience of a new kind of
sensibility altogether—that of us seeing nature as a projection of
our own half-understood quest for eternity. Isaac would argue that
in doing so we have lost sight of the forest for the trees. We have
fallen into the age-old pharaonic trap of believing that we can man-
ufacture eternity simply by rearranging nature to suit our purpose.

"To release ourselves from such an illusion," Lazarus remarked
one afternoon when I broached with him the idea of the confusion
we have about the manipulation of nature and our desire for immortality, "we need to understand what Isaac meant by purification."

"Did he propose a system?" I asked.

"He spoke of three purifications. The first being a bodily one.
We need to cleanse the body of its attachment to the passions. Excessive food, sexual activity, and a love of luxury are a barrier to
bodily purity. This is why we anchorites practice such austerities.[9]
We are trying to break the hold our passions have on our body."

"Is this what Isaac means by heaviness of flesh?" I inquired.

"The body must be elevated to a level of transparency," Lazarus
continued. "We know this by the fact that men such as Arsenius
were perceived to be surrounded by fire, even as they lived. It is at
such a point that we must consider the second purity—what Isaac
calls psychic purity. The soul must now be released from hidden affections of the spirit. I think the great man means that we have to
remove from our thoughts all wrongfulness, all sense of animosity
felt toward others and ourselves. Instead we must become absolutely
open and uncritical toward our fellow human beings. Isaac likens
this condition to that of a child."

"And the third purity?" I asked.

"Purity of the mind," replied Lazarus, "is to be free from all hidden affections residing in the spirit. Through revelations, or thoughtful encounters with the deepest aspect of our selves, we are able to withdraw from any emotion directed toward those things that lie in the domain of the senses. It is derived from perfection in training in heavenly contemplation. The mind, divorced from the senses, is stimulated by certain spiritual powers emanating from the manifold worlds above us."

"Which may be seen as none other than achieving a state of *apatheia*," I countered.

"A state that can only be realized when the bonds pinioning the mind are finally untied," Lazarus said. "To do this, Isaac urges us to seek after wisdom, which he says has no limit. Its very limitlessness leads to a purity of mind that considers all natural knowledge as relative. When we become free of this knowledge to such an extent that we reach the original simplicity and integrity of nature, then we have returned to the ways of a child. A child's face, after all, is not yet molded by language; it is a face outside time. I think Isaac is trying to say that science cannot be the repository of wisdom, nor can the scientist be a sage."

"Isaac called such an interior state of recognition the 'crucifixion of the mind,'" I recalled.

"He did indeed. He wanted us to understand the degree of suffering that we must endure in order to be free. There's no getting away from the fact that we cannot avoid suffering. It is like heating a piece of iron in a forge to a point where it can be made malleable. Only then is it able to be fashioned into something of value. Turning one's gaze away from nature, and constantly directing it toward God, may realize this transformation. Isaac put it more poetically when he remarked: 'Place in me the pure metal of your love, so that, following you, I become alienated from the world.' Worldly exile is thus the key to our ascent on the cross."

"Is it possible to achieve such purity of heart that a person no longer belongs to this world?"

"I have seen it in a man only once," Lazarus admitted. "One time I traveled to Saint Catherine's monastery on Mount Sinai to pay my respects to the saint's relics. Her skull is there and possesses healing properties, so I was told. While I was staying in the monastery, I met an anchorite living at the foot of Mount Sinai in his cave. He had reached such a state of perfection, this old man, that he was in the habit of forgetting whether he had eaten or not. The serenity that radiated from his face reminded me of a baby's. I was informed by one of the monks in the monastery that they often had to bring him down from the mountain to attend liturgy in the church because he thought he'd actually attended it earlier! This blessed man was so very pure and serene in all his actions that he had no idea whether he had eaten or whether he had partaken of the Eucharist— or whether, indeed, he was alive at all! I really do think that he was so out of this world that his bodily presence meant nothing to him."

"It is as if the old anchorite had made a palimpsest of his mind," I suggested. "His whole life had been written upon it, but nothing was actually registered. Everything that summed up his psychic life had been erased."

Lazarus nodded.

"A lifetime of ascetic practice had removed him from the influence of time, or a need for nourishment, or any knowledge of where he lived," he remarked.

"I am reminded of the state of perfectionlessness that Dionysius the Areopagite spoke of," I replied. "Those that are truly perfect transcend the idea of perfection itself, since perfection implies an object or purpose achieved. The old anchorite that you met had obviously arrived at such a state because he had managed to overcome the distinction between self and nonself. In a sense, he had become *alter Christus*, another Christ."[10]

"I think the good Dionysius also spoke of it as the power of imitating angels, [aggelomimetos]." It is the supreme mental attitude of unknowing when the mind becomes emptied of its own powers, and so acquires a knowledge whose scope and activity is outside itself."

"Dionysius also called it 'a state of darkness which is beyond light,'" I added. "He argued that we must attain to a vision through the loss of sight and knowledge, which, in ceasing to see or to know all that is beyond perception and understanding, leads us to strip away those qualities pertaining to a knowledge of unknowing itself."[12]

How easy it was to become absorbed into the rarified world of thinkers like Dionysius! His talent for exploring the outer reaches of ecstatic experience made him one of the most profound of all mystics. That he may have been a Syrian monk influenced by the writings of the pagan philosopher Proclus, sometime during the fifth century, in no way robs his work of its originality. What we can surmise, however, is that in studying Proclus, who in turn was influenced by Plotinus, we find ourselves journeying as far eastward as India. Although Plotinus never actually reached the subcontinent, it is generally believed that he had encountered aspects of Indian philosophy during his sojourn in Alexandria, and possibly even Edessa. It may be argued that many of Dionysius's ideas, therefore, bear a distant relationship to those of the Vedas. It's no accident that the *Manu-smrti* (ca. AD 200) describes ascetic practice in a similar way to Anthony and his friends.[13]

The fact was that Anthony and his friends had attempted to change the very basis of intellectual perception as it had existed throughout the classical period. It was as if they had seen a radical flaw in the Hellenic view of matter, grounded as it was in sensual apperception, and wanted to impose a more radical criterion for engaging in a dialogue with the world. They were no longer content to accept the world as it is but, rather, wanted to return to a primary understanding of creation in the hope of discovering a different, more essential method of determining reality. Isaac himself called this the second creation, thus implying that the revolutionary Christian experience had in some way broken through the screen of matter by undermining man's allegiance to it through the medium of his own flesh. In doing so, the ascetic was proposing a mode of life beyond anything the philosophers of old might have envisaged. As Isaac remarked:

> And how suddenly this wonderful order will be destroyed, and how a new world will begin in which no recollection whatever of the first creation will occur to any man's mind, in which there will be a different mode of life, different deliberations, and different thoughts. Then human nature will no longer recollect this world nor the former way of life in it. For the gaze of their mind will be captivated by the sight of that new order, and it will not be able to turn in its memory toward the races of flesh and blood; for as soon as this world is destroyed, the new one will begin.
>
> O mother who has suddenly been forgotten by the sons that she has born and educated and instructed—and in a twinkling of an eye they are gathered unto another bosom, and have become real sons of the barren one that has never been born. Rejoice, O barren one, you that did not bear, that the son which the earth has born to you. And the mind thinks in amazement, of how a new world will take the place of this, and of when its beginning will be; and how long these bodies will lie in that state, body and dust mingled together; and how that life will be; and in what likeness this nature will arise, and in what way it will come to the second creation.[14]

Isaac instinctively knows that it is impossible to repeat the first creation, so he suggests a moving-toward what he calls the second creation. To do this, however, one must engage in a rapprochement with man's thinking past in order to hear the voice of the future. In a sense, all progress in spiritual growth must align itself with a stepping-away from the first creation toward the second creation. But one thing becomes evident: the second creation represents a fundamental shift in values that inspires a "different mode of life" for everyone who partakes of the spiritual genesis implied. Isaac's view of the future suggests that he believed in a true *eschaton,* or divinely ordered climax to history. He knows that there can be no turning back to the old pagan belief in the Good as a basis for life.

The "wonderful order" that he sees as being destroyed is that of the material world considered as mere *physis.* For a man to enter the abode of the second creation, such a radical severance is not only necessary but unavoidable. Man must be prepared to abandon his reliance on old, outmoded ideologies and cultural behavior so that he might begin to comprehend the essence of truth. The key to this act of severance is in forgetting the past and in distancing one-self from the old order. Nonrecollection, crossing the river Lethe, as it was known to those of antiquity, was seen as the only way of breaking with the past. This past, it must be emphasized, embodied all that held a man to his old ways, be they familial, economic, or material.

But Isaac goes further in his plea. He suggests that the sons of this world must gather in the bosom of another, the so-called bar-ren one, an epithet he gives to what may be termed the Divine Mother—that is, the female embodiment of Christ as ungendered Being. It is a complex analogy, and probably a dangerous one in terms of Christian orthodoxy, but one that Isaac pursues anyway in his attempt to reconcile material man with his spiritual metamor-phosis. In a sense, the new man is conceived of on this earth through an act of spiritual insemination. Man's womb is the world, with all its material limitations, into which God implants the inner light of his spirit, thus paving the way for a particular kind of rebirth.

Clearly this is an evocative, though possibly heretical (and Gnostical), notion, even if Isaac was never permanently branded as such by theologians.

What becomes clear is that Isaac wants to embrace a new *eschaton*. According to him, pagan values and the Stoic ideal of the Good, of virtue being pursued for its own sake, could lead only to a spiritual and intellectual impasse when compared with the *eschaton* posed by the advent of Christ. Isaac, like all the anchorites of those early years, further emphasized the break with the past by denying the importance of external goods altogether (the "natural things" that Antipater of Tarsus spoke of).[15] This, in part, is at the very root of asceticism: since the ancient ideal of happiness was linked to the possession of sufficient goods on which virtuous action was based, a man must break with such a concept if he is to realize Christ in this life. Happiness, for the ascetic, was thus determined by a denial of the Good in the Stoic sense, in favor of the *eschaton*. Man needs to recognize his role in the divine plan, not submerge himself in "natural things" as he had done in the past. The "barren one" did not conceive his sons; they conceived themselves by entering into communion with Christ by way of an act of ascesis. This, according to Isaac, is the ultimate demonstration of free will. A man needs to die to the world ("body and dust mingled together") in order that he might participate in the second creation.

Obviously Isaac had alerted me to an important fact I already half believed in, anyway: that today the mystery surrounding living beings goes unheeded because we have transferred our allegiance to psychology and science in the wake of our disillusionment with metaphysics, philosophy, and religion. Isaac also felt this to be the case in his own time. He sensed, however, that men wanted to reaffirm this mystery for themselves rather than accept the by then exhausted valuations of antiquity. Christ represented something uniquely different for humanity—a going beyond the idea of the

Good, and of Perfection, to a more open-ended view of man's spiritual possibilities. He recognized, as did Anthony and his contemporaries, that the world would be a richer place when mere *physis* was put back into its rightful place. Nature, he knew, was much *more* than the sum of its materiality; it was an ongoing realization that the mind had become contingent to being as never before. For the mind to be "captivated by the sight of that new order" was for every anchorite the beginning of a process of personal transformation.

On Mount Colzim it seemed that every conversation I enjoyed with Lazarus was rich in the humus of thought. It was as if the desert itself had joined us in our discussions. I was more than conscious, too, that the invisible presence of Isaac of Nineveh among us had made it possible to go beyond simple analysis and the limitations of rational discourse. "Different deliberations" had instead become the enlivening substance of our thoughts as they mingled with those of past generations. I began to appreciate the sheer adventure of thought that men such as Anthony, Isaac, Abdisho', and others had embarked on all those centuries before. They were not satisfied with preserving the status quo but, rather, were often prepared to die for their beliefs, just as the history of martyrdom during the first centuries of our era indicates. More important, perhaps, they were prepared to tread the path on the extreme edges of humanity as a whole in order to come to terms with their belief in a new vision for men. This took a significant amount of courage.

Of course, they had been empowered. Christ, the crucified man and God, had provided them with a concept of the inner man that was entirely otherworldly. By his actions alone he made humankind realize that the journey to the home of God was a thinking-out toward the beginning—and that each of us thinks the beginning insofar as we think of truth at all. To Anthony and his successors, ascesis was the elixir of truth. The task he had set himself, and by implication us, was to drink of this elixir and so regenerate the psychological sphere within himself, making it into an orb of incorporeal light that shone on everyone in the process. As Isaac wrote, "Our deliberations are divine impulses. The motions of the pure mind are quiet voices with which they secretly chant psalms to the Invisible One."[16] This is the language of a new impetus toward spiritual realization. Song had at last become the "secret chant" of all ascetic activity among those desert anchorites after all.

twelve

GARNERING THE PEARL

Song. Ultimately this is what Anthony and his contemporaries had struggled to come to terms with all
their lives. *Apatheia,* they discovered, was the only way
to enter into the stillness of unutterable speech. In another way it accounted for why those early anchorites
wrote so little. They had yet to discover a language to
express the depth and wonderment that they had experienced on the road to spiritual understanding. Ascetic practice had taught them that words owe their
allegiance less to the certainty of their articulation
than to the mystery of the inexpressible—that they
were, in the fullest sense, tethered to the divine.[1] More-

over, through their prolonged encounter with silence, these men and women of the desert learned to understand that the most important thing is not how one expresses experience but the degree of intensity with which one lives it. Such was the new language of ascesis: in order for a person to sustain plenitude he must set his mind to living a divine life, to dreaming it.

This was the "priceless pearl" that Ephraim the Syrian so eloquently wrote about in one of his hymns:

> On a certain day I found a pearl, my friends
> In which I saw the mysteries of the Kingdom
> Its forms and types expressing His Majesty;
> A fountain where I drank of the Son's glory.
>
> Upon the palm of my hand I placed this gem
> In order to study it carefully:
> When I looked at the pearl from one side
> It proved to be the same from all sides.
> Thus was the Son's incomprehensibility
> Revealed, since He is wholly light.
>
> In the pearl's brightness I saw the Bright One
> Whose countenance cannot be clouded,
> Its purity containing a great mystery—
> That of the Body of Our Lord, so well refined
> Is undivided, just as the Truth
> Which is also undivided.
>
> In this pure conception I saw the Church
> Containing the Son within her
> Like a cloud, bearing Him
> As if in the skein of heaven
> His gracious radiance shining forth from her.

Therein I saw his Trophies, his Victories
His glorious Crowns. I saw the richness
Of his helpful and overflowing graces,
His hidden things amid those that are revealed.[2]

This is the language not of theology but of poetry. For Anthony and his friends, truth's meaning was a task taken on to accomplish through silence, the interior silence of the cave. From a lifetime of asceticism Ephraim managed to arrive at a state whereby he was so dominated by an overwhelming experience of divinity that the very fabric of his personality was torn apart. He became, in a sense, a purely conceived pearl able to reflect the multisided nature of divinity itself. In so doing he was transformed into one of Christ's trophies, a living example of man's ability to surpass himself by way of a prolonged act of physical and psychic disengagement. Asceticism was the oyster, he the grain of sand inserted in its shell, and the pearl of the new man the result of a lifetime of mental, physical, and spiritual aggravation.

My studies in the monastery library, and or course my discussions with Lazarus, had all helped me to come to terms with an issue that had always troubled me about Christianity: its too great reliance on doctrinal orthodoxy as a means to understanding the depths of divine sobriety. I suppose I had grown tired of its entrenched moralism, its desire to mold man into some kind of polite entity devoid of the essence of poetry and extreme life. More than anything, I still wanted to encounter all the power of the elemental in the conduct of my inner life. Indeed, I wanted to place myself within the domain of measureless experience whenever I contemplated what Holderlin called the "supreme form," a term he devised to explain the supremacy of poetic reality over that of reason.[3] I had come to the conclusion that Anthony understood the nature of chaos as a liberating event. He saw it as a primeval force that afforded him nothing to lean on, or to brace himself against, whenever he tried to order existence. For him it was none other than the power of the immediate designed to check him before he slipped into that zone of security we associate with everyday life. I suspect that Anthony really had discovered the origin of eternity in the nature of fracture.

A man's soul is like a volcano: it must achieve a state of extinction wherein it becomes extinct to itself and thus extinct to its own extinction. In the act of becoming unconscious of itself and unconscious of its own unconsciousness, the soul is able to enter into a state of *katastasis*, that state of supreme stillness so much sought after by the anchorites. It may be argued that such a condition represents a turning away from life, a regression into a womblike existence. It is a charge that was leveled at many a hesychast, whose practices were often derisively labeled as navel gazing because they were in the habit of concentrating their gaze on the abdominal region during long periods of meditation.[4] It is, however, to view such effacement in terms of our own obsession with egoic behavior. Anthony, I'm sure, sought to break the chain that bound his inner life to the contingencies of the world. He wanted, above all, to forge a new link with what Ephraim called the "beauty of the Word" being reflected in the beauty within himself:

> *In the beauty of the Word your beauty*
> *Is mirrored, supremely precious this Word on High!*
> *As the ear is a leaf, the flesh a tree,*
> *In the midst of it you are fruit of light*
> *And to the womb that brings forth Light*
> *You are the angel that points.*[5]

So the Anchorites were trying to establish a connection between the Word and the word. They were perhaps the first thinkers of their age to recognize that the divine Word and language were in fact separate, that in order to experience the former, one needed to establish a new language to describe God's absence. As Simon of Taibutheh remarked, "'Divinity' is only [a word] applied to the Divine Essence in which is hidden a mystery: that of God and of the man from us, who is called God horizontally."[6] What Simon seems to be saying is that in the so-called horizontal domain of rationality, words are often used to describe what is essentially a mystery. For him, the "Kingdom of Heaven" is not a place but the knowledge of "sublime spiritual theory of the intelligible natures of the heavenly hosts."[7] This is another way of saying that the "Kingdom of Heaven" is none other than a metaphor to describe the inner state of the hesychast.

As a student of ascetic activity, I felt that I was beginning to understand the subtle nature of Anthony's spiritual endeavor. Whereas at one time I might have regarded his long sojourn in a cave on Mount Colzim, or in his tomb outside Pispir, as a sign of a certain social and spiritual derangement, now I knew otherwise. Though I had always been fascinated by his life, in the past something inside had made me draw back from granting him the ultimate accolade: that he was a genius, an example of the supreme spiritual prototype. Echoes of Edward Gibbon and his dismissal of those early Christian ascetics as representative of a cultural decline still lingered. The idea that a half-naked man, lice ridden and verging on the anorexic, could embody a resurgence of the human condition seemed absurd. The ascetics were not men but animals, not explorers of the spirit but inverts.

But to my credit, I had managed to slough off these prejudices. I was beginning to see men like Anthony in a new light. They were life's renegades, men in whom the spirit of denial was proof of their commitment to abandoning the worn-out husk of classicism that had for so long held men in its sway. The philosophers had run out of answers. The academies were filled with dialecticians content to pick over the tailings left by the great gold diggers of old. The long line of thinkers from Pythagorus through Heraclitus, Parmenides, Anaxagoras, Empedocles, and Zeno, down to Plato, Aristotle, and Plotinus, had finally become frayed. No one had yet been able to answer satisfactorily the question of Being. Instead it had been left to an unlettered carpenter from Nazareth to propound a new metaphysic and a new reason for living. It was this man who made his own death into an event rich in symbolic meaning: if a man could die to being, then he could become like unto a God in Being. It was the message for the future. Christ had become a manifestation of a vast, unused sweetness that now bathed the world in the perfume of flowers. His death was the dew that slaked the thirst of the world.

It may be argued, too, that Anthony and his contemporaries had set out to make their bodies into poems. When we come across remarks by Athanasius such as "His face had a great and marvellous grace," or "It was not his physical dimensions that distinguished him from the rest, but his stability of character and the purity of his soul," or "His soul being free of confusion, he held his outer senses undisturbed, so that from the soul's joy his face was cheerful as well, and from the movements of the body it was possible to sense and perceive the stable condition of his soul,"[8] we become aware of a desire to portray the ascetic as a deeply edifying spectacle, as a living poem. In a fresco of a virgin martyr in the oratory at Abou-Girgeh in Egypt, for example, we see a woman rising like a ghost from a field of flowers. She has become, in a sense, a flower blooming in a flower-strewn field of paradise. The emaciated body of this anchorite or martyr is thus transformed into a living embodiment of Christ on the cross. By an act of inversion, martyrdom, emaciation, and crucifixion these become supreme gestures of reproach against the cult of the perfect body. What such configurations reveal is a desire to preempt the body's corruptibility by revealing it in its true role—that of sacrifice. Anthony, like Christ before him, seems to be telling us that the body *must be abandoned* if one is to enter into the deified state. It's not for nothing that Paulinus of Nola described a person who had achieved such a condition as "living dust."[9]

"This is the model for the beginnings of a new way of life," Anthony insisted in one of his letters. "I castigate my body and bring it into subjection," he further elaborated, echoing the words of Saint Paul.[10] He knew what he was saying. He also knew that such remarks were in conflict with those of the classical philosophers who treated the body as a perfectly proportioned object. Harmony and balance in all things. They, after all, only *looked* at nature and did not enter into its mystery.[11] But such was Anthony's psychological acumen that he recognized where this attitude might lead: into a kind of unthinking self-satisfaction that ultimately manifested itself in man as consumer. To those who wished to "resurrect their minds," there was but one alternative: to moderate the power of the body. Anthony's asceticism was singularly directed toward the realization of what he called spiritual essence. And spiritual essence could be achieved only through "oneness." Above all, he maintained, a man has no obligation toward bodily life anyway.

This struck me as a rather provocative statement. What did Anthony mean? It was self-evident that one could not live without the body. It was also clear that he regarded the corruptible nature of flesh as an inhibition in the pursuit of pure being. Demonic activity he undoubtedly associated with the passions that he saw as the outward manifestation of corruptibility. Therefore, to deny the passions and bodily appetites was to neutralize the process of corruption and thus to diminish the hold that the demons have over us. In order to realize man's true essence, it was incumbent on him to deny these demons their hegemony over the body. Though they are never visible, Anthony insisted that they feed on our unwieldy temperaments, sucking them dry like vampires. All ascetic activity was thus designed to cut off their supply of nutriment at its source. It follows that *apatheia* came as a result of the distillation of the heart and mind into its primary essence, that of nothingness.[12] For Anthony, it appears, it is between thorns that God blooms.

Considering Anthony's journey into the desert in his quest for intimacy with God (*parresia*), I could not help equating his life to that of another seeker, the Marquis de Sade. For all de Sade's devotion to excess, there are similarities in these men. In its own way de Sade's debauchee resembles Anthony's recluse. "He [i.e. the debauchee] is thoughtful, concentrated in himself, and incapable of being moved by anything whatsoever," wrote de Sade. A solitary, he is unable to endure noise or laughter: nothing should distract him: "Apathy, indifference, stoicism, and inner solitude are the pitch to which he must lift his soul." De Sade further insisted that if passion were to be transformed into energy, then it had to be compressed in order to pass through a necessary moment of insensitiveness. "My passions concentrated on a single point are like the rays of the sun collected by a magnifying glass," one of his characters declared. For de Sade, negation is power in man, and man's whole future depends on this negation's being pushed to its limit.

Is not this Anthony's view? But, of course, with one difference. While de Sade may have seen passion as a transformative energy, Anthony saw its denial as the principle of the transformative energy he sought. While de Sade might have seen the complete man as he who completely asserts himself and is destroyed, Anthony saw the complete man as he who utterly negates himself and so "self"-destructs. Such polarities harbor a hidden nexus, however. The essential difference between the two men lies in their view of God. For de Sade, God is man's unpardonable fault, his original sin, the proof of his nothingness, and so an authorization and justification for crime. Whereas for Anthony, God is the name given to that void of vitality lying at the heart of ascesis. The more one dies in the flesh and in time (eternity is, after all, death of and in the body), the closer we are to him. The absolute is realized only through the exorcising of those private demons. But for both men, it seems power is achieved in solitude; it is not only a state but a choice and conquest.

I was beginning to realize why Anthony so fascinated me. He embodied a complexity, a distance, and a presence all in one. Far from being that disembodied image witnessed in so many paintings of him doing battle with demons, a man in league with his own weaknesses, I now saw Anthony as someone who had confronted the spiritual malaise of his age and set about seeking ways to cure it. Like a scientist analyzing his results, Anthony had tried to discover a workable hypothesis for the spiritual life. And like the scientist, he probably made a number of incorrect assessments as he trod the path toward enlightenment. There was no exact mathematical equation to guide him toward *parresia*. Like all pioneers, he was forced to work out his own set of laws to uncover the secrets of transcendent life. That he did so, and with such overwhelming significance in the spiritual life of those who came after him, is a tribute to his courage in the face of extreme adversity. The Roman state had no love for a man who viewed village life as antithetical, or who preferred a life as a self-appointed hunter on a mountainside "stalking his god."[13] Here was a blueprint for social collapse.

According to Anthony, the aim of the ascetic life, and by implication the life of the spirit, was to transcend earthly life and so prepare oneself for death. It was not a new concept: Plato had propounded a similar idea in relation to the importance of philosophy as a bridge between life and death. But where the ascetic and the philosopher differed is in their emphasis on the value of the physical life. Plato barely addressed it as an impediment to the realization of transcendent existence. Anthony, on the other hand, insisted that physis held back the soul from realizing itself. This was the point where classicism and Christianity parted. A new interiority had entered the world, and Anthony paved the way for its realization with his work in the desert. His cave had become a temple of the spirit. The difference between the two men, it seems, is that Plato wanted to live *next* to the flames, while Anthony want to live *in* them.

The fact is that I suspected Anthony of retreating into his cave on Mount Colzim for other reasons than those of simple ascesis. In a sense, he was a failed mystic who wanted to defeat time and individuation. Moreover, he wanted to preside over a new eruption of the absolute in history, one that echoed Christ. No other Christian before him had been so conscious of the value of Christ's engagement with history. As God and man, he had imposed a revolutionary eschatology on man's progress in the world. Henceforth, he who embraced Christianity embraced a world end that prefigured the culmination of matter in the form of its own limitation. What the Christian was concerned with—or should be, at least in Anthony's view—was the realization of a spiritual condition that operated outside such a limitation. Man, in his solitude, must somehow learn to stand up to God in order to contest this ground. In his agonic passion on the cross, Christ had paved the way to reaching the divine. Divinity was the seed of suffering from which the blue flower of ascesis was born.

By his actions Anthony acknowledged this seismic shift. Retreating to a cave in a mountain was more than just a symbolic gesture; it was his way of passing judgment on noneschatological existence. There was no way out of history save through a concerted attempt to posit an *eschaton* beyond it. Moreover, the old harmonies and cyclic trauma of ancient religions and thought had been exhausted. A man must stand up to God, not in any egoic way, but in the sense that a kind of divine exhaustion might ensue, as in the case of Jacob wrestling with the angel. According to Anthony, this was the mark of a true man: that he could contend with God over the nature of being, in order to discover the divine depths of Being.

So I was dealing not with an illiterate Egyptian but with an aging recluse scarred by history who had found himself living in the impasse of antiquity. He who spoke so often of the "great wound" knew full well that to stanch it required something more than a visit to the local temple or attendance at some cleansing ritual presided over by priests. That was the old way of doing things. Anthony had glimpsed something profound during his long sojourn in the desert. The veil of appearance that had for so long concealed the numen, and left it imprisoned in the temples of Egypt in the form of wooden statues of the gods, was finally lifted. He saw what few men in the history of mankind have witnessed: that the ultimate source of existence was not God as such but a divine negation, a prolonged utterance that came forth from cosmic silence in the form of the Word rising up from the depths of that fathomless sea of mysteries. We know this to be true of Anthony from the writings of Athanasius:

> Once while he sat working, he went into ecstasy . . . , and he groaned a great deal during the spectacle. Then, turning to his companions after a while, he moaned as he trembled; and then he prayed and, bending his knees, he remained there for a long time. When he rose the old man was weeping. Those who knew him now began to tremble, and greatly frightened, they begged to learn from him what it was. And they pressed him a great deal until, being forced, he spoke. And so with much groaning he said: "My children. It is better for you to die before the things in the vision take place."[14]

What was in that vision? Athanasius argues that Anthony had seen the impending desecration of the infant Church, threatened as it was by various heresies. But it may well have been more. His ecstasies were such that he found it impossible to articulate what was happening. It may be that he saw further, and deeper, than any man before him. It is no accident that he *knew* of his impending death: men who live in the realm of the timeless are acutely aware of where their bodies lie in relation to cessation. For them it is not an issue. It is as though they have some inner knowledge of their body's mechanism—and they, in fact, are able to determine when and where they might give up the ghost. It seems that Anthony was able to travel between the physical and spiritual as if he were in possession of some suprasensory gift. Perhaps he was. Perhaps he had learned how to defy corruptible nature by circumventing it. As Athanasius relates, "even his death had become something imitable."[15] In other words, he simply willed it.

> When he learned from providence about his death, he spoke
> to the brothers, saying: "This is the last visitation that I shall
> make to you, and I wonder whether we shall see one another
> again in this life. Now it is time for me to perish, for I am
> nearly one hundred and five years old." When they heard him
> they wept and embraced and kissed the old man. But he, *like
> one sailing from a foreign city to his own,* talked cheerfully and
> exhorted them not to lose heart in their labours, nor to grow
> weary in the discipline, but to live as though dying daily. He
> told them, "Be zealous in protecting the soul from dark
> thoughts as I said before, and compete with the saints." . . .
>   When the brothers pressed him to stay with them and die
> there, he refused for a number of reasons, as he *indicated while
> remaining silent,* but because of one in particular. The
> Egyptians love to honor with burial rites and to wrap in
> linens the bodies of their worthy dead, and especially of the
> holy martyrs, not burying them in the earth, but placing
> them on low beds and keeping them with them inside. . . .

But Anthony, aware of this practice and afraid that they might perform it for his body, pressed on, departing from the monks in the outer mountain. He entered the inner mountain to stay there as usual, and in a few months became ill.[16]

We are left with a vision of an old man completely in charge of his own death. Indeed, he was orchestrating it. He was sailing to a foreign city, a celestial city, a city not of this world. There is something unnerving about his certitude. Here is a man who has abandoned all rites, all procedures, all allegiance to those age-old sympathies that were normally accorded to the dead. He wanted none of it. Ever the stranger, the outsider, the solitary man, he did not wish to see his body become an object of veneration. He wanted to slip quietly from this world, from the temporary home of his body, and journey to the land of the Fathers, to their "eternal habitations."

One senses a tremendous pressure on him. He is not a man like others. He has subjected himself to a searching scrutiny over a period of more than seventy-five years, living as he did in solitude. It is a lifetime. He has pressed himself against that wall of silence that is his own self-effacement. He has subjected his body to the most excruciating afflictions. He has allowed his mind to become one interminable night of theater, the theater of deep and unremitting perturbation. No man before him has fought so hard for a liberty outside the self. He has become self-less, the incarnation of no-man, the bodily apotheosis of someone who has escaped altogether the concept of man-ness. He is now free. His body has become as living dust, the crushed remnant of being masquerading as stone. This is the fullness of his persona: to become just another rock on Mount Colzim vying with the heat, the cold, the bone-cracking nights of midwinter, when every star is frosted over with light.

I begin to identify with his predicament. I see in his quest something more than the eternal song of ascesis. Here is a man who has defied the odds, who has pitted himself against culture, against the timeless inundations of a river, against the ageless promise of personal fulfillment that they might offer. He has set about founding a new culture, a culture of the spirit, one that might overreach flood and fire, drought and deluge, death and taxes, the hopes and dreams of a people wedded to the simple expectations of survival. This is not for him. He has gone beyond such an uncomplicated paradigm of human consciousness. Instead he has dived deep into the waters of the gulf in search of Ephraim's pearl, that glimmering nacre of consciousness that is both spherical and indivisible. He has witnessed, if only ever momentarily, undividedness. He has allowed himself to be bathed in the glow of the infinite that is Christ.

In the end, his only concession to common humanity is to bestow on Athanasius a sheepskin cloak that his biographer had kindly given him many years before. Even at the last he makes sure that he owns nothing at his death. It is typical of the man. A worn-out sheepskin must not come between him and the prospect of annihilation. For a man who has devoured the world and contrived all his life to remain alone, only God should be allowed to appear from behind his screen of nothingness. It is as though some inner flame had refined his physical resistance to such an extent that there is nothing left of his body except the immateriality of ecstasy. Death holds no terror for someone who has managed to diminish the dimensions of matter. I am thus dealing with a man who has gone beyond appearances, who has found saintliness in an act of disembodiment.

I am secretly aghast at these admissions. Who would have imagined that one day I might find myself *identifying* with Anthony! At the beginning of my journey into the desert, all I had on my mind was the thought that perhaps I might glean some useful information about ascetic behavior to help me in my own life. I had never imagined that such a journey would lead me to this—to actually sympathizing with an irascible old ascetic whose only contribution to society was to deny it. Miracles do happen. In this respect I kept thinking back over some lines I had read by Isaac of Nineveh, commenting on the value and difficulty of words to describe the growth of spiritual understanding. He said, "Those who in their way of life are led by divine grace to be enlightened are always aware of something like a noetic ray running between the written lines which enable the mind to distinguish words spoken simply from those spoken with great meaning for the soul's enlightenment."[17] I suddenly realized that Anthony was my "noetic ray" shining on me. He had enabled me to concentrate my interior gaze on the workings of the soul as my principal concern. I had become an amateur hesychast! In any event, Athanasius assures us that Anthony was like a lamp to everyone, so my inclusion is not so surprising.

Today it is said that he is buried under the floor of the ancient Church of Saint Anthony, in front of the iconostasis. I do not know whether this is true, nor does it matter. Almost daily I have lit a candle to his memory and said a prayer before his fresco on the wall in this church. The woolen rosary that Lazarus so kindly gave me has helped in my meditations. Each knot reminds me of the descent we all make, into the deep waters of Ephraim's gulf, hoping to discover some pearl. And in a pendentive above, I observed the highbrowed image of Athanasius, who reminds me of the contiguity between saint and word. It is true: a spiritual genius does need a scribe to record his actions. Without Athanasius's pen, would we know of Anthony? This is conjecture, I know.

I am now at the mercy of the ascetic impulse. It moves me deeply. I know that it is one of the greatest gifts that humankind can bestow on itself. Those who see it as some life-destroying activity have not experienced its power to transform a life. I am reminded of a remark made by 'Ain al-Qudat when he said, "Fear is the clairvoyance of the believer, for he sees by the light of God."[18] Without fear, a fear of the inestimable depths of the infinite, no light can shine. The same argument can be laid in support of the ascetic impulse. It is fear put into practice. It is the light that shines on everyone who wishes to break free from his or her physical confinement in order to experience the eternal pulsations of the spirit.

thirteen

THE PARTING

This is a story about three men—no, four, if I include myself. I am thinking first of Anthony, of course, his biographer Athanasius, and Lazarus, my compatriot and friend. But it is also a story of countless men and women who have chosen to live the ascetic life in the anonymous reaches of the desert. Most of all, it is a story about how we are capable of transforming the lives of one another. Without Athanasius, we know that Anthony might not have come to our notice. Conversely, without my drawing attention to his existence, Lazarus might well remain on Mount Colzim, a solitary anchorite content to emulate the life of his hero. Either way, anonymity and notoriety are wayfarers on this long journey through life.

It is true that Lazarus had not asked for me to be present in his life. We had met by accident on a mountain, which is itself an important nodal point in the history of Western spirituality. Clearly, thinking men are drawn to such summits in their desire to deepen their understanding of the invisible. After nearly seventeen hundred years, Anthony's cave on the mountainside still harbors its powers of renewal for us all. A man lived here, and died, even as others bore his message to the world. I, along with Lazarus, am merely the last of a long line of pilgrims that have made the ascent to his haven.

Ascesis is like a blue flower; it blooms with the mysterious glow of phosphorescence. We are enamored by its radiance. I for one have journeyed to some of the most remote ascetic communities in the world in order to observe it. Morocco, Greece, Japan, Italy, Egypt, India, and Turkey are but a few of the countries I have visited in my quest to know and understand more about why men choose to remove themselves from the world. In every place, I have met ascetics that have impressed me with their dedication to a life that is considered to be inimical to the modern world. This is not to say that its value is diminished. It is simply to state a fact: that modernity is suspicious of solitude because in some way it calls into question the entire premise by which we live.

Nonetheless these lonely warriors of the spirit are important to us. I will go so far as to say that they represent the very ground of culture. Without them, without their prayers and lives of meditation on our behalf, the secular world would soon wither and die. They cultivate the flame of the spirit for everyone. Lazarus may at present be the last anchorite to inhabit Mount Colzim, but until he passes, the memory of Anthony will live on. I'm sure that someone will replace him, so that the tradition of holy ascesis will never die out. On Mount Athos, for example, many of the monasteries are undergoing a renaissance. Young men from all over the Orthodox

world are adopting the habit in a genuine spirit of renewal. It is as
though we were witnessing a kind of spontaneous combustion in
the ascetic life of the West. I recall once visiting a monastery populated by young French monks on a hilltop in Umbria. Here they
practiced absolute silence in emulation of Anthony. These are not
isolated incidents. In Australia, in a monastery in the Blue Mountains west of Sydney, I met a solitary monk tending his church. In
time, he insisted, others will join him. I also met an anchorite living
beside a church in a valley not far from where I live, and heard of
another residing above a shop in a coastal village. Such men and
women are probably the tip of an iceberg.

Coming to terms with this new dimension to my life had been a
major step for me. I felt that I had begun to understand the ascetic
impulse that had drawn men to a life in the desert, and its contribution to the deepening of consciousness. What was it Athanasius
had said? "Their cells in the hills were like tents filled with divine
choirs." One can picture these rustic communities spread across the
desert—caves, reed huts, mud-brick cells, small compounds gathered around a tiny chapel—each in its own style housing men and
women intent on attaining to some inner realization. The absent
figure in attendance in all these communities, of course, was Jesus
Christ. He walked among them, a silent witness to the gathering
momentum of those bent on attaining to a condition of *apatheia*.
For them, as for him, dying was a manner of encountering the invisible.

Those weeks in the monastery library had changed me. Delving
into the world of those Eastern ascetic writers had been a revelation. Who would have imagined that buried in the libraries of these
ancient monasteries of the East were works of such significance to
the development of early Christianity? Men such as Isaac of Nineveh, Dadisho' Katraya, John Climacus, Dionysius the Areopagite,
Ephraim the Syrian, Simon of Taibutheh, and my beloved Evagrius

Ponticus, as well as many others, had opened my eyes to a deep vein of mysticism running through the region. Truly it was a land of devotion and righteousness, as Athanasius so aptly remarked. It was as though the great expanse of sand that makes up the Middle East had become a vast accumulation of spirit. Indeed, it has been said that a grain of sand is but the sheen of the infinite.[1]

What had I learned from them? Everything and nothing, I suppose. I suspect it was the flavor of their thought that attracted me most. It seemed so free of dogma, so palpable and yet so abstract, and so rich in human insight. None of these thinkers and poets ever resorted to proof to bolster their argument. I gained the impression that they were in league with such a powerful insight into the way the world worked that it was fruitless on their part to address man's failure to understand in anything other than the language of love and humility. These men were not philosophers or theologians but seekers like myself. At some point in their lives they had set out to find answers to the question of being, just like me. They had trod the road of confusion, of doubt, and of disbelief, much as I had. In other words, they had risked everything on a roll of the dice. But in their case the dice were made up not of numbers but of the either/or of appearance versus reality. Who would have imagined them playing such a game?

Until now I certainly hadn't. The monastery library at Saint Anthony's was like a volcano of thought. Until I had entered its rooms, it had remained more or less dormant. The aging Psalters and bound vellum folios, the finely executed Coptic manuscripts with their Kells-like imagery coruscating on every page, each had managed to bestow its magic on me during the course of my visits. They had released their fiery spirit into the air. The library seemed to be perfumed not by mold so much as by the heady aroma of ideas. One thing was certain: those Eastern thinkers had been committed to developing a system of thought that went beyond philosophy, beyond even the concept of religion itself. They had set themselves the task of renovating the way men thought about issues of the spirit, so that later generations of thinkers might begin to build a new set of criteria for comprehending man's relation to the infinite.

Anthony and his successors were pioneers of the spirit. They had journeyed into a wilderness of forms. Was it any wonder that Anthony suffered so much from his encounter with demons? These were none other than the outpourings of his own tired intellect confronting for the first time that age-old edifice of appearance crumbling before his eyes. He had no idea how to deal with such a metaphysical disaster. The ancient pharaonic culture that he was heir to possessed no equipment to deal with it. Nor did Greek philosophy, whose only siege engine was too heavy a reliance on the rational. Alone in his cave, he had been left to deal with the voices of his own imagining and the crude phantoms of spiritual disengagement. In those early years of ascetic apprenticeship, Anthony had been forced to devise a method of dealing with those demons of irresolution and defiance for himself.

Such is our inheritance. We who classify ourselves as Christians, whether nominally or otherwise, must accept what Anthony and his friends have bestowed. The ascetic impulse is his gift to us. We may not like it; we may even deny its relevance in the modern world, but it remains a constant in the formation and continuing development of the Western tradition. Without asceticism there would be no monasteries, cathedrals, crusades, popes, mystical literature, religious reformers, wandering clerks, translators, scribes, manuscript illustrators, artists, religious pageants, inquisitors, saints, theologians, military orders, missionaries, or even heretics. Every aspect of Christian society has been influenced by the ascetic ideal devised by Anthony and his friends in the Egyptian desert. It is here that Christ's legacy was fashioned into a social reality that has affected us ever since. The desert offers us the deepest expression of individual space, solitude, interiority, and mystical identity that serves to underpin our every gesture in the fields of law and social obligation, even today. It seems that we carry the desert into our every action, however much we might attempt to honor the tropical nature of our senses.

I suppose my encounter with Anthony and his friends had alerted me to the vitality of the mystical tradition within Eastern Christianity. The desert anchorites had lived within a subtle envelope of nihilation that had made it possible for them to explore the outer reaches of the spirit in a way that had never been done before. A near-naked man living on bread and water for half a century became a singular denouncement of the idea of excess as a preferred mode of existence. Anthony's conduct was an act of supreme eco-centricity, a method of defining one's existence by how little one might encroach on nature and the world. It was as if Anthony recognized that in order for a man to be crowned king of his domain, he must first reduce that domain to its essence. Only then could he govern the unruly nature of his heart and mind. I think he would have agreed with Abu Ya'qub al-Zabuli when he said that realizing a state of *apatheia* was to obliterate the essence of humanity within, together with all signs of whereness. Nonwhereness is a condition of the anchorite. He lives in a world not of things, or of place or social obligation, but of theophanic forms, the wholly other, that which is beyond the sphere of the usual.

Anthony taught me also that by confining the parameters of one's existence it was possible to cultivate a rich imaginative terrain wholly given over to what Rudolf Otto calls *empty distance*.[2] This is a condition where the wide-stretching desert, with its boundless uniformity, provokes the sense of a remote vacancy that is both sublime and palpable all at once. It acts as a mirror in which we can view deep into ourselves in a way that normally would not be possible. The ascetics of old seemed to be able to conjure up this condition whenever they wished. I suspect, too, that it is another reason why they were suspicious of language, which, after all, is the product of urban space rather than desert. It was as if these men wanted to draw out of speech the silence that they most desired. This in turn led them into a superb world where their thoughts and their nightmares were given the force of an obligatory existence. An ascetic became like a spiritual menhir in a land populated by invisible lines of concordance. They alone had discovered the hidden geometry of such a state and were able to preserve its ley lines intact.

How else can I explain what happened to me on Mount Colzim? When I arrived at the monastery I had not journeyed back in time so much as into that "superb world" of Anthony and his friends. As soon as I took up residence in my room overlooking the palm garden, I knew that I had entered what can only be described as a mystical precinct. Even the palms outside appeared to collude with the energy that swept down from the mountain. The spring, too, that life-giving spring that had slaked the thirst of countless anchorites, bubbled forth with unremitting enthusiasm as it filled the cistern. That water, I had come to the conclusion, was surely the living waters of the spirit. I had come home at last. The monastery was an oasis of calm in a chaotic world.

At the outset I had asked myself whether it was possible to practice a form of asceticism of the mind, given that the monastic state does not always appeal to everyone. I asked myself, too, whether it might be possible to become an anchorite in one's own head. Was this the next stage in the growth of consciousness that those early anchorites had struggled so hard to realize? Are we able to wear a hair shirt over our thoughts and experience the aggravation of discomfort that such ascetic behavior implies? As strange as it may seem, I think such questions should be asked—and if possible answered. The mind may well need to be strapped into a kind of spiritual straitjacket, there to fulminate against its loss of freedom. Because it may be that the very excess of freedom that we enjoy today distances us from the true goal of ascetic life, that of charity. As Evagrius noted, "the ascetical life is the spiritual method for cleansing the affective part of the soul."[3]

Now that I was due to end my stay at Saint Anthony's, it was time to climb Mount Colzim again and pay my respects to Lazarus. We hadn't seen one another during the past week, since he had decided to concentrate more on prayer and meditation, in the light of his recent period of wall building and painting on the edge of his terrace. Pleading to return to his solitude, he asked me not to come up until he had completed what he called the fast of "seven days." This included regular all-night vigils in Saint Anthony's cave farther up the mountain. Physical fatigue was the mistress of such a taxing regime, and he told me that he needed to catch up on his sleep during the day.

At the end of the week, however, I packed a rucksack full of bread and a few vegetables, then started up the hill to say good-bye to Lazarus. I had mixed emotions, of course; I was to leave Egypt in a few days in order to return home. The thought of not gazing out over the wadi and seeing the brown hills of the desert as I climbed this holy mountain pained me. I kept stopping en route to take in the scene before me, hoping to print it indelibly on my memory. More than anything I wanted to carry away from Mount Colzim a vision of its solitary grandeur in the midst of what I liked to think of as nature's *apatheia*: its power to negate movement and so realize an endless silence.

Nearing Lazarus's cell, I called out to let him know that I was coming. His head peered over the newly built wall, and a hand waved me on up. Reaching the terrace, I found myself gazing at a man whose face bore an expression of deep tranquillity, as if he had returned from a prolonged inward journey. It seemed that the fast of the seven days had prepared Lazarus well for his return to the sage slopes of Mount Colzim.

"Welcome," Lazarus remarked, still half removed from his body.

"I'm to return home in a few days, unfortunately," I replied.

"Then it is appropriate that we spend this time together. We have explored much during the past weeks. I feel that I have been accompanying you on your travels among the Eastern Fathers."

"They have changed my life," I confessed. "In their presence I begin to think that I have stepped into another world."

Lazarus smiled almost wistfully, I thought.

"It's the world of the spirit," he said, "where visible things become less substantial. Isaac of Nineveh considered this world to be supranatural, a place that he felt was one of 'knowledge-transcending.'"

"From memory, Isaac also saw such knowledge as the product of the raising of the intellect above everything. It's as though the intellect were equipped with wings to fly above the passional nature that governs our knowledge of things. Tell me, Lazarus," I finally asked, "is it possible that we might learn how to practice an asceticism of the mind to help us reach a state of *apatheia*? I pose this question in light of the difficulties encountered by attempting to live the full anchoritic life during these troubled times. Though I acknowledge that some people such as you have found a way to do so."

"It's a question that I have often attempted to resolve," Lazarus replied, sitting down on the seat at the back of his terrace to ponder my remarks. "The early Fathers escaped into the desert because they saw it as an acceptable metaphor for where they wanted to be, at least historically. We need to ask ourselves whether those conditions exist for us today. I suspect they do not. Late antiquity, with its declining affluence and loss of social cohesion, is a far cry from the burgeoning and often illusory nature of modern society. I think we must accept that to become a Desert Father today is a retrogressive statement about the kind of spirituality we might wish to embrace for the future."

"Even though you are prepared to live here yourself," I countered.

"I live on Mount Colzim in order to continue the tradition only. I don't see my actions as those that should be followed by others, except the rare few like me who wish to maintain the tradition of desert anchoritism for its own sake. It is our choice, and not to be recommended to the many who are desperate to nourish their souls and alleviate their spiritual anxiety. I can't imagine, nor would I like to see it happen, that the desert would become once more populated by thousands of hermits living in caves. This would be to *repeat* history rather than to honor its gift. No, my dear friend, I feel we must find a new way to embrace the spirit of anchoritism. You speak of an asceticism of the mind. I do think it worthy of investigation, yes."

"Which means that we need to imagine a desert within us. A place where we can dig out our own cave of the heart."

"Such a cave must include a spiritual depth that can be derived only from appropriate ascetic behavior," Lazarus responded. "We must recognize what ascesis truly means; it is the spirit of restraint, and we need to understand that it's only through self-imposed aggravation that a pearl is produced. Those old Qatar pearl divers like Ephraim certainly knew what they were talking about!"

"We must therefore learn how to practice asceticism even as we live a normal life. We need to find a way to impose on ourselves a certain aggravation."

"The hair shirt can be made of other things besides the skin of a camel or a goat."

"What, may I ask?"

"Let me read you a piece that I feel might answer this question for you," Lazarus replied, rising from the seat and entering his cell. Presently he appeared, carrying a small book, which he opened on a previously selected a page.

"John Cassian, one of Anthony's most notable successors in the ascetic life, as you know, made some interesting remarks on the subject." Slowly he began to read:

We believe that discretion is the true light of the body. It is our sole guidance for life. We call it our divine council. Like a city that has its walls destroyed and is not fenced in, so is a man who does anything without council. Our inward house cannot be built without discretion. Herein lies wisdom, intelligence, and understanding. A house is built with wisdom, and again it is set up with intelligence. With understanding, the storehouses are filled with all the precious riches and good things. The blessed Anthony maintained that discretion leads us in stages to God. It is the mother of all virtues.[4]

"Discretion is a quality of the mind and of the soul," Lazarus elaborated, after he had closed the book. "If we look on it as a kind of hair shirt—that is, if we choose to practice discretion in all things—then we may begin to ascend in stages toward a higher level of consciousness. Inner asceticism is achieved by wearing the hair shirt of discretion. Does this make sense?"

"I think it does," I replied, "so long as we remain clear that the object of such restraint is the attainment of genuine spiritual knowledge."

"Cassian speaks of it as a kind of ripening of judgment. To achieve it, however, we must also address those seven principal errors of behavior that cloud such judgment. We cannot escape the reality that all our actions are governed in varying degrees by them. The early Fathers did not beat about the bush when they named them, either. And even today, though we may resort to psychology to explain our motives, the plain fact is that these faults in our character need to be acknowledged."

"You mean they shouldn't be put to one side but actually named."

"Cassian did so, so why can't we? They haven't lost any of their power to diminish our sensibility, nor our spiritual growth, simply because we refuse to do so. In many ways I think we are afraid of naming the old strictures these days, simply because we believe we have outgrown them. It is as if we have lost the ability to gaze directly at ourselves and prefer instead to view ourselves as though through a prism, thus breaking up our self-image into many different permutations, so many subtle hues. It is clearly as a result of our penchant for psychoanalysis, which distorts even the *value* of our flaws."

"What you are suggesting is that we have achieved a state of lukewarmness in relation to the way we conduct ourselves," I suggested. "There is no heat in our convictions because we have allowed our inner lives to grow cold."

"Putting it that way suggests that we have not understood the need to chart a middle course through the shoals of extremes. Rather, we delight in subjecting ourselves to such extremes. This is not the path of discretion," replied Lazarus.

"Quite the contrary," I agreed. "We have become saturated in ineffectual decorative feelings and activities without aim. Discretion is opposed to this. It is opposed to the pleasurable and picturesque."

"It's the reason the Desert Fathers turned their back on normal human activity, I believe. They felt it was impossible to achieve a genuine spiritual understanding in the world. But in those days they saw the world as an objective reality. We know otherwise. Today we know that the so-called 'world' is a projection of our inner condition. To deny this reality is to enter the true desert. It's why I feel we must conjure up our own inner desert. Even here, on Mount Colzim, I'm much occupied with the question of this interior desert. It's not for nothing that Anthony called such a place the inner mountain. He knew, I'm sure, that he was merely playing with metaphors."

"Then the inner mountain is also made up of our flaws."

"Inasmuch as they are acknowledged, yes."

"Yet you still haven't named them. Is it from want of certainty on your part?"

"My dear friend, you and I come from the same country. It is the land of emptiness. Our accident of birth is immaterial to the main issue: that we have both, in our different ways, been drawn to this mountain. I'm sure it is for the same reason. I came here because I realized that I had not taken charge of my inner life and that I had yet to address the primary nature of my being. Perhaps it is so for you also," Lazarus added.

"I'm beginning to accept that as 'I,' I have joined myself to my restrictions," I replied. "In this sense I am condemned to being myself. This was enough to make me want to climb Mount Colzim in the first place. I somehow believed that in doing so, I might free myself from such a restriction."

"To do so you need to have tremendous spiritual conviction. I recall a story that Evagrius related in this respect. He spoke of a man who, while praying one day, felt a snake, a viper no less, laying hold of his foot. He did not so much as lower his arms until he had finished praying. Not surprisingly, he suffered no harm. The snake had no power over such a man who loved God more than his own self."[5]

"How can I argue with that? It seems that even the venom of evil cannot penetrate a pure heart."

Lazarus allowed himself a smile.

"When you return home, what will you do?" he asked.

"Begin to fashion for myself a new type of hair shirt, I suppose."

"Then you will need to practice discretion in all that you do."

"Without knowing the principal faults, how can I?"

"I will tell you what they are," Lazarus responded, "only if you agree to accept that these faults are the manifestation of an unbounded inner lassitude. They are not in themselves real but, rather, are the product of a tendency toward spiritual disintegration. You must treat them as you might the full force of resistance that causes a meteor to break up on entering the earth's atmosphere. They pulverize the sensibilities, causing a man to lose his density and form. This is why our faults are so demeaning: they allow us to lose contact with our essential self."

"I accept what you are saying, Lazarus. Now, can you tell me what they are?"

"Let me tell you, then. The seven principal faults as outlined by Cassian are what we most abhor in ourselves. They are anger, avarice, lust, dejection, boredom, vainglory, and pride. Taken as a whole they amount to the complete destruction of being. No one, not even the most resolved of men, is able to resist their poison. This is why it took Anthony so many years in his tomb outside Pispir to overcome his demons. Each one had to be acknowledged, wrestled with, and finally put to the sword. Let no one assume that he did not suffer terribly in pursuing victory."

"I have no doubt that Anthony experienced more deeply than anyone before him the anguish of reappraisal," I admitted. "It cost him the young man who was once a farmer on the Nile."

"And gained him the old man who could move mountains," replied Lazarus. Then he added, sensing that I felt it time to leave, "I'm afraid that I have nothing to give you, not even a sheepskin, as Anthony gave to his friend Athanasius."

We gazed at one another, conscious of the pleasant irony of his remark. Was there an echo in our lives of theirs?

"If only it were possible to re-create that momentous parting," I said.

"Wait, I do have something for you," Lazarus added, rising and reentering his cell. Again he appeared, this time clutching a small icon in the folds of his habit. "Take it as a mark of my respect. It is a copy of a sixth-century Christ from the Monastery of Saint Catherine on Mount Sinai."

I accepted the icon. It was a portrait of Jesus Christ depicted as a man in full possession of his youth. His neck and shoulders were strong, capable of bearing the weight of any cross. His gaze was direct, penetrating, yet filled with an enormous sense of life. This was no God of suffering, no man afraid of sacrificing his life. Rather, I found myself looking at a figure who was aggressively himself. The portrait, one of the earliest we have of Christ, revealed a man reveling in the perfection of his being. No wonder he saw himself as God: he had surmounted all obstacles on the road to transcendence.

"Thank you, Lazarus. I shall cherish it," I said, unable to shift my gaze from this powerful evocation.

"Go, my friend. Journey back to the world. Allow the spirit of ascesis to settle about your shoulders like a cloak."

"I have one more place to go before I descend to the monastery and take my leave of the monks there," I said.

Lazarus followed my gaze up the mountainside.

"Ah, to Anthony's cave. Yes, it is a fitting place to visit. The old man will welcome you, I'm sure."

We parted with a handshake, I to climb Mount Colzim, and Lazarus to attend to evening prayer.

POSTSCRIPT

I climbed Mount Colzim and slowly made my way along the narrow trail below the ridge. The entrance to Anthony's cave was vaguely visible behind a vertical block of stone emerging from the hillside. Below me, a carpet of shale and small stones reached into the wadi. The reddish hills in the distance retained their solitary glow. I felt so small there, carefully treading that path, watching my every step. This was a journey of leave-taking and the final encounter between myself and Anthony. I knew how Athanasius must have felt when he climbed this hill to interview his erstwhile hero and to bestow on him a sheepskin cloak.

I reached the cave at last. Behind me the narrow entrance disappeared into the depths of the mountain. Instead of entering it immediately, I sat on a rock nearby and gazed at the view. At once I felt settled, not at all out of breath. I sensed that I belonged here too, that I had finally served my apprenticeship in knowledge of the ascetic life. Anthony and his friends had done their work well; they had taught me how to embrace the idea of discretion in my bid to become a more complete and resolved person. An asceticism of the mind was possible, I told myself. All it required was for me to replace the desert that they knew so well with its psychic equivalent, that of a genuine aridity of consciousness of my own. I kept telling myself that were God a Cyclops in an earlier existence, then this cave was surely his eye.

Those few minutes of contemplation made me feel that I was conversing with Anthony. He sat nearby, his aging limbs protruding from his rough cotton habit. His face, deeply lined with suffering, radiated stillness. Father, I found myself thinking, the persistence in which you allowed God to enter your inner space ended up nullifying him. Over forty years of engaging him in this lonely spot in the desert caused God to fall, like an overripe piece of fruit, into the garden of your solitude. You became, in the end, a *positive* expression of his nothingness. This, Father, was your singular achievement: you made it possible for others to recognize that the road to *apatheia* requires us to make of our souls a tabula rasa and so strive toward achieving a psychological blankness. To reject the world, at least inwardly, is to come to terms with an elusive yet fecund emptiness.

We are all of us caught up in the net of disbelief in one way or another. It is difficult for us to submit to the idea that the divine operates outside ourselves and therefore manipulates us according to its whim. But Anthony had taught me that it was possible to overcome our lot as mere creatures in the scientific scheme of things and so to reposition the divine within ourselves. Anthony's victory over temptations made it possible. He cleared away all the psychological debris that had marooned humankind on an island of fear, superstition, and despair. He showed us that wanting to be in league with the divine was not something affirmed by either belief or disbelief—that these were only words issuing forth from our own need to determine reality in accordance with rational explanation. By his actions Anthony had made it possible to lead a thoroughly dangerous life without any apparent purpose, save that of freeing himself from the superfluous.

But equally I knew that he was only an innovator, that he did not invent the ascetic life. His model was Christ. I could not forget that it was Christ who had made it possible for him to abandon appearance in his pursuit of *apatheia*. Though Christ's unique message may be attributed to his being the Son of God, we must also remember that he spent some time in Egypt as a child, possibly a lengthy time (Muslims believe that the Holy Family remained more than six years there, fleeing from the agents of Herod). Could it be that this ancient and fertile river valley bounded by desert instilled in the infant Christ a disposition toward inwardness? In other words, had this deeply spiritual land of Egypt attended the birth of Christianity as its midwife?

In any event, I was now heir to Anthony's vision—his, along with that of a number of Eastern ascetics that I had come to know and respect. These men chose to embark on a voyage into the unknown with only the memory of Christ as their compass. Were they any different from Columbus, Vasco da Gama, or even Captain Cook? I don't think so. Their instinct for spiritual discovery was as acute as any navigator's to reach his destination in the past, bent as they were on discovering some new world. Yet these Eastern ascetics managed to see beyond the settled horizon of commerce, trade, and colonization. They wanted to set up a colony not of this world—a colony, rather, rich in spiritual insight and grace. It was not an unrealistic expectation. We still live in the shade of their legacy, the great edifice of thought that they bestowed on their age and future ages.

Quietly contemplating the view outside Anthony's cave, I had come to the conclusion that in spite of everything, the ascetic life still has something to offer. It may not offer a diet of bread, dates, and water, or prolonged vigils and fasts, but it may offer a way to somehow *withstand* the incursions of the real. One must be thankful that such spiritual alternatives survive. Anthony took up residence in the desert not to escape the world but to reflect more intensely than others on the condition of man in his relation to matter. Ascetic practice was the essence of this process. As Simon of Taibutheh remarked, "Through these teachings and exertions, the mind is so much exercised and illuminated that it is not able to see a material object without immediately seeing, in its own context, the divine Providence which is hidden in it, and works secretly in it."[1] Thus matter, at least for those early ascetics, became the wax into which they implanted the seal of their spiritual endeavor. It was necessary, as Isaac of Nineveh wrote, "to free oneself from matter, for freedom from matter precedes the bonds in God."[2] I suspect that the relationship between matter and thought was like the challenge of understanding the workings of DNA: men wanted to discover whether the spirit imprisoned in matter could be set free by an act of ascesis.

Fortunately, I had found a way back to the heart of my own spirituality. Anthony had seen to that. The culture of the Church, its theology and dogma, its emphasis on morality at the expense of mysticism, now seemed less important to me in the wake of one man's bid to comprehend the teachings of Christ. Or should I say a school of men such as these Eastern ascetics who had carved out their own caves of consciousness in the desert. One thing was certain, though: I would return home to the teeming metropolis of men, knowing that I had experienced something unique on Mount Colzim. The monastery library, with its vellum-bound volumes and illuminations, was the lamp that lit my path. The vigils at dawn in the Church of the Four Living Creatures opened the way for me to enter into the solitude of the void. My daily walks in the palm grove, or to the spring at the rear of the monastery, made it possible for me to savor the fruit of silence. No wonder it had ripened.

In the end I did not wish to reenter Anthony's cave. I wanted to remember it as I had experienced it on the occasion of my first visit. I had no desire to recapture that feeling, since I had already moved on. Instead I withdrew from my pocket the icon that Lazarus had given to me. Gazing at it, I now saw the image of the One who had made it possible to storm the bastions of the real and raze its walls. This was the image I wanted to carry back with me. I wanted to carry a vision of youth even as it transformed the world.

Appendix

From A. Wensinck, Mystical Treatises of Isaac of Nineveh (Verh. KNAW, 1923).

If anyone, however, desires to give his body some rest, he must finish and turn toward the East. As long as he is sitting, he shall not allow his mind to be idle; but he shall meditate and think and deliberate on the greatness of his duty, and what his performance is; and how it is done, and how great his crown, and how glorious the fruit of his labour is; and what watchfulness it demands; and how the ancients had dealt with it, and of what things they have deemed worthy through the fulfilment of their struggles; and how by the mercy of Jesus he was turned from the world, he that was occupied with vain labours the end of which is destruction from God and reprehension through sins; and how this mercy brought to this performance of the angels, the hope of which is veracious hope, and its joy is a joy which is beyond the power of distress and its confidence a confidence which cannot be fallacious. For a man may work ever so much, his labours are small in comparison with that which he will receive at his end, in the pledge of good things, to the delight of his soul.

While these and similar deliberations are in his heart and he is astonished at them, he places his mind in the spiritual chariot, and lets it fly and be occupied with all the holy Fathers of all generations, the inheritance of whose behavior he possesses, thinking of how everyone of them has accomplished, with various distractions, this spiritual service; and how they had abandoned the inhabited world and mankind and have withdrawn themselves from the allurements of the world and the disturbances of life, and have gone and hidden themselves in mountains and caverns and removed and lonely places, because they saw that this course of life cannot be accomplished among men, on account of the many hindrances; and have become dead in their lifetime for the sake of life in God, erring through desert places and between rocks as those who have lost their way; people of such worth that every single one's glory is not equalled by the whole world. Some of them lived on rough and steep rocks, some at the foot of mountains, or in deep valleys; some in the caves of the ground and in caverns, as those who dig after foxes in order to surprise them; some in graves and mountain cliffs. Some have constructed a small hovel in the desert and passed there the rest of their life; some have built a small pen on the top of a mountain and have dwelt therein with pleasure as if in a royal palace. And because they did not care for their livelihood, they only thought of how each of them should please God and accomplish his struggle beautifully.

From Dana Miller, trans., The Ascetical Homilies of Saint Isaac the Syrian *(Holy Transfiguration Monastery: Boston, 1984).*

How can a man acquire humility. . . . By an unceasing remembrance of errors; by an anticipation of approaching death; by inexpensive clothing; by always preferring the last place; by always running to do the tasks that are the most insignificant and distasteful; by not being disobedient; by unceasing silence; by a dislike of gatherings; by desiring to be unknown and of no account; by never holding to one sort of work exclusively; by shunning conversations with numerous persons; by abhorrence of material gain; and, after these things, by raising the mind above the reproach and accusation of every man and above zealotry; by not being a man whose hand is against everyone and against whom is everyone's hand, but rather someone who remains alone, occupied with his own affairs; by having no concern for anyone in the world save himself. In brief, exile, poverty, and a solitary life give birth to humility and cleanse the heart.

From John Moschus, The Spiritual Meadow, *trans. John Wortley (Kalamazoo, Mich.: Cistercian Publications, 1992).*

THE FINDING OF THE CORPSE OF THE ANCHORITE JOHN THE HUMBLE

We went to an estate that was six miles from Rossos and there, two elders living in the world received us as guests in the church on their property. This estate lay at the foot of a mountain. They showed us some gravestones in the church and told us: "Christians, a great anchorite lies in this tomb." We asked them how they know this. "Seven years ago," they replied, "one night we who belong to this estate saw a light that looked like a fire on the summit of the mountain. We thought it was because of the wild beasts [that a fire had been lit there] but we saw it for many days. One day we went up there, but saw no evidence; no lights of anything whatsoever that had been burnt in the woods. Again, the following night we saw the same lights, and for three months after that. Then one night we took some local men armed with weapons (on account of the wild animals) and climbed up the mountain toward the light. We stayed there where the light was until dawn. At daybreak we noticed a little cave where the lights had appeared, and found the anchorite dead [inside]. He was wearing a hair shirt and a tunic of sackcloth. He was holding a gospel book and a silver cross. Beside him we found writing tablets inscribed thus: 'I, the unworthy John, died in the fifteenth indiction.' We calculated the time, and discovered that he had been dead for seven years—yet he was as though he had died that very day. We carried him down, and buried him in the church."

From Alexander A. Vasiliev, History of the Byzantine Empire, *vol. 2 (Madison: University of Wisconsin Press, 1952).*

Hesychasts ("they who live in quiet") devote themselves entirely to the knowledge and contemplation of God, and the attainment of unity with Him. And concentrate all their strength for this purpose. They retire from the whole world and all that reminds them of the world, and isolate themselves by means of the concentration and gathering of the mind in themselves. To attain this concentration the hesychast has to detach himself from all knowledge, all conceptions, all thoughts, and free his mind from all knowledge, in order to be able to freely, by an absolute independent flight, merge easily into the truly mystic darkness of ignorance. The highest, most sincere, and most perfect prayer of the perfect hesychast is an immediate intercourse with God, in which there exist no thoughts, ideas, images of the present, recollection of the past. This is the highest contemplation—the contemplation of God one and alone, the perfect ecstasy of mind, and withdrawal from matter. No thought is more perfect or higher than such a prayer. It is a state of ecstasy, a mystic unity with God, deification (apotheosis). In this state the mind wholly transcends the limits of matter, frees itself from all thought, requires a complete insensibility to outward impressions, and becomes deaf and mute. Not only is the Hesychast entirely cut off from outward impressions, but he also transcends his individuality and loses consciousness of himself, being wholly absorbed in the contemplation of God. Therefore he who has reached ecstasy no longer lives a personal and individual life; his spiritual and corporeal life stops, his mind remains immovable, attached to the object of contemplation. Thus, the basis and center of *hesychia* is the love of God from soul, heart, and mind, and the desire for divine contemplation through the abnegation of everything, however small and remote, which might recall the world and its contents. The goal of the hesychast is attained by absolute silence, by the "care of the heart" and mortification of the mind, continuous penance, abundant tears, the memory of God and death, and the constant repetition of an "inner" prayer [namely, the Jesus Prayer]: "Lord Jesus Christ, Son of God, have mercy on me."

Notes

Introduction

1. See John of Ruysbroeck, *The Sparkling Stone*, trans. by C. A. Wynschenk DOM. (n.d.). "By each act, the spirit rises upwards to a new union. And so activity and union perpetually renew themselves; and this perpetual renewal in activity and in union is a ghostly life."

One: Toward the Inner Mountain

1. The monastic movement was founded by John Cassian (360–435), who was born in Scythia. Probably Roman by origin, he became a monk at Bethlehem before visiting the hermits of Egypt. He later traveled to France, where he founded the first monastery, the famous abbey of Saint-Victor at Marseille. His writings on the Desert Fathers formed the basis of the monastic rule throughout Europe. He maintained that the so-called ripened judgment of these remarkable men of the desert stemmed from their unique ascetic practice, pursuing what he called the "light of the body."

2. I am reminded of John of Ruysbroeck's remarks on such a dramatic change of life, which he likened to "prevenient grace." Such grace "touches a man from without and within. From without through sickness; or through the loss of external goods, of kinsmen and of friends; or through public disgrace." See John of Ruysbroeck, *The Sparkling Stone*.

3. Isaac of Nineveh, a sixth-century Syrian ascetic who wrote with subtlety and insight on the mystical life, coined this expression to mean "a kind of influence which possesses the mind. And when a man is deemed worthy of this *maggenanutha*, the mind is snatched away in ecstasy and so expanded in some divine revelation."

4. Evagrius Ponticus (346–399), a uniquely gifted theologian and desert anchorite, regarded *katastasis*, or "still state of the soul," as an important technical term for describing a certain fixed degree of perfection and a quality of peace that extends even into the unconscious.

5. This is a reference to Saint Anselm when he wrote "I do not seek to understand that I may believe, but I believe that I might understand." He further went on to suggest that "those who try to understand before they believe are like bats that, seeing only the sky at night, presume to argue with eagles about the midday sun."

6. Evagrius expressed it succinctly: "When the spirit begins to see its own light, when it remains in a state of tranquillity in the presence of the images it has during sleep, [then] it maintains its calm as it beholds the affairs of life." See Evagrius Ponticus, *The Praktikos, Chapters on Prayer* (Kalamazoo, Mich.: Cistercian Publications, 1981), 64.

7. I am reminded here of the remarks made by Dadisho' Katraya (d. 690), an east Syriac writer and monk in the monastery of Rab-Kinnare, in the Qatar district of the Persian Gulf: "When a man begins with the exercise of the mind and with the struggle against the passions in his life of solitude . . . he goes forward, till he reaches purity of heart." Alphonse Mingana, ed., *Woodbrooke Studies*, "Treatise on Solitude."

Notes

TWO: WELCOME, THE STRANGER

1. Athanasius, *The Life of Anthony and the Letter to Marcellinus*, trans. Robert C. Gregg (Mahwah, N.J.: Paulist Press, 1980), 2.

2. See Peter Brown, "The Rise and Function of the Holy Man in Late Antiquity," in *Society and the Holy in Late Antiquity* (Berkeley, Calif.: University of California Press, 1982).

3. Matt. 6:34.

4. I am thinking here of men like Apollonius of Tyana, a Cappadocian holy man and miracle worker who became a mythological hero to the Greek writer Flauvius Philostratus. It has been speculated that Apollonius was a literary creation designed to counteract the influence of early Christian holy men such as Anthony. Making him into a "neo-Pythagorean" further enhanced his classical pedigree in the eyes of those who wanted to see Christianity stamped out.

5. Palladius (ca. 363–before 431), a Galatian monk and chronicler, whose *Lausiac History* (New York: MacMillan and Co., n.d.) gives a lively account of the early Christian anchorites of Egypt, wrote, "while the Great One [Antony] is still alive . . . go to him . . . and wait until he comes out from his cave and refer the case to him. And what he says to you, go by his decision, for God speaks to you through him."

6. We are left with an interesting example of this: "As the holy man with the crowd approached the palace of Hebdomon, a Goth leant out the window and, seeing the holy man carried along by the crowd, dissolved with laughter and shouted: 'See, here is our new consul!'" He fell from the window to his death. (H. Delahaye, ed., "Vita Danielis," in *Les saints stylites*, Brussels, 1923.)

7. Hilarion Alfeyev, *The Spiritual World of Isaac the Syrian* (Kalamazoo, Mich.: Cistercian Publications, 2000).

8. Ibid.

9. This story is told by F. Halkin in "Saint Antoine le Jeune et Petronus vainqueur des Arabs en 863," *Analecta Bollandiana*, 62 (1944).

10. Arius, a fourth-century Alexandrian presbyter, argued that Christ was not truly divine but a created being. His basic premise was that the uniqueness of God is that he alone is self-existent and immutable. Christ, therefore, who is not self-existent, cannot be God. Athanasius condemned such teaching because it reduced Christ to being a demigod, thus reintroducing the idea of polytheism. According to him, Arius reduced faith to a dried-out abstract construction.

11. As Athanasius recounts it, Anthony's watchfulness was such "that he often passed the entire night without sleep. . . . He ate only once daily, after sunset, but there were times when he received food every second and frequently every fourth day." See Athanasius, *The Life of Anthony and the Letter to Marcellinus*.

12. Ibid.

13. Ibid.

14. Charles H. Kahn, *The Art and Thought of Heraclitus: A New Arrangement and Translation of the Fragments with Literary and Philosophical Comments* (Cambridge, UK: Cambridge University Press, 1995), fragment 125.

15. This is clearly reinforced by the following remark: "Some say of Abba Antony that he became a bearer of the Holy Spirit, but he did not wish to speak of this because of men, for he could see all that passed in this world, and could tell all that would come to pass."

16. Athanasius, *The Life of Anthony and the Letter to Marcellinus*.

17. See Samuel Rubenson, trans., *The Letters of Saint Anthony* (Minneapolis: Fortress Press, 1975), a selection of letters attributed to the saint. This is taken from one of the unauthenticated letters of Anthony that I mentioned earlier. However, the thought sounds genuine enough. I am reminded, too, of the statement by Ibn al-'Arabi, a medieval Islamic theologian much influenced by early Christian mysticism and ascetic practice, when he said: "He who knows himself knows his Lord." Ibn al-'Arabi took this concept even further when he suggested that "by knowing Him, I in turn caused Him to exist." No Christian would have gone this far, but the idea is intriguing nonetheless.

18. Athanasius, *The Life of Anthony and the Letter to Marcellinus.*

19. This story is reminiscent of Saint Teresa's near-death experience when she fell unconscious for four days after a fit. Her grave was even dug in the grounds of her monastery, and nuns came to her father's house to watch over the corpse. She would have been buried had not her father insisted that there was still life in her. When she returned to consciousness, she found blobs of wax on her eyelids from the funeral candles.

20. See Charles H. Kahn, *The Art and Thought of Heraclitus.* This point is further emphasized by one of the Sayings of the Fathers (*Apophthegmata Patrum*): "Abraham, the disciple of Abba Agatho, questioned Abba Poemen, saying: 'How do the demons fight against me?' Abba Poemen said to him: 'The demons fight against you? Our own wills become the demons, and it is these that attack us in order that we might fulfil them.'" Note here that the demons were always associated with deviant mental attitudes rather than objectively existing in themselves.

THREE: LIFE OF AN ANCHORITE

1. René Daumal, *The Powers of the Word: Selected Essays and Notes, 1927–1943*, trans. Mark Polizzotti (San Francisco: City Lights Books, 1991).

2. Christopher Donaldson, *Martin of Tours* (London: Routledge and Kegan Paul, 1980).

3. Seventy-two is considered a sacred number in traditional cosmology. It is said, for example, that seventy-two scholars translated the Hebrew Scriptures, each working separately for seventy-two days on the Isle of Paros, and all producing identically the same version.

4. See chapter seven.

5. Gregory Palamas intimates this qualitative difference when he says, "Although the angels are superior to us in many ways, yet in some respects they fall short of us.... Angels only carry out the commands of God, whereas man, a terrestrial being composed of body and soul, was created to be lord and ruler over all creation."

6. Dionysius the Areopagite, *The Divine Names and the Mystical Theology*, trans. C. E. Rolt (SPCK Publishing, 1972), ch. 1. para. 1.

7. Ibid. Dionysius goes on to remark, "Concerning the Super-Essential Godhead we must not dare, as I have said, to speak, or even to form any conception Thereof, except those things which are divinely revealed to us."

8. As Cassian remarked of another monk that he met: "The sparseness of those who at that time dwelt in the Desert was gracious to us as a caress; it lavished liberty upon us, in the far-flowing vastness of that solitude." For this man, as for Anthony, solitude became the creative condition of genius.

9. Helen Waddell, *The Desert Fathers: Translations from the Latin* (Fontana Library, 1965).

10. Benedicta Ward, trans., *The Sayings of the Desert Fathers* (Kalamazoo, MI: Cistercian Publications, 1975).

Four: Citizen of Heaven

1. The *tau* later became the symbol for another great ascetic, Francis of Assisi, in the thirteenth century.

2. Eusebius (fourth century) claimed that he was present in the Thebaid, home to many anchorites, and witnessed as many as one hundred monks being put to death in a single day, the executioners becoming exhausted and their axes dulled. The last official martyrdom was of Patriarch Peter, who was put to death in 310, though deaths did continue until two years after the overthrow of Maximinus Daia sometime in 313.

3. Origen (ca. 185–ca. 254) greatly influenced Christian thought in Egypt, including that of Anthony. So intense was his commitment to Christ that he castrated himself in order to make himself a "eunuch of the Lord," and also to protect himself from any scandal associated with teaching young female aspirants for baptism at the catechetical school, of which Clement was the head. One of his greatest achievements was to produce a new edition of the Old Testament, a task that took him nearly twenty years. He died in exile in Tyre.

4. Valentinus was a second-century thinker who founded the Alexandrian and Roman schools of Gnosticism. He was also a baptized Christian who developed a mythically derived religious philosophy that achieved a fusion of Christian theology and Gnostic principles. Basilides was also a second-century thinker and the founder of his own Basilidian school in Alexandria. He claimed to have received a secret tradition on which he based his gnosis, or esoteric knowledge. He wrote a number of commentaries (heretical) on the Gospels.

5. Pachomius (ca. 290–346) was the founder of cenobitic monasticism. He had been a member of the Roman army before retiring into the desert in 314 near his hometown of Thebes. There he established a community of solitaries on the east bank of the Nile, which eventually became a fully enclosed monastery. He drew up a communal program of work and prayer that formed the guide for other monastic rules, notably Cassian's.

6. John Climacus, *The Ladder of Divine Ascent* (Willits, Calif.: Eastern Orthodox Books, 1969). John Climacus (ca. 579–ca. 649) lived the anchoritic life in a cave five miles from Saint Catherine's monastery, Mount Sinai, for forty-five years. His book *Climax tou paradeisou* (The Ladder of Divine Ascent, also known as The Ladder), is considered to be one of the great classics of ascetic literature.

7. J. P. Migne, *Patrologica Graeca*, 170.

8. Ibid., 150, 1108 C. Gregory Palamas (1296–1359), a Greek of noble family, renounced a promising political career in Constantinople to become a monk on Mount Athos, the spiritual center of Orthodoxy. He spent twenty-five years mastering the mystical discipline of *hesychia* before expounding its subtleties in a number of important works. He detailed a theory of Inner Light, which will be explored in a later chapter.

FIVE: THE LAW OF PROMISE

1. See Peter Brown, *The Body and Society: Men, Women, and Sexual Renunciation in Early Christianity* (New York: Columbia University Press, 1988) for a further elucidation of these ideas.

2. Athanasius relates Anthony's injunction: "As we rise daily, let us suppose that we shall not survive until evening. And again, as we prepare

for sleep, let us consider that we shall not awaken." See Athanasius, *The Life of Anthony and the Letter to Marcellinus.*

3. Derwas J. Chitty, *The Desert a City: An Introduction to the Study of Egyptian and Palestinian Monasticism under the Christian Empire* (Crestwood, NY: SVS Press, 1966). Athanasius gives us an equally vivid picture of Anthony: "Receiving bread from the brothers, he sat by the banks of the river, looking to see a boat would come by, so that boarding it he might leave with them."

4. Jean Coppin, *Egyptian Journey* (1686).

5. Simone Weil, *First and Last Notebooks*, trans. Richard Rees (Oxford: Oxford University Press, 1970). vol. 2, 592.

6. See Samuel Rubenson, trans., *The Letters of Saint Anthony.* In "Letter One" of his *Letters,* Anthony tells us: "And when the mind accepts this struggle, then it prays in the Spirit and begins to expel the afflictions of the soul which have come upon it through its own greed. *The soul is then in communion with the Spirit* [italics added], since it keeps the commandments that it receives."

7. As Plato remarks in *Phaedrus* (*Collected Dialogues*, Bollingen LXXI, Princeton): "Let it [nature] be likened to the union of powers in a team of winged steeds and their winged charioteer [the mind]. Now all the gods' steeds and all their charioteers are good, and of good stock, but with other beings it is not wholly so. With us men, in the first place, it is a pair of steeds that the charioteer controls [that is, body and mind]; moreover one of them is noble and good, and of good stock, while the other has the opposite character. Hence the task of our charioteer is difficult and troublesome."

8. Samuel Rubenson, trans., *The Letters of Saint Anthony.* "Letter One."

9. Ibid., "Letter Three." Cf. "Letter Five": "Then, too, the council of the prophets built upon the foundation of Moses, but they were unable to heal the great wound of their members, and realized that their power had ceased."

10. Ibid. In "Letter Four" he relates: "My beloved in the Lord, know yourselves! Those who know themselves know their time, and those who

know their time are able to stand upright without being moved by shifty tongues."

11. Isaac of Nineveh wrote: "This first class is called the Initiated, not because they see spiritually by the intermediary of the various apperceptible symbols, or because from spiritual writings they have acquired understanding concerning the Essence; but because they are full of the exalted light of the whole of immaterial knowledge and have been saturated with the essential contemplation of the threefold rays of the beauty that creates all beauties, so far as it has been permitted to them." See Wensinck, A. J., *Mystical Treatises of Isaac of Nineveh* (Amsterdam: K.N.A.W., 1923).

SIX: A WORDLESS JOURNEY

1. See John of Apamea, "Letter to Hesychius," in *The Syriac Fathers of Prayer and the Spiritual Life*, 89, para. 33. John of Apamea, or John the Solitary, lived in the first half of the fifth century, possibly in the monastery of Nikertai in Syria. One of his tenets was that of "self-emptying" (Syr., *msarrquta*), a level of spiritual practice that ultimately leads to "purity of soul." He argued that purity of soul makes possible "luminosity or transparency of soul," which is a condition of receptivity to the light of the revelation of divine mysteries.

2. I am reminded of Isaac of Nineveh in this respect, when he wrote: "God has never perceptibly shown his action except in a region of stillness, in the desert, and in places bereft of chance encounters with men and the turbulence of their habitations." See Wensinck, A. J., *Mystical Treatises of Isaac of Nineveh*. Surely he was thinking of a place like Megaspelion, even if he had never visited it.

3. Hilarion Alfeyev, *The Spiritual World of Isaac the Syrian*. Kalamazoo, Mich.: Cistercian Publications, 2000, 204.

4. See Miller, *Ascetical Homilies of Saint Isaac*, in the appendix.

5. Sebastian Brock, *The Syriac Fathers on Prayer and the Spiritual Life*. Kalamazoo, Mich.: Cistercian Publications, 1987.

6. In Isaac's time, the scientific view was that a pearl is born in the oyster as a result of lightning penetrating the oyster when the shell is open. A

pearl was therefore made of congealed lightning. See Wensinck, A. J., *Mystical Treatises of Isaac of Nineveh.*

7. Ibid.

8. Samuel Rubenson, trans., *The Letters of Saint Anthony.*

SEVEN: CROSSING THE BORDER

1. The other Cappadocian Fathers were Basil the Great and his brother Gregory of Nyssa. These three friends represent one of the high points of early Christianity by reason of their holiness, character, and culture. Evagrius was indebted to each of them for much of his doctrine.

2. Palladius rendered it more succinctly: "Now it happened that this man, who was held in high honor by the whole city, was congealed by an image of the desire of a woman." See Palladius, *The Lausiac History*, Trans. W. K. Lowther Clarke (Society for Promoting Christian Knowledge. New York: MacMillan and Co., n.d.)

3. Ibid.

4. Macarius the Egyptian (ca. 300–ca. 390), also called Macarius the Great, retired to Scete near Nitria at the age of thirty. Palladius tells us that he possessed such discernment that his followers call him the "aged youth." A Coptic camel driver by birth, he was deeply influenced by Anthony, whom he met on a number of occasions, and so represented his more primitive strain of Christianity. In later life it was said of Macarius that he spent more time in a state of ecstasy than he did contemplating the things of this earth. The line of transmission from Anthony through Macarius to Evagrius is therefore pertinent.

5. This did occur at the council in 553, where Evagrius was charged with being a Gnostic. He was later absolved of these charges, though for many centuries his work was promulgated under the name of Saint Nilus the Ascetic in order to forestall suspicion.

6. Viz., "Given these insights, that becoming has no goal and that underneath all becoming there is no grand unity in which the individual could immerse himself completely as in an element of supreme value, one escape remains: to pass sentence on this whole world of becoming as a deception and to invent a world beyond it, a *true* world." Again:

"At bottom, man has lost faith in his own value when no infinitely valuable whole works through him; i.e., he conceived such a whole in order to be able to believe in his own value." (Friedrich Nietzsche, *Will to Power*, trans. Oscar Levy (London: T. N. Foulis, 1914), 12A.

7. Evagrius Ponticus, *The Praktikos, Chapters on Prayer*, 68.

8. Ibid., 58.

9. Ibid., 38.

10. Ibid., 57.

11. Ludwig Wittgenstein, *Tractatus Logico-Philosophicus* (New York: Routledge, 1974), 6.373/4.

12. Evagrius Ponticus, *The Praktikos, Chapters on Prayer*, 84.

13. J. P. Migne, *Patrologia Graeca* 150,1233 D.

14. For information on this extremely interesting topic, see Basil Krivosheine, "The Ascetical and Theological Teaching of Gregory Palamas," *Eastern Churches Quarterly* 4 (1938).

15. John Cassian echoes Evagrius's remarks in his *Conferences* (9:31) by way of an allusion to Anthony: "I will give you not my own opinion but that of the blessed Antony: whom we have known sometimes to have been so persistent in prayer that often as he was praying in a transport of mind, when the sunrise began to appear, we have heard him in the fervor of his spirit declaiming: 'Why do you hinder me, O sun, who art arising for this very purpose; viz., to withdraw me from the brightness of this true light?'" Ibid. And his also is this heavenly and more than human utterance on the end of prayer: "That is not," said he, "a perfect prayer, wherein a monk *understands himself and the words which he prays.*" It is this wordless encounter with prayer that both Anthony and Evagrius support as the essence of pure prayer.

16. "Hesychia is the standing still of the mind and of the world, forgetfulness of what is below, initiation into secret knowledge of what is above, the putting aside of thoughts for what is better than they; this is the true activity, the ascent to the true contemplation" (Migne, *Patrologia Graeca*, 170–71).

17. Evagrius relates in this respect a story about Anthony that he heard: "A certain member of what was then considered the circle of the wise

once approached the just Antony and asked him: 'How do you ever manage to carry on, Father, deprived as you are of the consolation of books?' His reply: 'My book, sir philosopher, is the nature of created things, and it is always at hand when I wish to read the words of God.'" One senses immediately the irony in Anthony's reply: he intends to denigrate philosophic discussion that is purely a product of intellectual discourse. "The nature of created things" is clearly a euphemism for meditative knowledge derived from ascetic practice.

18. Plotinus, *The Enneads*, trans. Stephen MacKenna (New York: Faber and Faber, 1969), 1.3.5, where it is also says that "philosophy is supremely precious."

19. The other two subjects were grammar and logic. The quadrivium made up the balance of the liberal arts in classical education: geometry, arithmetic, music, and astronomy.

EIGHT: EYE OF THE OSTRICH

1. See Robert Curzon, *Visits to the Monasteries in the Levant* (London: Century Travellers, 1983).

2. Quoted by James Howard Wellard in *Desert Pilgrimage: Journeys to the Egyptian and Sinai Deserts* (London: Hutchinson, 1970).

3. Amoun, the third of the great founders of Egyptian monasticism, along with Anthony and Pachomius, died in 352. According to the *Apothegms*, Anthony came to him one day on the mountain of Nitria. When they met, Amoun said to him: "Thanks to your prayers, our brothers have become very numerous, so that some of them would like to build cells at a distance, so as to have more peace. Now, what do you say should be the distance between their cells and the ones here?" Anthony replied: "Let us eat at the ninth hour, then go out and walk in the desert, looking for a place." When they had walked in the desert until sunset, Abbot Anthony said to Abbot Amoun: "Let us pray and set up a cross here; this is where those who wish to do so shall found (their cells). Thus those from yonder (Nitria), when they come to visit those here in (Kellia), will come after having taken their

small meal at the ninth hour; and the same for those here who go there. In that way they will be able to come and visit more easily!" See Helen Waddell, trans., *The Desert Fathers: Translations from the Latin*, ed. John F. Thorton (London: Fontana Books, 1965).

4. In 1707 Elias Assemani, a Maronite in the service of Pope Clement XI, arrived at Suryani with orders to buy up as many manuscripts as he could lay his hands on. Fearful of anathemas that might fall on those found guilty of removing manuscripts from a rightful owner, the monks turned a deaf ear to the papal envoy. In the end they parted with only thirty-four manuscripts. The curse, however, came to fruition, as Assemani's boat sank on the Nile en route to Cairo and the envoy drowned. A few books were fished out of the river and brought to Rome much the worse for their immersion.

NINE: IN THE CRUCIBLE OF FIRE

1. The morning office usually starts before dawn and includes chanting parts of the Psalms while standing in the church.

2. Vladimir Lossky, *The Vision of God* (Clayton, Wis.: Faith Press, 1973): "The intellect must be trained for the knowledge of God in creation, for physical gnosis or *theoria*, the gnosis of sensible and intelligible natures. We have here an arena of exercise, a gymnasium of the intellect."

3. See Wensinck, *Mystical Treatises of Isaac of Nineveh*.

4. According to Diogenes Laertius, however, Pythagoras was also an advocate of restraint when it came to food: "Drinking . . . is a snare, and he discountenances all excess, saying that no one should go beyond due proportion either in drinking or eating. Of sexual indulgence, too, he says, 'Keep to the winter for sexual pleasures, in summer abstain.'" Laertius Diogenes, Loeb Classical Library, vol. VIII, trans. R. D. Hicks (Cambridge, MA: Harvard University Press, 1995), 8–10. Like the anchorites, Pythagoras encouraged the eating of uncooked foods and no meat.

5. See Brown, *The Body and Society*.

6. Gregory Palamas argued that the distinction between Creator and creature could disappear altogether during prayer: "If we could partake

of the divine substance itself, then everyone who partook of it, either of the whole of it or its minutest part, would become omnipotent since, because of its indivisibility, the divine substance would be communicated together with all its powers." See Krivosheine, "The Ascetical and Theological Teachings of Gregory Palamas."

7. Examples of "hidden activity" are often alluded to in Benedicta Ward, trans., *Sayings of the Desert Fathers*. "The bee, wherever it goes, makes honey; the monk, wherever he finds himself, carries out God's work." And "The heart of the palm tree is but one; it is white and encompasses the whole activity of the palm tree. This is what we find among the just: their heart is unique and simple, looking out towards God."

8. A story about Arsenius amply describes this new alphabet: "One day Abba Arsenius consulted an old Egyptian monk about his own thoughts. Someone noticed this and said to him: 'Abba Arsenius, how is it that you with such a good Latin and Greek education, ask this peasant about your thoughts?' He replied, 'I have indeed been taught Latin and Greek, but I do not even know the alphabet of this peasant.'"

9. See Wensinck, *Mystical Treatises of Isaac of Nineveh*.

10. Plotinus, *The Enneads*, trans. Stephen MacKenna (London: Faber and Faber, 1969), VI, 7.34, said: "No longer can we wonder that the principle evoking such longing should be utterly free from shape, even shape Intellectual. The very soul, once it has conceived the straining love towards this, lays aside all the shape it has taken, even to the Intellectual shape that has informed it. There is no vision, no union, for those handling or acting by anything other; the soul must see before it neither evil nor good nor anything else, that alone it may receive the Alone."

11. See Wensinck, *Mystical Treatises of Isaac of Nineveh*.

12. Henry Corbin, *The Man of Light in Iranian Sufism*, trans. Nancy Pearson (Boulder, Colo.: Shambhala Publications, 1978), 112.

13. Patricia Cox Miller, "The Little Blue Flower Is Red: Relics and the Poeticizing of the Body," *Journal of Early Christian Studies* 8 (2000): 213–236.

14. I am reminded of a certain Abba Julian, an elder in the monastery of the Egyptians in the Nitria Desert, who lived for seventy years in a cave with little more than a hair shirt, a bowl, a cloak, and a book of Gospels in his possession. John Moschus (ca. 550–619), in his *Spiritual Meadow*, trans. John Wortley (Kalamazoo, Mich.: Cistercian Publications, 1992), tells us that "all his life long he never lit a lamp to give light, for at night-time a light shone upon him from heaven sufficient for him to discern the sequence of letters when he was reading." (See Moschus, *Spiritual Meadow*, in the appendix for details on the discovery of the corpse of John the Humble in this respect.)

15. Palladius, *Lausiac History*, ch. 48.

TEN: THE LION'S MOUTH

1. Jerome, St., *Selected Letters.* (Cambridge 1980), 125–29.

2. See Dadisho' Katraya, "A Treatise on Solitude," in *Woodbrooke Studies*, vol. 7., ed. and trans. Alphonse Mingana (Cambridge University Press: Cambridge, 1934), 98.

3. Ibid.

4. Ibid., 150.

5. "How can there ever be," Abdisho' says, "while the mind does not know and does not distinguish its own self from the glory of that light which has no image, and in which its spirituality is swallowed up?"

6. We find echoes of the sphere of serenity of Abdisho' in the thought of F. W. J. Schelling in the nineteenth century: "It can readily be seen that in the tension of longing necessary to bring things completely to birth, the innermost nexus of the forces can only be released in a graded evolution, and at every stage in the division of forces there is developed out of nature a new being whose soul must be all the more perfect the more differentiatedly it contains what was left undifferentiated in the others. It is the task of a complete philosophy of nature to show how each successive process more closely approaches the essence of nature, until in the highest division of forces the innermost center is disclosed" (F. W. J. Schelling, *Philosophical Inquiries into the Nature of Human Freedom* [Chicago: Open Court Classics, 1986]).

7. *Woodbrooke Studies*, v. 7, 160.
8. See *Woodbrooke Studies*, vol. 7.
9. Ibid., 167.
10. See *Woodbrooke Studies*, vol. 7.
11. Ibid.
12. Ibid.
13. Ibid.
14. Ibid.
15. Ibid.
16. "The poet must make himself a *visionary* through a long, prodigious and rational disordering of *all* the senses. Every form of love, of suffering, of madness; he searches himself, he consumes all the poisons in him, keeping only their quintessence. Ineffable torture in which he will need all his faith and superhuman strength, the great criminal, the great sickness, the accursed—and the supreme Savant!" Quoted from Arthur Rimbaud, *Illuminations*, trans. Louise Varese (New York: New Directions, 1957).

ELEVEN: CONVERSATIONS IN THE DESERT

1. See Wensinck, *Mystical Treatises of Isaac of Nineveh*.
2. Ibid. There is some suggestion that he left for Scete in the Egyptian desert, though it has never been proven. It may be that the chroniclers wanted to link Isaac's name with the tradition of the great ascetics of the past.
3. *Studia Syriaca*, vol. 1, 33. Quoted by Hilarion Alfeyev in *The Spiritual World of Isaac the Syrian* (Kalamazoo, Mich.: Cistercian Publications, 2000).
4. Ibid.
5. See Wensinck, *Mystical Treatises of Isaac of Nineveh*, 203–204.
6. Isaac was adamant in this respect. He wrote: "How small psychic life is when compared with the hope preserved for eternities." (Ibid., 266.)
7. Ibid., 202.
8. Comparisons may be made with the metaphysical aspects of the Tao and the desire of the *hsien*, or adept, to forestall death by the practice

of asceticism. In the *Inner Chapters* of Pao P'u Tzu we read: "Worldly pleasures shorten human life; we ought to discard them, otherwise even worship is without effect. . . . If one takes care of one's health by avoiding worldly pleasures, he will live long. People who know nothing about the art of *hsien* but who attain to old age are very rare" (*Proceedings of the American Academy of Arts and Sciences* 74, (1935) no. 10). In another text, by Yun Tsu Ts'ung, we read: "The fate of life is like a bubble floating on water. Those who know nothing but income, emolument, fame, and rank will soon see their faces turning pale and their bodies degenerating" (*Proceedings of the American Academy of Arts and Sciences* 73, (1939) no. 5).

9. Cf. Diodore of Tarsus: "To support the body in softness and luxury, quickly imparts to the soul a sensation of suffering."

10. Dionysius wrote: "It is Perfectionless (Gr. *atelis*) in those that are perfect as transcending and anticipating their Perfection" (Dionysius, *Divine Names*, 77). In Sufism, this state is known as *fana*, or "annihilation," where consciousness is negated. The highest possible state is known as *fana dar fana*, "the annihilation of the annihilation," which corresponds to *epiptelis*, or the state "beyond perfection." (See Henry Corbin, *Creative Imagination in the Sufism of Ibn Arabi* [Princeton, N.J.: Princeton University Press, Bollingen Press, 1969], 202–3.)

11. Dionysius wrote: "For the angels, too, are said by Scripture to know the things upon earth not through sense-perception of them (though they are such that may be perceived this way), but through a faculty and nature inherent in a Godlike Intelligence." Dionysius the Areopagite, *The Celestial Hierarchies*, 151.

12. ". . . that we may begin to see that super-essential Darkness which is hidden by all the light that is in existent things" (ibid., 196).

13. Cf. "Studying the Veda, practising austerities, the acquisition of true knowledge, the subjugation of the organs, abstention from doing injury, and serving the Guru are the best means for obtaining supreme bliss" (*Manu-smrti XII*).

14. Ibid., 172–73.

15. Antipater of Tarsus argued that the sole end of life was "doing all in one's power to obtain the prime natural things." In this case "natural things" could also be things such as good health and social standing, aside from external goods pertinent to pursuing a profession, as Aristotle maintained.

16. See Wensinck, *Mystical Treatises of Isaac of Nineveh.*

Twelve: Garnering the Pearl

1. Cf. Anthony's "Letter Seven": "Hence, all bodily spirit fails them, when they receive the teachings of the Holy Spirit."

2. Ephraim the Syrian, *The Pearl: Seven Hymns on the Faith,* trans. J. B. Morris (The Saint Pachomius Orthodox Learning Center). Known as the Harp of the Holy Spirit. Ephraim the Syrian (ca. 306–373) composed some three million lines in his long career as a poet, theologian, hymnist, and doctor of the Church in the city of Edessa, where he lived. His graphic description of heaven and hell contributed to the inspiration of Dante's *Divine Comedy.*

3. Holderlin said: *"Die hochste Form im hochten Leben"* (In extreme life, supreme form).

4. See Vasiliev, *History of the Byzantine Empire,* in the appendix for details on hesychastic doctrine and practice.

5. See Ephraim the Syrian, *The Pearl.*

6. Simon of Taibutheh, "Medico-Mystical Work," *Woodbrooke Studies,* vol. 7.

7. Ibid.

8. See Athanasius, *The Life of St. Anthony and the Letter to Marcellinus.*

9. Cf. Paulinus, describing the relics in the churches of Nola: "The ashes even of the apostles have been set beneath that table of heaven, and consecrated amongst other holy offerings, they emit a fragrance pleasing to Christ from their living dust."

10. Anthony's words are from Samuel Rubenson, trans., *The Letters of St. Anthony,* Letter One. They are also echoed in 1 Cor. 9:27.

11. I am reminded of Schopenhauer's remark: "The Greeks and Romans ... were still entirely absorbed in life, and did not seriously

look beyond this." Schopenhauer, *Essays and Aphorisms*. London: Penguin Classics, 1970.

12. Cf. "Letter Six": "We are all created from one invisible essence, having a beginning and no end; thus, they who know themselves know that the essence of unity is immortal."

13. See Athanasius, *The Life of St. Anthony and the Letter to Marcellinus*.

14. Ibid.

15. See Athanasius, *The Life of St. Anthony and the Letter to Marcellinus*. One is reminded here of Socrates' general disposition in the face of his own death: "Death is one of two things. Either it is annihilation, and the dead have no consciousness of anything, or, as we are told, it is really a change—a migration of the soul from this place to another. . . . Now it is time that we were going. I to die and you to live, but which of us has the happier prospect is unknown to anyone except God." (Plato, "Socrates' Defense." *Collected Dialogues*, Bollingen Series LXXI. [Princeton: Princeton University Press, 1961].)

16. Theodoret, *Historia Religiosa Graeca* LXXXII.

17. See Wensinck, *Mystical Treatises of Isaac of Nineveh*.

18. 'Ain al-Qudat, *A Sufi Martyr: The Apologia of 'Ain al-Qudat al Hamadhani*, trans. A. J. Arberry (London: George Allen and Unwin, Ltd., 1969). 'Ain al-Qudat was a Sufi mystic who wrote his *Apologia* while awaiting execution for heresy in a Baghdad prison in 1131. He was thirty-three years old. It was he who said: "Philosophers deny such states [that is, ecstatic states] because they are imprisoned in the narrow defile of reason. The term 'prophet' for them means a man who has attained to the furthest degree of reason. That, however, has nothing in common with faith in prophethood. Prophethood in fact consists in a variety of perfections that supervene in a stage beyond the stage of sainthood. The stage of sainthood itself transcends the stage of reason." He also said. "Wisdom is not the fruit of wordy discussion; on the contrary, it is the heritage of silence." 'Ain al-Qudat. *A Sufi Martyr*. Surely Anthony would have agreed.

THIRTEEN: THE PARTING

1. Edmond Jabès, *The Book of Questions*.
2. Rudolf Otto, *The Idea of the Holy*, trans. John W. Harvey (Oxford University Press: Oxford, 1958).
3. Evagrius also regarded charity as a "killer of snakes" in that it helped to bridle anger. See Evagrius Ponticus, *The Praktikos*, 38.
4. Cassian, *Conferences*, 2:4.
5. Evagrius Ponticus, *The Praktikos*, 108.

POSTSCRIPT

1. *Woodbrooke Studies*, "Medici-Mystical Work," vol. 7.
2. See Wensinck, *Mystical Treatises of Isaac of Nineveh*.

GLOSSARY OF TERMS

Agape: "To love," in Greek; a meeting of men or women wishing to celebrate the Christian mysteries in a state of fraternity and love.

Agnosia: A state of unknowing where one may know him who is above every possible object of knowledge. The rational faculties have been stilled.

Anachoresis: Literally, "to withdraw," in Greek. A condition of spiritual and social disengagement.

Anchorite: "To withdraw"; a man who removes himself from society to live an eremitical life in the desert.

Apatheia: A state of serenity, when all passions are stilled. For the early Christians in the East, it represented the beginning of deification. For Ponticus it reflected a state of impassability.

Apophaticism: The isolation of the qualities of God by pointing out who or what he is not. The practice of negative theology was popular among mystics, especially Dionysius the Areopagite.

Apostasis: A complete and resolved state of ascetic renunciation.

Arianism: A fourth-century heresy promulgated by Arius that advanced the idea that Christ was a created being and not born of man.

Ascesis: Literally, "exercise" or "training"; a condition of voluntary restraint in all actions pertaining to bodily pleasure. The practice of spiritual self-discipline.

Ataraxia: A state of untroubled calm.

Autarkism: To live in a state of absolute self-sufficiency, outside social structures.

Baraka: An Arabic word implying spiritual energy or attributes (grace) usually associated with holy men.

Copts: Indigenous Egyptian Christians as distinct from Greek or Latin Christians living in Egypt.

Desert Fathers: Name denoting the early fathers of the Egyptian church who lived in the Nitria Desert north of modern-day Cairo and in certain regions along the Nile. These men formulated the early statutes for eremitical and monastic living.

Diakrisis: The gift of discernment, detachment, and discrimination; also known as discretion.

Eschatology: The knowledge of Last Things, usually associated with life after death.

Eschaton: The condition of the Last Things, or the ideal (heavenly) time after death.

Eudaemonia: A state of bliss, being in the proximity of God.

Five Signs: Stages of renunciation of the world central to the hidden activity of ascetic behavior. They correspond to the elimination of sense activity, the attainment of humility, tearfulness, recollection, and, finally, knowledge of intelligible nature.

Four Living Creatures: Those creatures traditionally associated with the Gospels: the lion, the ox, the eagle, and the angel.

Geronte: Spiritual advisor or mentor.

Gnosis: Spiritual knowledge. The term *Gnostic* was also applied to a dualist heresy in the early Christian Church known as Gnosticism.

Hesychasm: A meditative practice designed to invoke a condition of "holy quiet" and the suspension of all appetitive qualities. Literally, a turning inward. It involves the repetition of the Jesus *Prayer:* "Jesus Christ, Son of God, have mercy on me."

Isochristoi: A state of oneness and equality with Christ. Another way of saying *Theos Anir,* the perfect man.

Katastasis: Another word implying a state of stillness in the soul; tranquillity or peace.

Kosmikos: A man of the world who understands and accepts the spirit in his life.

Laura: The name given to a loose community of monks that is not yet a monastery.

Maggenanutha: Syriac word for a state of ecstasy or bliss, an "overshadowing" of the higher power on a lower. It is the sanctification that is received through divine grace.

Marabout: The tomb of an Islamic holy man or saint.

Nag Hammadi texts: A collection of Gnostic texts found in Upper Egypt in 1945. Monks, wanting to save their heretical texts from the fire after they had been banned, buried them in earthenware jars. Today they are housed in the Coptic Museum in Cairo.

Nomos: A rule or a series of directions for living.

Parresia: A state of intimacy with God.

Prophetus: A sage or wise man, a prophet.

Proteleios: A state of perfectionlessness, or a going beyond perfection.

Theophany: The visible manifestation of God to humankind.

Theos anir: The divine, or perfect, man; a man deified.

Wadi: The Arabic word for dry riverbed or gully.

Xeniteia: The process of social disengagement toward "living as a stranger"; a voluntary state of exile.

▲▲▲▲▲

GLOSSARY OF NAMES AND PLACES

Alexandria: The capital of Greco-Roman Egypt, located near the mouth of the Nile. Home to Neoplatonic philosophers such as Plotinus and Porphyry and the great early Christian theologians such as Tertullian, Origen, and Athanasius.

Amoun: Born in the delta region of the Nile, Amoun gave up the marriage bed on the eve of his betrothal in order to devote his life to chastity. He was one of the first anchorites to retreat to the Nitria Desert, where he lived as a solitary for twenty-two years.

Anthony (ca. 251–356): Founder and father of Christian monasticism. A disciple of Paul of Thebes, he lived much of his life as a hermit in remote places such as Mount Colzim. He was the first religious to embark on a program of psycho-spiritual cleansing in a bid to attain to a state of stillness and calm *(apatheia)*. His so-called Temptations in religious art have become a part of the European canon, denoting the battle against the sins of externality and physical excess. His influence on European monasticism and religious thought was profound.

Athanasius (293–373): An Alexandrian theologian, advisor to bishops, and key figure in the battle against heretical teachings then beginning to influence early Christian thought. Greatly influenced by Clement and Origen, he later went on to propound a theory of Christian salvation known as *theopoesis* (apotheosis), which emphasized the need to wait for salvation to occur. He was exiled on a number of occasions for his beliefs, to the point where Emperor Justinian called him a "disturber of the peace and enemy of the gods."

Cappadocia: A region of central Turkey and an early Christian stronghold. At places such as Goreme, Christian monasteries were built by communities of monks, who dug their monasteries out of the soft tufa limestone hills. Often called the Valley of a Thousand Churches.

Cassian, John (360–435): Probably of Roman birth, Cassian became a monk at Bethlehem, from where he later visited the monks in Egypt. His major work, *Conferences of the Egyptian Monks,* was influential in the further development of Western monasticism.

Climacus, John (ca. 579–ca. 649): Lived some forty years as an anchorite on Mount Sinai before becoming the abbot of Saint Catherine's monastery there. Little is known of his early life, but his use of secular metaphors in his great work *The Ladder of Divine Ascent* suggests that he had traveled widely in his youth. A man of vital personality, shrewdness, and human understanding, he brought to early Christian thinking a sharp, ascetic mind.

Dionysius the Areopagite: One of the great mystical thinkers of early Christianity, probably of Syrian origin, Dionysius likely lived in Palestine during the late fifth century. His writings include *On the Divine Names* and *On the Celestial Hierarchies,* both extensive studies of the hierarchical nature of the Godhead. His work powerfully influenced such writers as Erigena, Thomas Aquinas, and John of Ruysbroeck, thus determining the mystical theology of both the Eastern and Western churches.

Dorotheus of Gaza: Little is known of the man except that he was born in Antioch in 506 and received his education there. He probably came from a fairly wealthy Christian family. His eremitical life was spent in a monastery in Gaza, where he wrote his *Discourses.*

Erigena, John Scotus (ca. 810–ca. 877): Irish theologian and translator whose work was deeply influenced by Greek and Neoplatonist thought. He attempted to reconcile the Neoplatonist doctrine of emanation with the Christian tenet of creation. The Church later condemned his work as pantheistic.

Evagrius Ponticus: (346–399) Produced the first major philosophical-theological exposition of Christian monasticism. His *Gnostic Centuries* emphasized that the essential function of spiritual beings is to experience union with God, expressed as pure light. He is considered among Eastern Christians as a great mystical doctor of theology whose ideas today are sometimes seen as analogous to those of Zen Buddhism.

Gregory of Sinai (d. 1346): Greek Orthodox monk, theologian, and mystic and a prominent advocate of Hesychasm. He joined the community at Mount Sinai, where he became a devotee of John Climacus. Later, on Mount Athos in Greece, he devised a more moderate form of Hesychasm. His *Spiritual Meditations* extended the Hesychasm movement throughout Europe and the Byzantine world. Realization of the "Divine Light" was for him analogous to Christ's transfiguration on Mount Tabor.

Gregory of Tours (538–595): French bishop and writer whose books include the *History of the Franks* and *Lives of the Fathers.* His chronicle of the Franks is an unforgettable portrait of Europe just after the breakup of the western Roman Empire.

Hazzaya, Abdisho' (d. ca. 690): A Syriac monk who lived much of his life in the monastery of Maragna. Born in Nimrod, Mesopotamia, he was an advocate of the realization of a certain mystical light, which he called the fiery impulse, in any man who had reached a high level of spiritual attainment.

Jerome (ca. 347–420): Born in Slovenia and educated in Rome, Jerome spent twenty years living in different places before traveling to Palestine, where he entered a monastery in the Chalcis Desert. He later visited Egypt and met many of the anchorites there. A noted scholar, Jerome went on to translate the Vulgate Latin version of the Bible. His influence on Western theology was marked, given his knowledge of Eastern Christianity.

Mark the Ascetic: A late-fourth-century ascetic of Egyptian origin known for his quiet and meek disposition. His strict life and purity of heart raised him to a high degree of spiritual perfection.

Moschus, John: A wandering monk, possibly born in Damascus around 550. He was tonsured at a monastery near Bethlehem, but spent a good deal of his life moving from one monastery to another in Palestine. He wrote the *Pratum spirituale,* or *Spiritual Meadow,* a compendium of stories and sayings from the lives of the early Christian fathers of that region.

Mount Athos: Also known as the Holy Mountain; also the republic that is inhabited by the largest and most important community of Eastern Orthodox monks in the world. It consists of twenty monasteries, a dozen sketes, and numerous small hermitages. The oldest monastery, the Great Lavra, was founded in 963.

Nilus of Sinai (ca. 370–ca. 430): Belonged to a wealthy family from Antioch. His noble birth and special gifts raised him to the rank of prefect in Constantinople. Eventually, after an agreement with his wife, he renounced the world and settled at Mount Sinai. He lived as an anchorite for more than sixty years. He was a pupil of John Chrysostom, an early Orthodox theologian.

Origen (185–254): Theological and biblical scholar who was born a pagan and lived in Alexandria. As a young man he castrated himself in order to work more freely instructing young women at the Didascaleon or catechetical school. He later traveled to Asia Minor, where he was persecuted and thrown into prison under Emperor Decius. His theology ultimately turns on the goodness of God and the attribute of free will. His writings influenced both Evagrius and John Cassian.

Pachomius (ca. 290–346): Born a pagan in the Thebaid of Egypt, he was conscripted into the army and taken to Luxor, on the Nile, where he came under the influence of local Christians. On his release from the army, he returned to the Thebaid and was baptized. He is credited with establishing the first cenobitic monastery at Tabennisi.

Palamas, Gregory (1296–1359): Greek Orthodox monk, theologian, and intellectual leader of the Hesychasm movement. Born in Constantinople with ties to the imperial court, he became a monk on Mount Athos, the spiritual center of Greek Orthodoxy. In his writings he resisted the influence of rational humanism, which he believed undermined the mystical nature of Orthodox belief.

Palladius (ca. 363–ca. 431): Took up the ascetic life first at the Mount of Olives outside Jerusalem, then in the Nitria Desert of Egypt. There he met with Macarius the Egyptian and Evagrius Ponticus. His writings include the *Lausiac History*, a fusion of personal experiences with secondary accounts of desert monasticism.

Philo of Alexandria (ca. 15 BC–between AD 45 and 50): Greek-speaking Jewish philosopher from Palestine. He moved to Alexandria, where he became an important representative of Hellenistic Judaism. Also regarded by Christians as a forerunner of Christian theology.

Plotinus (205–270): Ancient Neoplatonic philosopher; though born in Egypt, was probably of Greek parents. He became the center of an influential circle of intellectuals in third-century Rome. Central to his teachings was the quest for mystical union with the Good through the exercise of pure intellect. His ideas show traces of Indian religious philosophy that he may have come in contact with in Mesopotamia during a military campaign.

Porphyry (ca. 234–ca. 305): Neoplatonist philosopher and editor and biographer of Plotinus. Born in Lebanon, he studied philosophy in Rome under Plotinus. After experiencing a suicidal depression, he was persuaded by Plotinus to travel in order to free up his mind. Later, he systemized the *Enneads* for his teacher. He also wrote a life of Pythagoras. He was a fierce critic of Christianity.

Pythagoras (580–500 BC): Greek philosopher and mathematician; founder of the Pythagorean brotherhood at Croton in Italy, which formulated principles that influenced the thought of Plato and Aristotle. He propounded a theory of numbers in the objective world, and in music, that paved the way for the development of the science of geometry and diatonic harmony. He was said to have studied under the tutelage of Egyptian temple priests, who taught him all that they knew.

Ruysbroeck, John of (1293–1381): Flemish mystic whose writings deeply influenced men such as Tauler and Groote. He viewed the relationship of the soul to God as similar to that between the lover and the beloved. He founded the monastery of Groenendaal, where he spent much of his life.

Thebiad: A region northwest of Cairo, and some thirty-five miles southeast of Alexandria, that embraced the desert known as Scete. It was here that many monastic and hermit communities sprang into existence during the fourth century. Amoun and Macarius the Egyptian, who followed the rule laid down by Antony, founded these colonies.

Valentinus: Second-century Egyptian philosopher and founder of the Alexandrian school of Gnosticism. Though baptized a Christian, he left the church in Rome to settle in Alexandria, where he further developed his system of mythically derived religious philosophy. His writings were considered to be heretical and have not survived except in the works of others.

SELECTED BIBLIOGRAPHY

Alfeyev, Hilarion. *The Spiritual World of Isaac the Syrian*. Kalamazoo, MI: Cistercian Publications, 2000.

Arberry, A. J. *A Sufi Martyr: The Apologia of 'Ain al-Qudat al-Hamadhani*. London: George Allen and Unwin, 1969.

Athanasius. *The Life of Anthony and the Letter to M-arcellinus*. Trans. Robert C. Gregg. Mahwah, NJ: Paulist Press, 1980.

Augustine. *Confessions*. London: Penguin Classics, 1970.

Aurelius, Marcus. *Meditations*. Trans. Maxwell Staniforth. London: Penguin Books, 1964.

Bettenson, Henry Scowcroft, comp. *The Later Christian Fathers: A Selection from the Writings of the Fathers from Saint Cyril of Jerusalem to Saint Leo the Great*. London: Penguin Classics, 1972.

Bevan, Edwyn R. *Hellenism and Christianity*. London: Allen and Unwin, 1921.

Boethius. *The Consolation of Philosophy*. Trans. V. E. Watts. London: Penguin Classics, 1969.

Brock, Sebastian. *The Syriac Fathers on Prayer and the Spiritual Life*. Kalamazoo, MI: Cistercian Publications, 1987.

Brown, Peter. *The Body and Society: Men, Women, and Sexual Renunciation in Early Christianity*. New York: Columbia University Press, 1988.

⸺. *The Cult of the Saints: Its Rise and Function in Latin Christianity*. Chicago: University of Chicago Press, 1984.

⸺. "The Rise and Function of the Holy Man in Late Antiquity." In *Society and the Holy in Late Antiquity*. Berkeley, CA: University of California Press, 1982.

Byron, Robert. *The Station: Athos; Treasures and Men*. London: Duckworth, 1928.

Cavarnos, Constantine. *Byzantine Thought and Art*. Belmont, MA: Institute for Byzantine and Modern Greek Studies, 1986.

⸺, ed. and trans. *The Icon: Its Spiritual Basis and Purpose*. Belmont, MA: Institute for Byzantine and Modern Greek Studies, 1956.

Chitty, Derwas James. *The Desert a City: An Introduction to the Study of Egyptian and Palestinian Monasticism under the Christian Empire*. Crestwood, NY: SVS Press, 1977.

Cioran, E. M. *Tears and Saints*. Trans. Ilinca Zarifopol-Johnston. Chicago: University of Chicago Press, 1995.

Climacus, John. *The Ladder of Divine Ascent*. Willits, CA: Eastern Orthodox Books, 1959.

Corbin, Henry. *Creative Imagination in the Sufism of Ibn Arabi*. Princeton, NJ: Princeton University Press, Bollingen Series XCI, 1969.

⸺. *The Man of Light in Iranian Sufism*. Trans. Nancy Pearson. Boulder, CO: Shambhala Publications, 1978.

Curzon, Robert. *Visits to the Monasteries in the Levant*. London: Century Travellers, 1983.

Daumal, René. *The Powers of the Word: Selected Essays and Notes, 1927–1943*. Trans. Mark Polizzotti. San Francisco: City Lights Books, 1991.

Diogenes, Laertius. Loeb Classical Library. Cambridge, MA: Harvard University Press, 1995.

Dionysius the Areopagite. *The Celestial Hierarchies*. London: Shrine of Wisdom, 1935, manual n. 15.

⸺. *The Divine Names and the Mystical Theology*. Trans. C. E. Rolt. London: SPCK Publishing, 1972.

Donaldson, Christopher. *Martin of Tours.* London: Routledge and Kegan Paul, 1980.

Doresse, Jean. *The Secret Books of the Egyptian Gnostics: An Introduction to the Gnostic Coptic Manuscripts Discovered at Chenoboskion.* Rochester, VT: Inner Traditions, 1986.

Dorotheus of Gaza. *Discourses and Sayings.* Trans. Eric Wheeler. Kalamazoo, MI: Cistercian Publications, 1977.

Evagrius Ponticus. *The Praktikos, Chapters on Prayer.* Kalamazoo, MI: Cistercian Publications, 1981.

French, R. M. trans. *The Way of a Pilgrim.* London: SPCK Publishing, 1973.

Gilson, Etienne Henry. *The Elements of Christian Philosophy.* New York: Mentor-Omega Books, 1963.

Goodier, Alban. *An Introduction to the Study of Ascetical and Mystical Theology.* London: Burns, Oates, and Washbourne, 1938.

Hugel, Friedrich von. *Selected Writings.* London: Fontana Books, 1964.

Hugoye: Journal of Syriac Studies. Leiden University, 1998.

Jabès, Edmond. *The Book of Questions.* Vol. 1–2. Trans. Rosemarie Waldrop. Middletown, CT: Wesleyan University Press, 1991.

Kadloubovsky, E., and G. E. H. Palmer, trans. *Early Fathers from the Philokalia.* New York: Faber and Faber, 1969.

Kahn, Charles H. *The Art and Thought of Heraclitus: A New Arrangement and Translation of the Fragments with Literary and Philosophical Comments.* Cambridge, UK: Cambridge University Press, 1995.

Kamil, Jill. *Coptic Egypt: History and Guide.* Cairo: American University in Cairo Press, 1997.

———. *The Monastery of Saint Catherine in Sinai: History and Guide.* Cairo: American University in Cairo Press, 1996.

Kasser, Rudolf. *Le site monastique des Kellia.* Lovain: Editions Peeters, 1984.

Kaye, John. *Some Account of the Writings and Opinions of Clement of Alexandria.* London: Griffith Farran, 1888.

Kingsley, Charles. *The Hermits.* London: MacMillan and Co., 1879.

Krivosheine, Basil. "The Ascetical and Theological Teachings of Gregory Palamas." In *Eastern Churches Quarterly* 4 (1938).

Lacarriere, Jacques. *The Gnostics.* Trans. Nina Rootes. London: Peter Owen, 1977.

——. *The God-Possessed: On the Hermits and Desert Monks of Egypt, Palestine, and Syria.* London: George Allen and Unwin, 1963.

Leroy, Jules. *Monks and Monasteries of the Near East.* London: George G. Harrap and Co., 1963.

Levi, Peter. *The Frontiers of Paradise: A Study of Monks and Monasteries.* London: Collins Harvil, 1988.

Lewis, Naphtali. *Life in Egypt under Roman Rule.* New York: Oxford University Press, Clarendon Press, 1985.

Loch, Sydney. *Athos: The Holy Mountain.* London: Lutterworth Press, 1957.

Lossky, Vladimir. *The Mystical Theology of the Eastern Church.* London: James Clark, 1968.

——. *The Vision of God.* Clayton, WI: Faith Press, 1973.

Meinardos, Otto. *The Historic Coptic Churches of Cairo.* Cairo: Philopatron, 1994.

Mingana, Alphonse, ed. and trans. *Woodbrooke Studies: Christian Documents in Syriac, Arabic, and Garshuni.* Vols. 1–7. Cambridge University Press: Cambridge, 1934.

Monk of the Eastern Church, A. *On the Invocation of the Name of Jesus.* London: Fellowship of Saint Alban and Saint Sergius, 1950.

Nilsson, Martin Perrson. *A History of Greek Religion.* New York: Norton and Co., 1984.

O'Connor, Eugene Michael. *The Essential Epicurus: Letters, Principal Doctrines, Vatican Sayings, and Fragments.* Amherst, NY: Prometheus Books, 1993.

Otto, Rudolf. *The Idea of the Holy.* Trans. John W. Harvey. Oxford: Oxford University Press, 1958.

Pagels, Elaine. *The Gnostic Gospels.* London: Penguin Books, 1979.

Palladius. *The Lausiac History.* Trans. W. K. Lowther Clarke. Society for Promoting Christian Knowledge. New York: MacMillan Co., n.d.

Plato. *The Collected Dialogues.* Princeton, NJ: Princeton University Press, Bollingen Books, 1978.

Plotinus. *The Enneads.* Trans. Stephen MacKenna. New York: Faber and Faber, 1969.

Porphyry. *On the Cave of the Nymphs*. Trans. Thomas Taylor. Grand Rapids, MI, Phanes Press, 1991.

Regnault, Lucien. *The Day-to-Day Life of the Desert Fathers: In Fourth-Century Europe*. Trans. Etienne Poirier. Petersham, MA: Saint Bede's Publications, 1998.

Richardson, Dan. *Egypt: The Rough Guide*. London: Rough Guides, 1996.

Rimbaud, Arthur. *Illuminations*. Trans. Louise Varese. New York: New Directions, 1957.

Rist, J. M. *Stoic Philosophy*. Cambridge: Cambridge University Press, 1969.

Robinson, James M., ed. *Nag Hammadi Library*. New York: Harper-Collins, 1990.

Ruysbroeck, John of. *The Sparkling Stone*. Trans. C. A. Wynschenk DOM. n.d.

Sasaki, Ruth Fuller. *Rinzai Zen Study for Foreigners in Japan*. Kyoto: First Zen Institute of America in Japan, 1960.

Schelling, F. W. J. *Philosophical Inquiries into the Nature of Human Freedom*. Chicago: Open Court Classics, 1986.

Schopenhauer, Arthur. *Essays and Aphorisms*. London: Penguin Classics, 1970.

Silouan, Staretz. *Wisdom from Mount Athos: The Writings of Staretz Silouan, 1866–1938*. Trans. Rosemary Edmonds. London: Mowbrays, 1973.

Vasiliev, Alexander A. *History of the Byzantine Empire*. 2 vols. Madison: University of Wisconsin Press, 1952.

Waddell, Helen, trans. *The Desert Fathers: Translations from the Latin*. Ed. John F. Thorton. London: Fontana Books, 1965.

Wallis, Richard T., ed. *Neoplatonism*. New York: Charles Scribners and Sons, 1972.

Walsh, P. G., trans. *The 40 Poems of St. Paulinus of Nola*. Mahwah, NJ, Paulist Press, Newman Press, 1975.

Ward, Benedicta, trans. *The Sayings of the Desert Fathers*. Kalamazoo, MI: Cistercian Publications, 1984.

Watterson, Barbara. *Coptic Egypt*. Edinburgh: Scottish Academic Press, 1988.

Weil, Simone. *Intimations of Christianity among the Ancient Greeks*. London: Ark Paperbacks, 1982.

Wellard, James Howard. *Desert Pilgrimage: Journeys to the Egyptian and Sinai Deserts.* London: Hutchinson, 1970.

Wensinck, A. J. *Mystical Treatises of Isaac of Nineveh.* Amsterdam: K.N.A.W., 1923.

Wittgenstein, Ludwig. *Tractatus Logico-Philosophicus.* New York: Routledge, 1974.